APR 11 72 May 10, 1971

66-26315

March of America Facsimile Series

Number 47

Journal of Captain Cook's
Last Voyage to the Pacific Ocean

John Rickman

Journal of Captain Cook's Last Voyage to the Pacific Ocean

by John Rickman

ANN ARBOR

UNIVERSITY MICROFILMS, INC.

A Subsidiary of Xerox Corporation

Foreword

The three voyages around the world made by Captain James Cook between the years 1768 and 1779 resulted in an enormous advance in geographical knowledge of the whole Pacific region. Cook eliminated once and for all the notion that a great continent lay in the South Seas off the tip of South America. He discovered and mapped many of the island groups of the Pacific, including the Hawaiian Islands, and his third expedition, in which he was killed in Hawaii, mapped the northwestern coastline of the North American continent, including Alaska and the Siberian coast beyond. Not since Francis Drake first circumnavigated the globe for the English had exploring expeditions created more excitement in the British world, and many narratives of Cook's expeditions soon appeared. *The Journal of Captain Cook's Last Voyage to the Pacific Ocean* (1781), reproduced here, is not Cook's own journal, as the title would seem to imply, but a journal kept by John Rickman, a lieutenant on the *Discovery*, the ship which accompanied Cook's ship, the *Resolution*. Rickman was transferred to the *Resolution* in August, 1779.

The authorship of this *Journal* has been a mystery. As late as 1930, it was attributed to John Ledyard, an American who was corporal of British marines in the expedition. But further research has proved beyond a reasonable doubt that it was composed by Rickman. So popular was this *Journal* that a second edition appeared in London in 1781, followed by a pirated edition in Dublin the same year. In 1783, an edition was brought out in Philadelphia which has been wrongly attributed to William Ellis. In 1785, a new edition was published in London.

After a long introduction giving a summary of earlier exploration, Rickman begins his narrative on June 14, 1776, when the two ships were taking on stores at the mouth of the Thames. The *Resolution* sailed ahead of the *Discovery* and the two made a rendezvous at the Cape of Good Hope. Much of the narrative concerns the exploration of the South Pacific; the voyages through the various islands, including stops at Tahiti and other islands in that group; the behavior of Omai, who was being repatriated to his native Huahine after a triumphant visit to London; and the discovery of the Sandwich Islands (Hawaii). But the portions of most concern to Americans deal with the investigation of the west coast of the North American continent and the Russian coast beyond.

Rickman describes Cook's investigation of this coastline in the spring and summer of 1778. When the winter ice prevented any further exploration in the north, Cook returned to the Sandwich Islands where he planned to winter. After his death on February 14, 1779, Captain Charles Clarke (or Clerke) took command of the expedition and sailed again for the Bering Sea region to search for the Northwest Passage which mariners had been trying to find since Tudor times. Clarke was convinced that such a search was hopeless. He himself died on April 22, 1779, while exploring in Avatcha Bay.

Rickman provides interesting commentary on the people of the Alaskan and Siberian coasts. He corrects an error, previously stated, that the Asian and American coasts were joined and points out that a strait separates them. He also corrects the notion that Alaska was a great island and emphasizes that

"Bering is justly entitled to the honor of having discovered all that part of the N.W. continent of America that has been hitherto marked in our maps as parts unknown." For information about Cook and Clarke, see the *Dictionary of National Biography* or any one of the numerous studies of Cook's expeditions. Rickman's authorship of this *Journal* is made clear in Sir Maurice Holmes, *Captain James Cook, R.N., F.R.S.: A Bibliographical Excursion* (London, 1952), pp. 44-45.

Representation of the Murder of Captain Cook at O-Why-ee

JOURNAL

OF

CAPTAIN COOK's

LAST

VOYAGE

TO THE

PACIFIC OCEAN,

ON

DISCOVERY;

PERFORMED IN THE

YEARS 1776, 1777, 1778, 1779,

ILLUSTRATED WITH

Cuts, and a Chart, fhewing the Tracts of
the Ships employed in this Expedition.

Faithfully Narrated from the original MS.

LONDON:

Printed for E. Newbery, at the Corner of
St. Paul's Church Yard.

MDCCLXXXI.

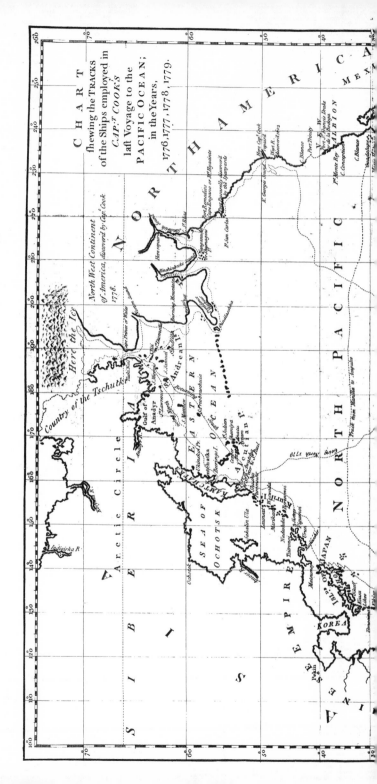

CHART shewing the TRACKS of the Ships employed in CAP.ᵗ COOK'S last Voyage to the PACIFIC OCEAN; in the Years, 1776, 1777, 1778, 1779.

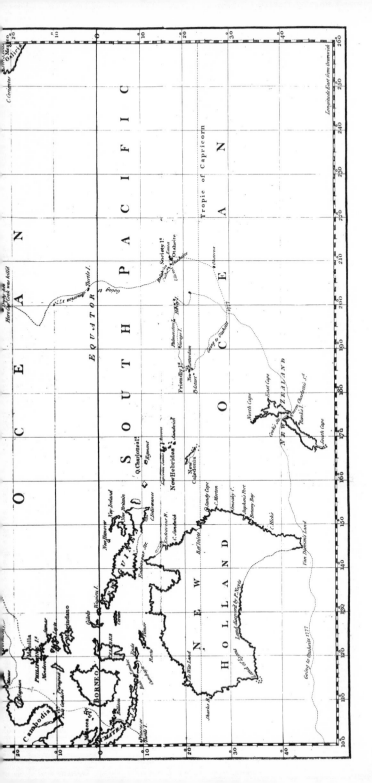

ADVERTISEMENT.

THE Editor of this Journal does not make himself answerable for all the facts that are related in it. There is certainly some allowance to be made to a man who has circumnavigated the globe oftener perhaps than once. And indeed there are many TRUTHS in nature, which till our ideas are enlarged by experience, appear to us incredible.

Thus much however the Editor may venture to affirm, that what immediately relates to the object of the Voyage, the places the ships visited, the distresses they met with, and the Discoveries of new Countries, new Inhabitants, new Customs Arts and Manufactures, so far as they could be learnt or apprehended during a short stay among people with whom the Journalist could converse only by signs; all these particulars are related with the strictest regard to truth, as is likewise the conduct and character of Omai, his reception and consequence at Otaheite, and the envy and jealousy which his riches and the favour shewn him by his patron and friend Capt. Cook excited among the Chiefs of his own country; these the Journalist seems to have noticed with particular attention.

But the Editor does not take upon him to say, that the Journalist has not upon some occasions exaggerated circumstances, nor that his

pre-

prejudices have not fometimes prevailed over his candour in reprefenting characters.

The Editor may have his errors too; but he hopes they are fuch as may be pardoned. Some have arifen from hafte, and fome from mifunderftanding the Journalift's Orthography, who, being at a great diftance, could not be confulted without retarding the Prefs. For thefe the intelligent Reader, he hopes, will accept of this apology. With refpect to language, fuffice it to fay, that he has affected no ornament. It was a plain tale he had to tell, and he has told it in a plain way.

The Chart that accompanies the Voyage illuftrates the courfe with as much accuracy as is neceffary even for Geographers, and it afforded no fmall pleafure to the Editor, when he found on comparifon, the latitudes and longitudes in the Journal corresponded with the obfervations of the late Spanifh Voyagers, fent out on the fame errand.

ERRATA.

Page 186, Line 7, *inftead of* * * * * * *, *add*, in Greece and Rome.

—— 273, —— 3, *for* the two lines beginning "had given the name of," *read* Alafkah, which we afterwards found to border on the American coaft. This bay, &c.

—— —— —— 9, *after the word* proved, *add* not.

—— 275, —— 1, *for* eaftward, *r.* weftward.

—— 282, ——10, *for* Helinifki, *r.* Alafkah.

—— 297, ——26, *for* 6 leagues, *r.* 20.

INTRODUCTION.

TWO illuftrious foreigners, Columbus and Magellan, rendered their names immortal, at an early period, by opening an immenfe field for difcovery and the improvement of Navigation; but it has been referved for a diftinguifhed native of this country and of this age, to fix the boundaries, and to complete the *ne plus ultra* of the nautical art. The two laft of thefe memorable Navigators fell in the profecution of their interefting projects—the firft furvived only to experience the viciffitudes of Fortune, and to *feel* the refentment of an ungrateful Court.

Columbus, by a perfeverance, of which there was then no precedent, very providentially furmounted every obftacle that oppofed his progrefs, and aftonifhed Europe with the production of a *new earth*; while much about the fame time Magellan, infpired by a like fpirit of enterprife, and animated by a magnanimity that defpifed danger while in the purfuit of glory, opened a paffage to a NEW SEA.

A brief recapitulation of the attempts made to improve this latter difcovery will fhew the importance of the prefent Voyage, and furnifh an idea of the vaftnefs of the undertaking —no lefs than to fix the boundaries of the two continents that form the grand divifions, which, tho' feparated to all human appearance, connect the Globe.

It

It was on the 6th of November, in the year, 1520 that Magellan entered the Straits, that have ever since born his name, and the 27th of the same month, when in a transport of joy he beheld the wished-for object of his pursuit, the GREAT SOUTHERN SEA. Elated with success, he proceeded chearfully for several days, with a favouring gale ; but the weather soon changing, and the sea growing boisterous, he altered his course from the high latitude in which he entered that almost boundless ocean, and directed his views to a more moderate climate. For 113 days he continued steering to the north-west, without seeing land or meeting with other supply except what water the sailors caught in the awnings, when the storms of thunder, which were frequent and dreadful, burst the clouds and let loose the rain. Having in that time crossed the line, he fell in with a range of islands, in the 12th degree of northern latitude, where with great difficulty he procured some refreshment for those of his followers who yet remained alive, most of them having perished by hunger and fatigue in that long run of tiresome navigation. Those who survived had fed some time upon tough hides, the leather of their shoes, and even that which surrounded the ropes, after having softened these dainties by soaking them in sea-water. Add to this, that many of them being attacked by the scurvy, the flesh of their gums had so envelop-

ped

ped their teeth, that unable to eat, they died famifhed in all the agonies of horror and defpair. The thievifh difpofition of the tropical iflanders in this ocean, to which Magellan now gave the name of PACIFIC, being new to the Spaniards, they were not at firft apprifed, that while they were abroad enjoying the fweetnefs of the refrefhing air at land, the natives were employed in ftripping the fhips of their iron, and whatever elfe was portable. It was in vain to punifh the delinquents, for where all were culpable thofe only could be made to fuffer, who were taken in the fact; and fuch was their dexterity that few were detected.

From thefe iflands, to which he gave the name of Ladrones, Magellan haftened his departure, and proceeding in fearch of the Maluccas, the chief object of his voyage, he found in his way many little iflands, where he was hofpitably received, and where a friendly correfpondence was eftablifhed, by which mutual civilities and mutual benefactions were reciprocally interchanged.

Thefe iflands were fituated between the Ladrones, and what are now known by the name of the Philippines, in one of which, named Nathan, Magellan, with 60 men, encountering a whole army, was firft wounded with a poifoned arrow, and then pierced with a bearded lance. His little fquadron, now reduced to two fhips, and not more than 80 men, departed haftily,

and

and after many difasters, in which only one, the Victory, escaped, she singly returned by the Cape of Good Hope, and was the first ship that ever went round the world. It may not be improper here to remark, that the death of our late gallant Commander Cook was not un-fimilar to that of Magellan, both originating from an over-confidence in their own confe-quences, which could avail them nothing when overpowered by numbers.

Other adventurers were not now wanting to trace the steps that had been pointed out by this intrepid Navigator; but we may venture to affert, that they were not all actuated by the fame paffion for glory; the hope of gain was their prevailing motive.

Alvarez de Mendamo, indeed, in 1567, was fent from Lima on purpofe for difcovery; he failed 800 leagues weftward from the coaft of Peru, and fell in with certain iflands in 11 de-grees fouth, inhabited by people of a yellowish colour, whose weapons were bows and arrows, and darts, and whose bodies were naked, but ftrangely punctuated. Here the Spaniards found hogs and little dogs, and fome domeftic fowls like thofe in Europe; and here likewife they found cloves, ginger, cinnamon, and fome gold, but it has yet been a queftion undecided to what groupe of iflands this difcovery is to be placed; for it is faid, that the Spaniards, *not feeking gold*, brought home, notwithftanding

40,000

40,000 pezoes [dollars] befides great ftore of cloves, ginger, and fome cinnamon ; none of which have yet been difcovered in the tropical iflands in the pacific fea. Capt. Cook inclines to the opinion, that they are the clufter which comprizes what has fince been called New Britain, &c.

Afterwards Mendamo difcovered the Archipelago of iflands, called the Iflands of Sólomon, of which great and fmall he counted thirty-three. He alfo difcovered the ifland of St. Chriftoval, in 1575, not far from the above Archipelago, in 7 deg. fouth, 110 leagues in circuit.

Sir Francis Drake in 1577, was the firft Englifhman that paffed the Streights already defcribed, and though his views were not the moft honourable, nor founded upon principles that could be ftrictly juftified, yet his difcoveries were no lefs important than if patronifed by his fovereign, and encouraged by the higheft authority. He difcovered the Ifland of California, which he named New Albion, having failed to the 43d deg. of northern latitude, with a defign to return by a north-eaft courfe, but was ftopt in his progrefs by the piercing cold. Other fmall iflands he difcovered in his route ; but as his fole view was to return with his booty, he paid no regard to objects of lefs concern. He arrived in England by the Cape of Good Hope, in 1580.

To

To him succeeded Sir Thomas Cavendish, who likewise passed the Streights of Magellan in 1586, and returned nearly by the same route pointed out by his predecessor, touching at the Ladrones, and making some stay at the Philippine Isles, of which on his return he gave an entertaining description.

In the mean time, namely in 1595, the Spaniards, intent upon discovery more than plunder, fitted out four ships, and gave the command to Alvaro Mendana de Neyra. This voyage proved unfortunate. The design was to have compleated the discovery of the Solomon islands, and to have made a settlement in one of the most plentiful. But most of those who embarked on this expedition either died miserably or were shipwrecked. His discoveries were the Marquesas, in lat. 10 south. Solitary Island, in 10 deg. 40 min. S. long. 178 deg. And lastly Santa Cruz, on which one of the fleet was afterwards found with all her sails set, and the people rotten. Soon after this miscarriage, it was resolved by the Spanish Court not to settle those islands, lest the English and other foreign adventurers, who might pass the Streights should in their passage home by the East-Indies be relieved by them. This resolution, however, we find soon after revoked in favour of Quiros.

In 1598, Oliver Van Noort passed the Straits; but his professed design being plunder, he made no discoveries. He touched to refresh, at one

of

of the Ladrone iflands, in his way to the Eaft-Indies, and afterwards refitted his fhips at the Philippines. It may here be neceffary to note, that in this year the Sebaldine iflands were difcovered by Sebald de Weert, the fame now known by the name of Falkland's Ifles.

In 1605, Pedro Fernando de Quiros, conceived the defign of difcovering a fouthern continent. He is fuppofed by Mr. Dalrymple and others, to have been the firft into whofe mind the exiftence of fuch a continent had ever entered. He failed from Calloa December 21ft, with two fhips and a tender. Luis Paz de Torres was entrufted with the command, and Quiros, from zeal for the fuccefs of the undertaking, was contented to act in the inferior ftation of pilot.

On the 21ft of December, the fame year, he fet fail from Caloa, and on the 26th of January following, they came in fight of a fmall flat ifland, about four leagues in circumference, with fome trees, but to all appearance uninhabited. It was juft 1000 leagues from Calloa, and in the 25th deg. S.

Finding it inacceffible, they purfued their voyage, and in two days fell in with another ifland, which Capt. Cook fuppofes the fame difcovered by Capt. Carteret, and by him called Pitcairn's Ifland.

On the 4th of February they difcovered an ifland, thirty leagues in circumference, that promifed

B 4   mifed

mifed fair to fupply their neceffities, which
now began to be very preffing; but this, like
the former, could not be approached. This
ifland, fituated in lat. 28. S. feemed to determine their courfe to the South; for on the
9th of February we find them in 18th deg.
South, and on the 12th in 17 deg. 10 min. in
conference with the inhabitants of a friendly
ifland, from whence with difficulty, they procured fome refrefhment, and on the 14th, continued their courfe. On the 21ft they difcovered an ifland, where they found plenty of
fifh but no water. It was uninhabited, and the
birds fo tame that they caught them with their
hands. They named this ifland St. Bernardo,
and is probably the fame which Capt. Carteret
calls the Ifland of Danger, in lat. 10 deg.
30 min. S.

The next ifland difcovered, they called Ifla
de la Gente Hermofa, or the Ifle of handfome
people. From thence they fteered for Santa
Cruz, already difcovered, where they were
kindly received; but could not leave it without
quarrelling with, and murdering fome of the
innocent inhabitants.

From this ifland they fteered their courfe
weftward, paffing feveral ftraggling iflands, till
they arrived on the 7th of April, at an ifland,
which by its high and black appearance, they
judged a Vulcano. Here they found a friendly reception, and in return carried off four of
their

their people, three of whom afterwards made their escape by watching their opportunity and jumping into the sea, the fourth accompanied them to New Spain. This island the Indians called Taumaco. Another island in 12 deg. S. named Tucopia, they passed, after some friendly intercourse with the inhabitants, and on the 25th of April, came in sight of an island which they named Nostra Signora de la Luz, in 14 deg. S. and presently after observed four other islands, one of which presented a most picturesque appearance, diversified with every beauty which Nature could display; rivers, pools of water, cascades, and every grace to decorate and dignify the prospect. Here the inhabitants were frank, as their country was abundant; but here the Spaniards could not help discovering their natural jealousy. The first who approached their boat, was a youth of graceful stature, him they thought to have secured by slyly throwing a chaim about his leg; but this the Indian snapt, and instantly made his escape, by jumping over-board; the next who came on board, they placed in the stocks, lest he too should make his escape in the same manner. Could it be wondered therefore, that the friends of these imprisoned youths should endeavour by fair appearances, to ensnare their enemies, and seek revenge. Making signs of peace, the Spaniards no sooner came within their reach than they let fly a volley of poisoned

arrows,

arrows, by which feveral of their company was wounded. Interpreting this as an act of treachery, without attending to the caufe that had produced it, they quitted the ifland in the night, and directing their courfe to the South-Weft, came in fight of an immenfe country, which had every appearance of the continent of which they were in fearch. They perceived an open bay, and on the beach, men of a gigantic fize, to which they made their approaches with inexpreffible joy, imagining that they had accomplifhed their wifhes, and that their labours would foon be rewarded with honour to themfelves, and advantage to their country.

On the 3d of May, they entered the harbour, having the day before given the name of St. Philip and St. James to the *bay*, with the fair appearance of which, they had been fo highly delighted. To the *port* they gave the name of La Vera Cruz, and to the *country* Austral del Esperita Santo. The harbour, fituated between two rivers, to which they gave the names of Jurdan and Salvador, was equally convenient and beautiful; the margin of the fhores was moft romantically interfperfed with flowers and plants odoriferous and fplendid; nor was the country lefs fruitful than it was pleafant. It abounded in all thofe delicious fruits which render the countries between the Tropics the happieft in the world; and there were befides great plenty of hogs, dogs, fowls

and

and birds of various kinds and colours. The inhabitants, indeed, were jealous of their approach ; and difcovered great uneafinefs at their attempting to land. The Spaniards, however, rather chufing to intimidate than conciliate the natives, made an excurfion into the country, furprized the unfufpecting people of a little village, and brought off a fupply of hogs ; but not without imminent danger to the party employed on that fervice, who were purfued to the waters edge, and fome of them wounded.

As Nature had dealt her bounty with a liberal hand to the inhabitants of this happy country, fhe had enriched her coafts with fifh as well as her land with fruits. In purfuit of the former, the Spaniards met with no interruption, but their fuccefs, which was very great, had like to have proved fatal to them. They caught large quantities of a moft beautiful fifh, which, though of a delicate flavour, was of fo poifonous a quality, that whoever eat of it was fuddenly feized with ficknefs and pain, for which there appeared no remedy. Every foldier and every failor was grievoufly affected ; the whole fhips companies were rendered incapable of their duty, and officers and people were alike alarmed with the apprehenfions of approaching death, till by degrees, the violence of the diforder began to abate, and in fix days all were reftored. It is worthy of note, that fome of the crew of the Refolution, in Capt. Cook's former voyage, who

had

had eaten of this fiſh, were ſeized in the ſame manner, and that ſome hogs and dogs, that had eaten the entrails and the bones actually died.

Quiros, for what reaſon does not appear, very ſoon quitted this *promiſed land*, and the two ſhips ſeparated as ſoon as they cleared the bay; Quiros with the Capitana, his own ſhip, ſhaped his courſe to the N E; and after ſuffering the greateſt hardſhips, returned to New Spain, while de Torres, in the Almiranta and the Tender, ſteered to the Weſt, and was, as Captain Cook obſerves, the firſt that ſailed between New Holland and New Guinea.

Quiros, ſoon after his return, preſented a Memorial to Philip II. of Spain, in which he enumerates twenty-three iſlands that he had diſcovered, namely, La Encarnacion, St. Juan-Bautiſta, Santelmo, Los 4 Coronades. St. Miguel Archangel, La Converſion de St. Paulo, La Dezena, La Sagitaria, La Fugitiva, La del Peregrino, Noſtra Signora del Soccoro, Monterey, Tucopia, St. Marcos, El Vergel, Laz Lagrimas De St. Pedro, Los Portales de Belen, El Pilar de Zaragoza, St. Raymunda, and La Iſla de la Virgin Maria, and adjoining to it the three parts of the country called Auſtralia del Eſpiritu Santo in which land were found the Bay of St. Philip and St. Jago, and part of Vera Cruz, where he remained with the three ſhips thirty-ſix days.

As

As this Memorial is very curious, and but in few hands, an extract from it, we are per-fuaded, will be highly acceptable to the intelligent reader.

" It is conceived," fays Queros, " that the three parts, laft mentioned, are only one large country, and that the river Jurdan, by its great-nefs, feems to confirm this conjecture, as is evident by an information made at Mexico, with ten witneffes of thofe who were with me, to which I refer.

" I further fay, Sir, that in an ifland named Taumaco, 1250 leagues diftant from Mexico, we continued at anchor ten days, and that the Lord of that ifland, whofe name is Tumay, a fenfible man, well made, of good prefence, and in complexion fomewhat brown, with beautiful eyes, fharp nofe, beard and hair long and curled, and in his manner grave; affifted us with his people to get wood and water, of which we were then in great want.

" This perfon came on board the fhip, and in it I examined him in the following manner :

" Firft, I fhewed him his ifland in the fea, and our fhips and people ; and pointed to all parts of the horizon, and made certain other figns, and by them afked him, if he had feen fhips and men like ours, and to this he replied, *No.*

" I afked him, if he knew of other lands far or near, inhabited or uninhabited ? and as foon as he underftood me, he named above 60 iflands,

iflands, and a large country, which he called
Manicolo. I, Sir, wrote down all ; having before me the compafs to know in what direction
each lay ; which were found to be from this
ifland to the S E ; S S E ; W; and N W. And
to explain which was fmall, he made fmall
circles ; and for the larger, he made larger
circles ; and for that vaft country he opened
both his arms, without joining them again,
fhewing that it extended without end. And to
make known which were the diftant, and which
were near, he pointed to the fun from E to W.
reclined the head on one hand, fhut his eyes,
and counted by his fingers the nights which
they flept on the way ; and by figns fhewed
which people were white, negroes and mulattoes, and which were friends and which enemies ; and that in fome iflands they eat human
flefh ; and by this he made figns by biting his
arm. And by this, and by means of other figns,
what he faid was underftood ; and it was repeated fo often that he feemed to be tired ; and
pointing with his hand to S. S. E. and other
points, gave them fully to underftand what
other lands there were. He fhewed a defire of
returning to his houfe. I gave him things that
he could carry, and he took leave, faluting me
on the cheek, with other marks of affection.

" Next day I went to his town, and to be better confirmed of what Tumay declared, I carried with me many Indians to the fhore, and
having

having a paper in my hand, and the compafs before me, afked all of them many times about the lands, of which Tumay gave the names; and in every thing all of them agreed, and gave information of others inhabited, all by people of the colours before mentioned; and alfo of that Great Country, wherein by proper figns, they faid, there were cows or buffaloes; and to make it underftood there were dogs, they barked; and for cocks and hens they crowed, and for hogs grunted: and in this manner they told what they wanted, and replied to whatever they afked. And becaufe they were fhewed pearls in the top of a rofary, they intimated that they had fuch. All thefe queftions and enquiries others of my companions made this day and other times of thefe and other Indians; and they always faid the fame; from whence it appeared they were people who fpeak truth.

"When I failed from this ifland of Taumaco I made them feize four very likely Indians; three of them fwam away; and the one who remained, and was afterwards named Pedro, declared at Acapulco, in the voyage, and in the city of Mexico, where he died, in prefence of the Marquis de Montefclaros, what follows:

"Firft, Pedro faid, that he was a native of the Ifland Chicayana, larger than that of Taumaco, where we found him; and that from one to the other is four days fail of their veffels; and that Chicayana is low land, very abundant in fruit,

and

and that the natives of it are of his good Indian colour, long lank hair ; and they punctuate themselves, as he was, a little in the face, arms, and breaft ; and that there are alfo white people, who have their hair red and very long ; and that there are mulattoes whofe hair is not curled, nor quite ftrait ; and that he was a weaver and a foldier-archer ; and that in his tongue he was called Luca, his wife Layna, and his fon Ley.

" He further faid, that from the ifland of Taumaco, at three days fail, and at two from Chicayana, there is another ifland, larger than the two above-mentioned, which is called Guaytopo, inhabited by people as white as ours are in common ; and that even fome of the men have red hair more or lefs, and alfo black ; and that they alfo punctuate their bellies, and at the navel, all in a circle ; and that all the three iflands are friends, and of one language ; that from this laft ifland a fhip, with more than fifty perfons, failed to another inhabited ifland, named Mecayrayla, to feek tortoife-fhell, of which they ufe to make ear-rings and other toys ; that being in fight of it, they met a contrary wind, which obliged them to fteer for their own ifland ; but when near it, the wind again became contrary ; and that in going backwards and forwards they fpent all their provifions, for want whereof forty perfons died of hunger and thirft ; and that he was in the

Ifland

Ifland Taumaco, where this fhip arrived there with only feven men, who were very white, except one who was brown; and with three women, white and beautiful as Spanifh, who had their hair red and very long; and that all three came covered from head to foot with a kind of veil, blue or black, and very fine, to which they gave the name of Foa-foa; and that of all thefe ten perfons only remained alive the Indian Olan, who related to him what he had faid of that ifland GUAYTOPO. And that he alfo faw come to his Ifland Chicayana, another fhip of theirs of two hulls full of people, white and beautiful, and with many very handfome girls; and counting on his fingers by ten and ten, he intimated they were in all 110 perfons.

" He farther faid, that from another ifland called Tucopia, (which is where the two Indians fwam away,) at the diftance of five days of their failing, is that great country, Manicolo, inhabited by many people, dun-coloured and mulattoes, in large towns; and to explain their fize, he pointed out Acapulco, and others larger; and on this, I afked him if there were towns as large as Mexico. He replied, *No*; but many people: and that they were friendly, and did not eat human flefh; nor could their languages be underftood; and that it was a country of very high mountains and large rivers: fome of them they could not ford, and could only pafs in canoes; and that to go from the ifland of

C   Tucopia,

Tucopia, to that country when the sun rises, they keep it on the left hand, which must be from South towards South East.

" I must add, that if this is as he says, it agrees well with the chain of mountains seen running to the Westward as we were driving about.

" Pedro much extolled the magnitude, populousness, fertility, and other things of this country; and that he and other Indians went to it in one of their embarkations, in quest of the trunk of a large tree of the many which are in it, to make a Piragua; and that he saw there a port, and intimated it was larger, but the entrance narrower, than that of the Bay of St. Philip and St. Jago; and that he observed the bottom was sand, and the shore shingles as the other I have described; and that it has within it four rivers, and many people; and that along the coast of that country they went to the Westward a greater way than from Acapulco to Mexico, without seeing the end of it, and returned to his island.

" By all that is above-mentioned, it appears clearly that there are only two large portions of the earth severed from this of Europe, Africa, and Asia. The first is America, which CHRISTOPHER COLON (Columbus) discovered; the second and last of the world is that which I have seen, and solicit to people, and completely to discover to your Majesty. This great object ought to be embraced, as well for what it promises mifes for the fervice of God, as that it will give a beginning to fo great a work, and to fo many and fo eminent benefits, that no other of its kind can be more, nor fo much at prefent nor heretofore as I can fhew, if I can be heard and queftioned."

Upon the authority of this Memorial, and others to the like purport, prefented by Quiros to Philip III. of Spain, future geographers have grounded their opinion of the reality of a Southern Continent, to the difcovery of which that vain Navigator boldly afferted an undoubted claim. "The magnitude of the countries " newly difcovered," fays he to his Sovereign, " by what I faw, is as much as that of all Eu- " rope, Afia Minor, the Cafpian Sea, and Per- " fia, with all the Mediterranean included." That an affertion like this fhould gain credit, at a time when nearly one quarter of the globe lay undifcovered, is not to be wondered ; but that a man could be found, upon fuch flender ground as the difcovery of a few infignificant iflands, lying, as it has lately appeared, within the narrow limits of fix degrees of latitude, and lefs of longitude; to impofe upon an enlightened Prince, and engage the attention of men of learning in every country throughout the globe, is matter of aftonifhment that, like other myfteries when they come to be difclofed, furprife only by their infignificance.

To this ideal object, however, every mari-

time

time power caft a jealous eye. No fooner was France apprifed of the intentions of the Britifh Court, to engage in earneft in the bufinefs of difcovery, than fhe fent a Navigator of her own to purfue the fame tract, who was foon after followed by another on the part of Spain. As the fuccefs which attended thefe firft enterprifes by no means anfwered the expectations of thofe by whom they were fet on foot, the two latter courts, who had profit only for their object, relinquifhed the project when they found themfelves difappointed in fharing the prize. The perfeverance of our amiable Sovereign, in the profecution of his liberal defigns, as it has enlightened, fo it has infpired every lover of Science at home and abroad, with a reverential regard for his priucely virtues, in promoting and patronifing ufeful arts. But to return.

In 1614, George Spitzbergen, with a ftrong fquadron of Dutch fhips, paffed the Streights of Magellan, and after cruizing for fome time with various fuccefs againft the Spaniards, fet fail from Port Nativity on the coaft of Peru, on his return home. In his paffage, in 19 deg. of North lat. and about 30 longit. from the Continent, he difcovered a mighty rock, and three days after, a new ifland with five hills, neither of which have fince been feen. The firft land he made was the Ladrones, already defcribed.

In 1615, *Schouten* and *Le Maire*, in the Unity of 360 tons, and the Hoorn of 110, failed from the Texel on the 14th of June, profeffedly for

the

the difcovery of a new paffage to the South Seas.
The fubjects of the States of Holland being
prohibited, by an exclufive charter to the Eaft-
India Company, from trading either to the
Eaftward by the Cape of Good Hope, or to the
Weftward by the Magelanic ftreights, fome
private merchants, confidering this prohibition
as a hardfhip, determined, if poffible, to trade
to the Southern countries by a tract never before
attempted. With this view they fitted out the
fhips already mentioned, one of which, the
Hoorn, was burnt in careening, at King's Ifland
on the coaft of Brazil, and the other left fingly
to purfue her voyage. Having faved what
ftores they could refcue from the flames, they
proceeded, directing their courfe to the South
Weft, till in lat. 54 deg. 46 min. they came in
fight of an opening, to which (having happily
paffed it) they gave the name of *Strait le Maire*
in compliment to the principal projector of
the voyage, though that honour was certainly
due to Schouten, who had the direction of the
fhip. Having foon after weathered the fouthernmoft point of the American Continent, they
called that promontary Cape Horne, or more
properly Hoorn, after the town in Holland
where the project was firft fecretly concerted ;
and two iflands which they had paffed, they
named Bernevelt Ifles. They had no fooner
cleared the land, than they changed their courfe

to

to the Northward, with a view to make some stay at Juan Fernandes to refit; but finding both islands inaccessible, by reason of the great swell, they were obliged to continue their voyage till a more favourable opportunity should offer to refresh the crew. The first land they made was a new discovery in lat. 15 degrees, 15 min. long. 136 deg. 30 min. W. and happened to be a small low island, which afforded them no other refreshment, except a scanty portion of scurvy-grass, but no water. They named this Dog Island, from a singular circumstance of finding in it dumb dogs that could neither bark nor snarl. About seven degrees further west, they fell in with another island, which they called *Sondre Ground*, because they sounded, but found no bottom. Still continuing their course to the Westward, they came to an island, to which they gave the name of *Waterland*, as it afforded them a fresh supply of water, of which they stood in much need. They likewise procured plenty of fresh herbs; but not being able to come to an anchor, they kept their course, and soon came in sight of a fourth island, in which they could perceive a stream of water, but, like the other islands which they had passed, it seemed difficult of access. They hoisted out their boat, and filled it with empty casks; but instead of water, the people in it returned covered with insects, which, though not so large as Musketoes,

Mufketoes, were by their numbers and their venom a thoufand times more troublefome. Such fwarms came from the fhore as covered the fhip as with a cafe, and it was more than three days before the crew could free themfelves and the veffel from thefe tormentors. This they named *Fly Ifland*.

In their courfe from this ifland an incident happened that is a reproach to humanity; an Indian bark fell in their way, to which, inftead of making fignals of peace to conciliate them, they fired a gun to bring them to. The bark was full of people male and female, who, frighted at the report, inftead of gueffing the intent, haftened to make their efcape. Prefently the pinnace was hoifted out, manned, and a purfuit commenced; the unhappy Indians, finding it in vain to fly, feveral being wounded in their flight, rather chofe to perifh in the o-cean, than truft to the mercy of their purfuers; moft of the men, juft as the Dutchmen were about to board their bark, jumped over-board, and with them they took their provifions; thofe who remained, chiefly women and children, and fuch as were wounded, fubmitted, and were kindly ufed, had their wounds dreffed and re-ftored to their bark; but furely nothing could excufe the brutal proceedings of the Dutch at their firft onfet, nor compenfate for the lives of the innocent fufferers.

Cocos

Cocos and *Traitors Islands* were the next they fell in with in their run from Fly Island. These were adjoining islands, and seemed to be composed of one people, and by joining cordially together to revenge the death of their unfortunate friends, they appear to have been of one mind. The Voyagers now began to feel distress, and to repent of their rash adventure; they held a consultation in what manner to proceed, being in want of almost every necessary. Fortune, however, did more in their favour than their own prowess; for after having passed the Island of *Hope*, (so called to express their feelings) where they were very roughly received, they arrived at a most delightful island, abounding with every blessing that nature could bestow; and inhabited by a people who seemed sensible of their own happy state, and ready to share with those who were in want of the good things which they themselves possessed, and which they so generously bestowed even to profusion. Here the Voyagers refitted their ships, recovered their sick, recruited their almost exhausted stock of provisions, by a plentiful supply of hogs, and with as large quantities of the delicious fruits with which the island was stored, as they could conveniently stowe. This proving a second home to them, they gave it the name of *Hoorn Island*, for the very reason already assigned. It is situated in lat. 14 deg. 56 min. South, long. 179 deg. 30 min. East, and

and in every refpect refembles the ifland of Otaheite, except in its naval ftrength, in which there is no competition.

Being now plentifully relieved, and the crew in high health, and having no hope of difcovering the Continent of which they came in fearch, they determined to return home by the neareft

k   tract : accordingly they altered their courfe to the North Weft, till they approached the line, and paffing many iflands, to which they gave names, as appearances or circumftances prefented, as Green Ifland, St. John's Ifland, &c. they coafted the North fide of New Britain, and arrived at Bantham, in the Eaft Indies, where their fhip was feized, and their cargo confifcated at the inftance of the Dutch Eaft-India Company, under pretence of being engaged in contraband trade. It is remarkable that hitherto they had only loft four men, one of whom died on their landing.

In 1623, Prince Maurice and the States of Holland, fitted out a fleet to diftrefs the Spaniards in the South Seas, and gave the command to Jaques Hermite : but as thefe returned by a direct courfe from Lima to the Ladrones, without making any difcoveries in what is called the Pacific Sea, it would be foreign to the defign of this Introduction to detain the reader by an unneceffary digreffion.

In 1642, Abel Tafman failed from Batavia in the Heemfkirk, accompanied by the Zee

Haan

Haan pink, with a profeffed defign of difcovering the Southern Continent. He directed his courfe to the Mauritius, and from thence, fteering to the Southward, the firft land he made was the Eaftern point of New Holland, fince known by the name of Van Dieman's Land, in lat. 42 deg. 25 min. long. 163 deg. 50 min. In this high latitude he proceeded to the Eaftward, till he fell in with the Wefternmoft coaft of New Zealand, where the greateft part of the boat's crew of the Zee Haan were murdered by the Savages in a bay, to which he gave the name of *Murderer's Bay*, now better known by that of Charlotte's Sound, fo called by our late Navigators. From Murderer's Bay, he fteered E. N. E. till he arrived at Three Kings Ifland, between which and the Continent he paffed, and run to the Eaftward, as far as the 220th degree of longitude; then turning to the Northward, till he came into the 17th degree of Southern latitude, he veered again to the Weftward, with a defign to reach Hoorn Ifland, difcovered by Schouten, in order to refit his fhip, and refrefh his men. But in his paffage he fell in with the ifles of Pylftaert, Amfterdam, Middleburg, and Rotterdam, at the latter of which iflands he found every accommodation which he expected to meet with at Hoorn Ifland, and embraced the prefent opportunity of fupplying his wants. This neceffary end accomplifhed, he relinquifhed his de-

fign

sign of visiting Traitors and Hoorn Islands, and directing his course to the N W; discovered eighteen or twenty small islands, in lat. 17 deg. 19 min. S. and long. 201 deg. 35 min. to which he gave the name of Prince William's Islands, and Hemskirk's banks. From thence pursued his course to New Guinea, without either discovering the continent he sought, or visiting the Solomon Isles, which were judged the key to the grand discovery. Thus leaving the whole in the same state of uncertainty as before, Tasman returned to Batavia on the 15th of June 1643.

In 1681, Dampier passed the Magellanic Straits; but in his return sailed 5975 miles in lat. 13 N. without seeing fish, fowl, or any living creature but what they had on board.

Next to him succeeded in 1683, Captain Cowley, who sailed from Virginia to the South Sea, but made no discoveries after he left the Western coasts of America; returning by the old tract to the East-Indies.

In 1699, Dampier made a second voyage on discovery, which was chiefly confined to New Holland, New Guinea, New Britain, and the islands adjacent. His discoveries were of infinite importance, but do not properly come within the limits of our enquiry.

In 1703, Dampier made a third voyage to the South Seas, but without making any new discoveries. He was accompanied in this voyage,

voyage, by Mr. Funnel to whom the circum-navigation of the globe is afcribed.

In 1708, the Duke and Duchefs failed from Briftol to the South Seas; but returned as all the Freebooters did, by the common tract.

In 1719, Captain Clipperton paffed the Straits with a view to enrich his owners by the fpoil of the Spaniards. He returned likewife through the Ladrone Iflands, confequently could make no difcoveries in the Pacific Seas.

In 1721, the Dutch Eaft-India Company, at the inftance of Captain Roggewein, fitted out a refpectable fleet, for the difcovery of that con-tinent, which lay hitherto undifcovered, though univerfally believed to exift. Three ftout fhips were appointed, and well provided for this fervice; the Eagle of 36 guns and 111 men, on board of which embarked Roggewein as Commodore, having under him Capt. Cofter, an experienced navigator; the Tienhoven of 28 guns, and 100 men, of which Capt. Bowman was commander; and the African Galley, com-manded by Capt. Rofenthall. From this voyage every thing was hoped. The equipment of the fhips, the appointment of the commanders, and above all, the hereditary zeal of the Com-modore which he inherited from his father, for the fervice, all contributed to raife the expecta-tions of Europe to the higheft pitch. Before they arrived at the Straits of Magellan, they had encountered the moft boifterous feas, and endured

endured the moſt intolerable hardſhips. They had ſooner entered the Straits, than they were again attacked by tempeſtuous weather; the ſtorm was ſcarce abated, when they were alarmed by the ſight of a veſſel, which they took either for a pirate or a Spaniſh ſhip of war, and as ſhe ſeemed to approach very faſt, were preparing for an engagement, when, to their agreeable ſurprize, they diſcovered it to be the Tienhoven's ſhallop, on board of which was Capt. Bowman, who had been ſeparated three months before, and it was concluded had been engulphed in the hurricane that happened when the Tienhoven loſt her main-top and mizen-maſts, and the Eagle her mainſail-yard. They mutually rejoiced at each others eſcape. Capt. Bowman thought they had periſhed in the ſtorm, and they had given him over for loſt. But their joy was of ſhort continuance; they had other dangers to encounter, and other hardſhips to undergo; they found the Magelanic Straits impracticable, and entered the Southern Ocean with difficulty, by the Strait le Maire. After recruiting their water at the Iſles of Fernandez, their firſt attempt was in ſearch of Davis's Land; which, it was imagined, from the deſcription given by the diſcoverer, would prove an Index to the continent of which they were in ſearch. They miſſed it where they expected to find it, but accident threw it in their way. It proved a ſmall iſland which they thought a new diſcovery, and

and becaufe they fell in with it on Eafter-day, they called it *Pafch*. We have juft to remark of this ifland, that as it was then full of people, and but few feen when laft explored, and among them only FIFTEEN women, it is more than probable that in lefs than another century, the whole ifland will be depopulated. From this ifland Raggewein purfued nearly the fame tract with that which Schuten had pointed out, till veering more to the North, he fell in with the iflands at which Commodore Byron firft landed, and where fome of the wreck of the African Galley was actually found. Here five of the crew deferted, and were left behind; and it would have been an object of curious enquiry for the Naturalifts who accompanied that voyage, to have endeavoured to trace a fimilitude of European features among the inhabitants of George's Ifland, as there is reafon to believe *that* to be the ifland on which the five Dutchmen chofe to fix their refidence. This ifland, which they place in the 15th degree of Southern latitude, they named Mifchievous Ifland, owing to their late difafter.

Eight leagues to the Weft of this ifland, they difcovered another, to which they gave the name of Aurora, from its fplendid appearance, gilded by the rays of the rifing fun. Another ifland difcovered in the evening of the fame day, they called *Vefper*. Purfuing their courfe to the Weftward, they difcovered a clufter of iflands,

iflands, undoubtedly the fame now called the *Friendly Ifles*, to which they gave the name of the Labyrinth, becaufe it was with difficulty they could clear them.

In a very few days fail after paffing the Labyrinth, they came in fight of a pleafant ifland, to which, from its fair appearance, they gave the name of the *Ifland of Recreation*. They were at firft hofpitably received; but in the end the natives endeavoured to furprize them by ftratagem, and to cut them off. They had fupplied the ftrangers with provifions, water, and wood, and they had affifted them in gathering greens, and in conveying them to the fhips; but one day feeing a party of them unarmed, and walking carelefly the field, charmed with the delights of the country, in a moment fome thoufands of the natives rufhed fuddenly upon them, and with fhowers of ftones, began an affault. The Dutch, from the fhips obferving a tumult, and fufpecting the worft, came haftily to the fupport of their comrades, when a general engagement enfued, in which many natives were fhot dead, fome of the Dutchmen killed, and not a few wounded. This proved baneful to the voyage. Few of the crews of either fhip, after this, would venture to go afhore for pleafure; moft of them became difcontented, and fome mutinous. It was therefore concluded at a general council of officers, to continue their courfe towards New Britain and New Guinea; and thence by the way of the Moluccas to the Eaſt Indies, which was accordingly carried into execution: and thus ended, like all the former, a voyage which was expected at leaſt to have ſolved the queſtion; but in fact it determined nothing. They who argued from the harmony that is obſervable in the works of Nature, inſiſted that ſomething was wanting to give one ſide of the globe a reſemblance to the other; while thoſe who reaſoned from experience, pronounced the whole ſyſtem the creature of a fertile brain.

In 1738, Lozier Bouvet was ſent by the French Eaſt-India Company, upon diſcovery in the South Atlantic Ocean. He ſailed from Port Le Orient on the 19th of July, on board the Eagle, accompanied by the Mary, and on the 1ſt of January following, he diſcovered, or thought he diſcovered land in lat 54 degrees South, long. 11 min. Eaſt. But this land being diligently ſought for by Capt. Cook, in his voyage for the diſcovery of the Southern Continent in 177 , without effect, there is reaſon to doubt if any ſuch land exiſts; or, if it does it is too remote from any known tract to be of uſe to trade or navigation. Bouvet purſued his courſe to the Eaſtward, in a high latitude, about 29 degrees farther, when in lat. 51 deg. South, the two ſhips parted, one going to the iſland of Mauritius, the other returning to France.

In 1742, Commodore Anſon traverſed the Great Pacific Ocean; but his buſineſs being
war,

war, he made no difcoveries within the limits
of our Review ; and his ftory is too well known
to need recapitulation.

Come we now to the Æra when his Majefty
formed the defign of making difcoveries, and
exploring the Southern Hemifphere, and when
in the year 1764, he directed it to be carried
into execution.

" Accordingly Commodore Byron having under his command the Dolphin and Tamar, failed
from the Downs on the 21ft of June the fame
year, and having vifited the Falkland Iflands,
paffed through the Streights of Magellan into
the Pacific Ocean, where he difcovered the
Iflands of Difappointment, George's, Prince of
Wales's, the Ifles of Danger, York and Byron's
Iflands. He returned to England the 9th of
May 1766.

" And in the month of Auguft following,
the Dolphin was again fent out under the command of Captain Wallis, with the Swallow,
commanded by Capt. Carteret.

" They proceeded together, till they came to
the Weft end of the Streights of Magellan, and
in fight of the Great South Sea, where they
were feparated.

" Captain Wallis directed his courfe more
wefterly than any Navigator had done before
him in fo high a latitude, but met with no land
till he got within the Tropic, where he difcovered the iflands Whitfunday, Queen Charlotte,

D Egmont,

Egmont, Duke of Gloucefter, Duke of Cumberland, Maitea, Otaheite, Eimeo, Tapamanou, Howe, Scilly, Bofcawen, Keppel, and Wallis; and returned to England, May 1768.

" His companion, Captain Carteret, kept a different route, in which he difcovered the iflands Ofnaburg, Gloucefter, Queen Charlotte's Ifles, Carteret's, Gower's, and the Streight between New Britain and New Ireland; and returned to England in 1769.

" In November 1767, Commodore Bougainville failed from France, in the frigate La Boudeufe, with the ftore-fhip l'Etoile. After fpending fome time on the coaft of Brazil, and at Falkland's Iflands, he got into the Pacific Sea by the Streights of Magellan, January 1768.

" In this Ocean he difcovered the four Facardines, the Ifle of Lanciers, and Harpe Ifland, (the fame afterwards named by Cook, Lagoon Ifland) Thrum Cap, and Bow Ifland. About twenty leagues farther to the Weft, he difcovered four other iflands; afterwards fell in with Martea, Otaheite, Ifles of Navigators, and Forlorn Hope, which to him were new difcoveries. He then paffed through between the Hebrides, which he calls the Great Cyclades, difcovered the Shoal of Diana, and fome others; the land of Cape Deliverance, feveral Iflands more to the North; paffed to the North of New Ireland, touched at Batavia, and arrived in France in March 1769.

" In

" In 1769, the Spaniards fent a fhip to trace
the difcoveries of the Englifh and French.
This fhip arrived at Otaheite in 1771, and in
her return difcovered fome iflands, in lat. 32
deg. S. and long. 130 deg. W. This fhip
touched at Eafter Ifland; but whether fhe returned to New or Old Spain remains undecided.

" In 1769, the French fitted out another
fhip from the Mauritius, under the command of
Capt. Kergulen, who, having difcovered fome
barren iflands between the Cape of Good Hope
and Van Dieman's Land, contented himfelf
with leaving fome Memorials there, which were
found by Captain Cook in the voyage which
we are about to narrate.

" This year was rendered remarkable by the
Tranfit of the planet Venus over the Sun's
Difk, a phænomenon of great importance to
Aftronomy, and which every where engaged
the attention of the learned in that Science.

" In the beginning of the year 1768, the
Royal Society prefented a Memorial to his
Majefty, fetting forth the advantages to be derived from accurate obfervations of this Tranfit
in different parts of the world, particularly from
a fet of fuch obfervations made in a Southern
latitude, between the 140th and 180th degrees
of longitude Weft from the Royal Obfervatory
at Greenwich; at the fame time reprefenting, that
veffels, properly equipped, would be neceffary to

convey

convey the obfervers to their deftined ftations; but that the Society were in no condition to defray the expence."

In confequence of this Memorial, the Admiralty were directed by his Majefty to provide proper veffels for that purpofe; and the Endeavour bark was accordingly purchafed, fitted out, and the command given to Capt. Cooke, who had already fignalized himfelf as an experienced Navigator; and Mr. Charles Green the Aftronomer was jointly, with the Captain, appointed to make the obfervations.

Otaheite being the Ifland preferred for the performance of that important fervice, Captain Cooke received orders to proceed directly; and his inftructions were, as foon as the Aftronomical obfervations were completed, to profecute the defign of making difcoveries in the South Pacific Ocean as far as the 40th degree of South latitude; and then, if no land fhould be difcovered, to fhape his courfe between lat. 40 and 35, till he fhould fall in with New Zealand, which he was to explore; and thence to return.

In the profecution of thefe inftructions he failed from Plymouth on the 26th of Auguft, 1768, and on the 13th of April following, arrived at Otaheite, having in his way difcovered Lagoon Ifland, Two Groups, Bird Ifland, and Chain Ifland.

At

At Otaheite he remained three months, and, (befides the Aftronomer Mr. Green), being accompanied by Mr. Banks a gentleman of fortune, and Dr. Solander one of the Librarians of the Britifh Mufeum, eminent both for his knowledge in Natural Hiftory, and in Botany; we have only to remark, that all Europe has already been benefited by the employment of their time.

The obfervations on the Tranfit being compleated with the wifht-for fuccefs, Capt. Cooke proceeded on difcovery; he vifited the Society-Ifles, and difcovered Oheteroa, fell in with the Eaftern coaft of New Zealand, and examined it; thence proceeding to New Holland, he furveyed the Eaftern fide of that vaft continent, which had never before been explored; difcovered the Streight between its Northern extremity and New Guinea; and returned home by Savu, Batavia, the Cape of Good Hope, and St. Helena, arriving in England the 12th of July 1771.

In 1769, Captain Surville made a trading voyage from fome port in the Eaft Indies by a new courfe. He paffed near New Britain, and fell in with fome land in lat. 10 deg. South, longit. 158 deg. Eaft, to which he gave his own name; then fhaping his courfe to the North Eaftward narrowly miffed New Caledonin, put into Doubtful Bay; and from thence fteered to the Eaft, between the latitudes of 35 and 41 deg. South, till he arrived on the

D 3　　　　coaft

coaft of America, a courfe never before navigated; and with that purfued by Captain Furneaux, between 48 and 52 degrees, and that afterwards by Captain Cooke, in a ftill higher latitude, confirms to demonftration the nonexiftence of a Southern Continent.

No fooner was Captain Cooke's voyage compleated, and his Journals examined, than another voyage was projected, the object of which was to compleat the difcovery of the Southern Hemifphere. Very extraordinary preparations were made for the equipment of this voyage, which required fhips of a particular conftruction to perform it, and fuch were purchafed; fome alterations likewife were neceffary in the fpecies of provifions ufual in the navy, and thefe were made. Add to this, that many extra articles were provided, fuch as Malt, Sour Krout, falted Cabbage, portable Soup, Saloup, Muftard, Marmalade, and feveral others, as well for food for convalefcents, as phyfic for the fick.

The fhips judged moft proper for the voyage were built for colliers, two of which were fitted up, and the command given to Captain Cook; the largeft of 562 tons, called the Refolution, had 112 men, officers included; the other, the Adventure of 336 tons, given to Captain Furneaux, fecond in command had only 81. To thefe were added, perfons well fkilled in Natural Hiftory, Aftronomy, Mathematics, and the liberal Arts of Painting, Drawing, &c. &c.

On

On the 13th of July the two ſhips ſailed from Plymouth, after having ſettled the latitude and longitude of the place by obſervation. This they did in order to regulate the time-pieces, of which they had four on board; three made by Mr. Arnold, and one by Mr. Kendal, on Mr. Harriſon's principles.

The great object of the Voyage was to determine to a certainty, the exiſtence or non-exiſtence of a Southern Continent, which, till then, had engaged the attention of moſt of the maritime powers, and about the reality of which Geographers of late ſeemed to have had but one belief.

Let it ſuffice, that this queſtion is at length decided : but before we enter upon the proofs neceſſary to decide that other queſtion, concerning the exiſtence or non-exiſtence of a N. W. or N. E. paſſage, it will be expected, that we ſhould not only lay before the Reader the facts that have appeared in the courſe of the Voyages made in the Pacific Ocean, which we are now about to relate, but thoſe alſo that are to be gathered from the Voyages made in the Atlantic Ocean for the like purpoſe.

Not only Navigators the moſt celebrated in their time, but even philoſophers and coſmographers of the firſt eminence have contended from analogy, that a communication between the Atlantic and great Pacific Ocean muſt exiſt ſomewhere in the Northern Hemiſ-

Hemisphere, in like manner as the same exists by the Straits of Magellan in the Southern Hemisphere; this appeared so certain to the Cabbots, the most renowned Navigators of the 15th century, that the younger Sebastian at the risque of life, proposed the discovery of that passage to Henry the VIIth; and though he failed by the mutiny of his crew, after he had sailed as high as the 68th degree of northern latitude, yet that prince was so well pleased with his endeavours, that he created a new office in his favour, and appointed him grand pilot of England, with a salary of 166 L. a year during life, which at that time was no inconsiderable sum.

He returned by the way of Newfoundland, bringing home with him two Esquimaux.

It was long, however, before a second attempt was made with the professed design of discovering a North-west passage. The attention of the nation was too much fixed on projects towards the South, to attend to any thing that had reference to enterprizes in the North.

Some there were however who held the object in view: and in 1576 Sir Martin Forbisher with 2 small ships attempted the Discovery; and having found a Strait on the Southernmost point of Groenland, through which he sailed about 50 leagues, with high land on both sides, he persuaded himself that he had succeeded in his enterprize; but after repeated trials, finding his error, he gave over the search.

In a few years after Sir Martin, Sir Humphrey Gilbert renewed the hopes of the Discovery by a Voyage to the North, which, tho' it failed in the main point, it proved of infinite advantage to the nation in another. He coasted along the Ameri-

can

can Continent from the 60th degree of Northern Latitude till he fell in with the Gulph of St. Lawrence, which he continued to navigate till he perceived the water to freshen; he then took possession of that vast continent, since called Canada by the French, in the name of his Sovereign; and was the first who projected the fishery in Newfoundland, and who promoted the establishment of it.

In proportion as the commerce to the East increased and became lucrative, the desire of engrossing the trade by shortening the passage thither increased also; thence arose an emulation among the merchants for discovering the passage of which we are speaking. Those in London had concerted a project for that purpose, and those in the West Country had a similar project in contemplation; but neither the one nor the other had managed their designs with so much secresy, but that each got acquainted with the other's intentions. This produced a coalition; both agreed to join in the expence; and both agreed in the appointment of Capt. John Davis, to conduct the Voyage.

In 1585 he embarked on board the Sunshine, a bark of about 60 tons and 23 men, attended by a vessel of 35 tons with 19 men to which he gave the name of the Moon-shine. He sailed from Dartmouth on the 7th of May. The first land he made was an Island near the Southernmost point of Groenland, which, from its horrid appearance, he named the Island of Desolation. In his progress he passed the Strait that still bears his name, and advanced as high as the latitude of 66 in an open sea, the coasts of which he examined till the approach of winter

ter obliged him to return, with every hope, however, of succeeding another year. On his arrival, his employers were so well pleased with the relation he gave and the progress he had made, that they next year augmented his force, and sent him out with four vessels, one of which, the Mermaid, of 120 tons burthen, he commanded himself, and the other three, (the Sun-shine, Moon-shine, and the North star a pinnace of 13 tons only) were furnished with masters of his own recommendation.

On the 7th of May he set sail from Dartmouth, and steered a strait course till he arrived in the 60th degree of latitude, when he divided his fleet, ordering the Sun-shine and North star to direct their search to the north-eastward as far as the 80th degree, N. while he with the Mermaid and Moon-shine should continue their former search to the N. W. where he had already contracted an acquaintance with the inhabitants in his former Voyage, from whom he hoped to receive considerable information. At first they expressed great joy at his return, but they soon shewed the cloven foot. They were fond of iron, and he gave them knives; knives did not content them, they wanted hatchets; when they got hatchets, they cut his cables, and stole one of his coasting anchors, which he never again recovered. He took one of the ring-leaders prisoner, who after some time proved a useful hand; but they surprized five of his men, of whom they killed two, grievously wounded two more, and the fifth made his escape by swimming to the ship with an arrow sticking in his arm. In this voyage he coasted the land, which he found to be an

Island

Island from the 67th to the 57th degree, N. and at length anchored in a fair harbour, eight leagues to the Northward of which he conceived the passage to lie, as a mighty sea was seen rushing between two headlands from the West: Into this sea he ardently wished to have sailed; but the wind and current both opposing his design, he was obliged, by the remonstrances of his people, to relinquish that savage coast, and, as the season was far advanced, to return home. When he arrived he met with the Sun-shine, but the North-star was never seen more.

His misfortunes did not abate his zeal. He was prepossessed with the certainty of a N. W. passage, and he prevailed upon other adventurers, in conjunction with some of his former friends, to enable him to make a third trial, which proved no less unfortunate than those he had attempted before; notwithstanding which, could he have raised friends to have advanced the money, he would have continued his researches till death had put an end to his labours.

These repeated disappointments threw a damp for a while on this favourite pursuit; and it was not till the year 1610, that the former spirit of discovery began to revive.

In that year, Mr. Henry Hudson projected a new course towards the N. W. which brought him to the mouth of the Strait that now bears his name. This he traced till he came into an open sea; but the season being past for making any farther progress at that time, he prevailed upon his crew, by flattering their avarice with the certainty of gain, to winter on that inhospitable coast, though destitute of provisions for a single month. While their provisions
lasted

lasted they were contented; and the tale of riches and glory that had been told them, cherished their hopes; but when famine and cold began to pinch, the ideal prospect vanished, and nothing but murmuring and mutiny succeeded, which ended in the tragical death of the Captain and seven of his sick followers, who, unable to make resistance, were set adrift in the boat, while those who were in better health seized the ship, and made the best of their way home, and on their return gave such an account of the certainty of the passage, as left no room to doubt of the discovery.

Accordingly, the very next year Sir Henry Button undertook the task, and steered directly to the new-discovered sea, in which he sailed more than 200 leagues farther to the S. W. than the Discoverer, wintered at Port Nelson, where he lost near half his men, and returned the next year, roundly asserting the existence of the passage, though he had not been so happy as to find it.

Sir Henry was scarce returned before James Hall and William Baffin set sail, with a view to share the honour of the Discovery.

In this attempt Hall fell by the hands of a savage, and Baffin soon returned, but with a full design to renew his pursuit, whenever he could find an opportunity so to do. This did not happen till the year 1615, when he examined the sea that communicates with Davis's straits, which he found to be no other than a great bay, with an inlet from the north, to which he gave the name of Smith's Sound, lat. 78.

About this time the Hudson's Bay Company was established, who by charter were obliged to pro-

profecute this difcovery, as were likewife thofe mafters of veffels that were employed in the whale fifhery; but neither the one nor the other paid much attention to the chief object of their eftablifhment.

In the year 1631 Luke Fox, commiffioned by king Charles the Firft, made a voyage in fearch of the fame paffage, but to as little purpofe as the reft.

He was followed by Capt. James, who after the moft elaborate fearch from one extremity to the other of the bay, changed his opinion, and declared that no fuch paffage exifted; and it was not till a hundred years after that Capt. Middleton undertook, upon the moft plaufible grounds, and at the inftance and by the recommendation of Arthur Dobbs, Efq; to make another attempt, and perhaps a final one, as the non-exiftence of a north weft paffage thro' Hudfon's Bay was then made almoft as certain as the non exiftence of a fouthern continent is now.

But it was not yet certain, that fuch a paffage might not be found on the weftern fide of America, as there is a remarkable note in Campbell's Voyages, on which that writer, who was a great advocate for the paffage in queftion, lays great ftrefs. He fays, that Capt. Lancafter, of the Dragon (afterwards Sir James) who commanded the firft fleet to the Eaft Indies, having heard a report while there, of another paffage to that country, and being on his return home overtaken by a ftorm, in which the Dragon loft her rudder, and was otherwife in danger of perifhing, yet being unwilling to defert her, he wrote a letter and fent it on board the Hector, to which was added the following P. S. " The paf-

paffage to the Eaft Indies lies in 62 deg. 30 min. by the N. W. on the American fide."—It was therefore to determine this queftion with as much certainty on one fide of America as it had been on the other, that our great naviga-tor was fent out on the late voyage, and it may now be fairly concluded on his examination, ad-ded to thofe of the late and former Spanifh Voyagers, and the Ruffian difcoveries, that no fuch paffage exifts, though it is remarkable, that in the lat. of 61 deg. 15 min. an open found was difcovered, which they traced till they came to a fhallow bay, impracticable for fhipping, into which a deep frefh water river emptied itfelf, with high land on both fides. This river Capt. Cook caufed to be examined with boats, but being more than 50 degrees of long. from the neareft coaft of Hudfon's Bay, there cannot be the leaft fhadow of reafon to fuppofe, that it can have any communication with that fea.

Let us now proceed to the Voyage.

A
VOYAGE,

PERFORMED IN HIS MAJESTY'S SHIP

DISCOVERY,

IN COMPANY WITH THE

RESOLUTION,

CAPTAIN COOK, COMMANDER.

HAVING taken in our guns at the Galleons, and what stores were wanting,

On the 14th of June 1776, both ships came to an anchor at the Nore; but our fresh provisions being nearly exhausted, we weighed next day, and left the Resolution waiting for her commander.

On the 16th, came too off Deal, and received on board a great quantity of beef and mutton for the ship's company, and a boat for the Captain's use. It blew hard in the night and all the next day.

On the 18th we weighed anchor and sailed; but we had no sooner entered the channel than a storm arose, by which we were driven into Portland Roads, where we received considerable damage. We had blowing weather till

The

The 26th, when we arrived at Plymouth. There we found a large fleet of men of war and tranſports with troops on board for America, and ſaluted the Admiral with 11 guns. They had been driven in by ſtreſs of weather, ſeveral of them much damaged. About 12 at noon we came to moorings in the Sound.

On the 30th the Reſolution arrived, ſaluted the Admiral, and came too and moored cloſe by us.

It was now found neceſſary to go into harbour to repair the damages our ſhip had received in the ſtorm of the 18th, and the Reſolution propoſed to wait till we were in readineſs; but it was with difficulty that an order was obtained for the carpenters to proceed, and when it was obtained, it was ſome time before it could be carried into execution. The repairs of the fleet for America being judged of greater conſequence than the repairs of a ſingle ſhip.

The Reſolution tired with delay, when the day came that ſhe ſet ſail on her former voyage, which was

On the 12th of July, the impatience of the ſhip's company, and the notion they had entertained of its being a lucky day, induced Captain Cook to comply with their importunities, and he accordingly ſet ſail, leaving orders with Capt. Clarke to follow him to St. Jago, one of the Cape de Verd Iſlands, and if he ſhould there

miſs

miſs of him, to purſue his courſe directly for the Cape of Good Hope.

This was unwelcome news to the ſhip's company of the Diſcovery, who were equally impatient to be gone, and who were not without their prognoſtics, their omens, and fancies, any more than their neighbours; but neceſſity, that irreſiſtible conqueror, to whoſe power all human paſſions muſt ſubmit, compelled their acquieſcence, though it could not remove their ſcruples.

During this tedious interval of unavoidable delay, a ſuccinct account of Omai, the native of Ulietea, who embarked with Captain Cook on board the Reſolution on his return home, will give thoſe who never ſaw him, ſome idea of his perſon and character. [Since the Writer's return home, he has been able to collect from the writings of the gentlemen, who had the beſt opportunities of knowing and converſing with Omai while in England, their ſentiments reſpecting him, which though not entirely correſponding with his own, (as will be ſeen in the ſequel) yet in juſtice to the public, he thinks it incumbent upon him to conceal nothing that has appeared in his favour. For which reaſon, if in the courſe of the Voyage, a different repreſentation ſhall be found of him, let it be remembered, that what is here ſaid is taken from hear-ſay only; but for what ſhall be ſaid hereafter, the Writer makes himſelf accountable.]

This

This man, it appears, by the teftimony of Captain Cook, had once fome property in his own country, of which he was difpoffeffed by the people of Bolabola.   Captain Cook at firft wondered that Capt. Furneaux would encumber himfelf with fo ordinary a perfon, who was not, in his opinion, a proper fample of the inhabitants of thofe happy iflands ; and Mr. Fofter fays, it is doing him no injuftice to affert, that among all the inhabitants of Otaheite and the Society Ifles, he had feen few individuals fo ill-favoured as Omai ; neither did he feem of eminence in rank or parts, any more than in fhape, figure, or complexion, to attract the notice of an enlightened nation, but feemed, adds Mr. Fofter, to be one of the common people ; and the rather as he did not afpire to the Captain's company, but preferred that of the armourer and common feamen ; yet, notwithftanding the contemptible opinion, which both thefe gentlemen feems to have entertained of him at firft, when he reached the Cape of Good Hope, and the Captain dreffed him in his own clothes, and introduced him to the beft company, he declared he was not a *towtow*, or one of the common clafs, but a *hoa*, or attendant on the King ; and Captain Cook acknowledges, that fince he arrived in England, he had his doubts whether any other of the natives would have given more general fatisfaction.   It will not, we prefume, be thought tedious if we add

his

his character, as drawn by Captain Cook and Mr. Foster, in their respective histories of the Voyage undertaken, to determine the existence or non-existence of an American Continent, in 1772.

" Omai," says Capt. Cook, " has most certainly a good understanding, quick parts, and honest principles; he has a natural good behaviour, which rendered him acceptable to the best company, and a proper degree of pride, which taught him to avoid the society of persons of inferior rank. He has passions of the same kind as other young men, but has judgement enough not to indulge them in any improper excess. I do not imagine (adds the Captain) that he has any dislike to liquor, and if he had fallen into company, where the person who drank the most met with the most approbation, I have no doubt but that he would have endeavoured to gain the applause of those with whom he associated; but fortunately for him, he perceived that drinking was very little in use but among inferior people; and as he was very watchful into the manners and conduct of the persons of rank who honoured him with their protection, he was sober and modest; and I never heard that during the whole time of his staying in England, which was two years, he ever once was disguised with wine, or ever shewed an inclination to go beyond the strictest rules of moderation.

" Soon

" Soon after his arrival in London, the Earl of Sandwich introduced him to his Majesty at Kew, where he met with a most gracious reception, and imbibed the strongest impressions of duty and gratitude to that great and amiable Prince, which I am persuaded he will preserve to the latest moment of his life. During his stay he was caressed by many of the chief Nobility ; but his principal patrons were the Earl of Sandwich, Mr. Banks, and Dr. Solander."

Captain Cook adds, " that though Omai lived in the midst of amusements during his residence in England, his return to his own country was always in his thoughts, and though he was not impatient to go, he expressed a satisfaction as the time of his return approached."

Thus far Capt. Cook ; and though there are some traits of this character to be found in that drawn by Mr. Foster, yet his good qualities are there so blended with childishness and folly, that one can hardly think it applicable to the same identical person.

" Omai," says Mr. Foster, " has been considered either as remarkably stupid or very intelligent, according to the different allowances which were made by those who judged of his abilities. His language, which is destitute of every harsh consonant, and where every word ends with a vowel, had so little exercised his organs of speech, that they were wholly unfit

to

to pronounce the more complicated Englifh founds; and this phyfical or rather habitual defect, has too often been mifconftrued. Upon his arrival in England, he was immediately introduced into general company, led to the moft fplendid entertainments, and prefented at court amidft a brillant circle of the firft nobility. He naturally imitated that eafy and elegant politenefs which is fo prevalent in all thofe places; he adopted the manners, the occupations, and amufements of his companions, and gave many proofs of a quick perception and lively fancy. Among the inftances of his intelligence, I need only mention his knowledge of the game of Chefs, in which he had made an amazing proficiency. The multiplicity of objects which crowded upon him, prevented his paying due attention to thofe particulars, which would have been beneficial to himfelf and his countrymen at his return. He was not able to form a general comprehenfive view of our whole civilized fyftem, and to abftract from thence what appeared moft ftrikingly ufeful and applicable to the improvement of his country. His fenfes were charmed by beauty, fymmetry, harmony, and magnificence; they called aloud for gratification, and he was accuftomed to obey their voice. The continued round of enjoyments left him no time to think of his future life; and being deftitute of the genius of a Tupaïa, whofe fuperior abilities would have

enabled

enabled him to form a plan for his own conduct, his underſtanding remained unimproved. After having ſpent near two years in England, Mr. Foſter adds, that his judgment was in its infant ſtate, and therefore (when he was preparing to return) he coveted almoſt every thing he ſaw, and particularly that which amuſed him by ſome unexpected effect: to gratify his childiſh inclinations, as it ſhould ſeem, rather than from any other motives, he was indulged with a portable organ, an electrical machine, a coat of mail, and a ſuit of armour."

Such is the account, and ſuch the character of this child of curioſity, who left his country and his connections to roam he did not know where nor for what, having no idea of improving the arts, manufactures, or commerce, of his country, or introducing one uſeful ſcience among them. He carried with him, beſides the articles above enumerated, a profuſion of almoſt every thing that can be named, axes, ſaws, chiſſels, and carpenters tools of every kind; all ſorts of Birmingham and Sheffield wares; guns, piſtols, cutlaſſes, powder and ammunition; needles, pins, fiſh-hooks, and various implements for ſport; nets of all ſorts; with hand engines, and a lathe for turning. He had likewiſe cloaths of different colours and different fabrics, laced and plain; ſome made in the ſtyle of his own country, and ſeveral after our manner: ſome of theſe laſt he bartered

with

with the petty officers (after he had paſſed New Zealand) for red feathers. He was likewiſe plentifully ſupplied with glaſs and china wares, with beads and baubles, ſome of great value; medals of various metals; a watch was preſented to him by a perſon of diſtinction: in ſhort, nothing was witheld from him that he required either for trade in his own country, or for curioſity.

When he came on board the Reſolution, he diſcovered uncommon ecſtaſy; but when he parted with the gentlemen who accompanied him, the tears, as Mr. Foſter obſerves, flowed plentifully; but they were childiſh tears; and the moment his old friends had left the ſhip, he was as lively and briſk as ever. He ſhewed no concern about leaving this country, but rather rejoiced at his going.

We ſhall ſee in the ſequel how he behaved on board, and in what manner he was received on his return home. And now having once more got our ſhip in readineſs, and every thing neceſſary re-imbarked,

On the 1ſt of Auguſt we weighed, and proceeded, with all ſails ſet, to join the Reſolution. While our ſhip was repairing, it was obſervable, that thoſe who had never been employed on diſcovery before, were more impatient to depart, than thoſe who had already experienced the ſeverities of a Southern Navigation near and within the polar circle; and it

E　　　　was

was diverting enough to listen to the ludicrous remarks of these last, on their fresh-water brethren as they called them, whom they ventured to foretel, would, like the Jews in the Wilderness, be the first to murmer and cry out for *the leeks and the onions of Egypt*; intimating thereby, that when these raw sailors came among the islands of ice in the frozen regions, to *feel* the effects of scanty fare and hard duty, they would then be the first to repent their impetuosity, and to sigh for the beef and the beer of the land they were now so desirous to leave.

We proceeded with a brisk gale till the 7th, when in sight of Cape Finisterre, the clouds began to darken, and the ocean to swell, and to threaten by every appearance an approaching tempest. Several ships were then in sight, and we could clearly discern that they were preparing, as well as ourselves, to meet the storm. For twenty four hours it blowed and rained incessantly; but on the 9th, a calm succeeded, which however was not of long continuance; for in the evening of the same day it thundered, lightened, and the rain poured down in torrents. The drops were such as no man on board had seen the like. To prevent the effects of the lightning, it was thought necessary to let fall the chain from the mast-head: a precaution which Capt. Clerke never omitted when there was danger from an accumulation of electricity in the atmosphere to be apprehended.

On

On the 20th, feeing a fhip to windward bearing down very faft, and fufpecting her to be an American privateer, all hands were ordered to quarters, to be in readinefs to engage. She proved to be a Lifbon trader, who by the violence of the gale the day before, had been driven many leagues to the Weftward of her courfe, and was in fome diftrefs. We fpared her thofe things of which fhe ftood moft in need, and purfued our Voyage.

Nothing remarkable till the 18th, when the fhip's company were put to fhort allowance of water, and the machine erected to diftil fea-water. This was occafionally made ufe of during the Voyage, and anfwered very well for fome particular purpofes, but was ill relifhed by the failors for boiling their meat. Thefe precautions were taken left the Refolution fhould have left St. Jago, and the Difcovery obliged to proceed to the Cape, without being able to procure a frefh fupply.

On the 19th we croffed the Tropic of Cancer for the firft time, and,

On the 28th, came in fight of St. Jago, bearing N W. diftant about fix or feven leagues. We bore away inftantly for the Bay, and at eight in the morning made land. An officer was fent afhore with all fpeed to make enquiry, who brought word back that the Refolution had touched at that Port; but had haftened her departure, as the rainy feafon was approaching, and it was unsafe to remain there long during its continuance. The same reasons that had induced the Resolution to proceed were doubly pressing upon us. It was now the time when the rainy season prevails, though we had as yet observed none of its approaches. It is generally preceded by a strong southerly wind, and a great swell. The sea comes rolling on, and dashing furiously against the rocky shore, causes a frightful surff. Sometimes tornadoes or violent whirlwinds arise near the coast, and greatly increase the danger. For this reason, from the middle of August till the month of November, Port Praya is but little frequented.

The officer was no sooner returned, and the boat hoisted on board, than we made sail with a gentle breeze, which continued till

September 1st, when a dreadful tempest arose, in which we every moment expected to be swallowed up. The thunder and lightening were not more alarming, than the sheets of rain, which fell so heavy as to endanger the sinking of the ship, and at the same time, though in the open day, involved us in a cloud of darkness, than which nothing could be more horrible: providentially the continuance of this tempest was but short; it began about nine in the morning, and before noon the whole atmosphere was perfectly serene, and not a spot nor a shade to be seen to mark the place of this elemental conflict. However, in this

this short period, our sufferings nearly kept pace with our apprehensions, having our main-top-gallant yard carried away in the slings, and the sail frittered in a thousand pieces; the jib and middle stay-sails torn clear off, and the ship so strained as to make all hands to the pumps necessary. The afternoon was employed in repairing the damages, and discharging the water which had been shipped as well from the heavens, as from the sea.

September 2, 3, 4, the weather continued squally, with rain; but as we approached the Line, a calm succeeded, and the sky became serene; but with a haziness and languor, as if the current of the air, like water upon an equipoise, moved only by its own impulse. Nothing could be more tedious and disagreeable than this calm; but fortunately it was of short continuance.

September 5th, at eight in the morning saw a sail, the second we had seen since we passed Cape Finisterre on the coast of Spain. We were at this time intent on fishing; and having hooked a shark of an enormous size, both officers and men were engaged in getting him on board. When he was cut up, there were six young ones found in his belly, about two feet long each. These were divided among the officers, and one was dressed for the great cabin. The old one was eaten by the ship's crew,

to

to whom freſh food of any kind was now become a dainty.

The weather continuing fine, the Captain ordered the great guns and ſmall arms to be exerciſed; the ſhip to be ſmoaked, and the bedding to be aired. Theſe laſt articles, it may be once for all neceſſary to obſerve, were never omitted during the whole courſe of the Voyage, when the weather would permit; but were more particularly neceſſary in croſſing the Line, as it has been obſerved that the whole wood-work between decks, in this low latitude, is more apt to become mouldy, and the iron to ruſt, than in higher latitudes, probably owing to that ſluggiſhneſs in the air that has been already noticed, and for which Nature ſeems to have provided a remedy by the frequent tempeſts and tornadoes, to which this part of the ocean is remarkably ſubject.

Nothing worth notice till the 17th, when we croſſed the line. The weather being ſqually, the uſual ceremony of keel-hawling the ſailors who had never croſſed it before, was omitted. This ceremony is ſo well known, that it were needleſs to deſcribe it.

On the 20th the weather became moderate, when upon examination, the ſtarboard main truſſel-tree was found to be ſprung.

On the 20th, George Harriſon, Corporal of Marines, ſitting careleſsly on the bowſprit diverting himſelf with the ſporting of the fiſhes,

fell

fell over-board. He was seen to fall, and the ship was instantly hove to, and the boats got out with all possible expedition; but he was never again seen to rise. His Dutch cap was taken up at the ship's stern; and as it was known that he could swim as well as any man on board, the boats made a large circuit round the ship, in hopes to recover him, but in vain. It is remarkable, that in Captain Cook's former Voyage, one Henry Smock, one of the Carpenter's mates, sitting on the skuttle, fell overboard about the same place, and much in the same manner, and shared the same fate. Both these were young men, sober, and of good characters. Their loss was regretted by the officers, but more particularly so by their comrades among the crew. It is more than probable that both were instantly swallowed up by sharks that constantly attend the ships.

On the 1st of August we caught a large shark, ten feet long, with several young dolphins in her belly : part of the entrails, when cleansed and dressed, were eaten in the great cabin, and the body given to those by whom it was caught. When fryed, it is tolerable meat; but the fat is very loathsome.

On the 15th a storm arose, accompanied with thunder, lightening, and rain. As it was not so violent as those we had before experienced, it proved more acceptable than alarming, as it supplied the ship's company with a good

E 4   quantity

quantity of fresh water, which they caught in blankets or by other contrivances, every one as he could. What was caught in the awnings was saved for the officers use.

On the 20th it blew a hurricane—handed the sails, and lay to all night under bare poles.

On the 25th, the storm abated, and the sky became clear; we observed a ship to the Southward, which by her course, we took for the Resolution: We crouded sail, stood after her, and soon came up with her. She proved to be a Dutch advice-boat bound to the Cape.

On the 28th our people began to look for land; and the appearance of some birds which are known never to go far from shore, confirmed them that the extremity of the African coast was at no great distance. Our Astronomer, however, was of a different opinion, and the event proved that he was right.

October 1st, having now been at sea just two months, without once setting foot on land, those who were unaccustomed to such long voyages, began to put on a very different aspect to that they wore at first setting out. They were, indeed, somewhat comforted by the chearfulness and vivacity which they observed to prevail in almost every countenance except their own; from whence they concluded, that many days could not elapse before the painful sensations of a solitary sea life would be recompensed by the pleasurable enjoyments they would find, when

they

they came on fhore. Such, perhaps, were the feelings, at that time, of the writer of this Journal.

October 3d, we ftill obferved a great variety of fifh and fowl to accompany the fhip, fome of which we had never noticed before; and we could not but remark the difference in this refpect, between the Weftern coafts of the Old Continent, and the Weftern coafts of the New, in the fame latitudes. No fooner had we croffed the Tropic of Cancer, than we were amufed by the fporting of the fifhes, or more properly, perhaps, by their unremitting labour in purfuit of their daily food. Flying fifh are generally the firft to attract the notice of thofe who never have been in thefe feas before, and it is curious to attend to their numberlefs windings and fhiftings to elude the attacks of the Dolphins and Bonitos, their declared enemies. Whatever may be the defign of Providence in the formation of thefe creatures, one cannot help confidering their exiftence as a ftate of perpetual punifhment. While they remain in the water their enemies are there, and tho' nature has given them the power to quit that element, and to fly for refuge to the open air, yet other perfecutors are there alfo in wait for them no lefs cruel than thofe they have efcaped. Boobies, Man of War birds, and other Sea-fowls are continually watching to make the Flying-fifh their prey, while the ravenous Sharks are no less vigilant in making reprisals on the Dolphins and Bonitos. Thus, a passage through the tropical latitudes in this sea, exhibits one continued scene of warfare; while in the other sea all is peace and uniform tranquillity. These reflections naturally occur when the mind, unoccupied with variety, is disposed for contemplation.

On the 4th of August, we too contributed to fill up one act of this tragic drama, and by catching a Shark, left one tyrant the less to vex the ocean.

On the 7th, at six in the morning, the man at the mast-head, called out land; and at eight we could all see it involved in a misty cloud. It proved to be Table Land, bearing S W, at the distance of about ten leagues, which induced us to change our course from E S E; to S S W.

On the 10th we entered Table Bay, and

On the 11th, came to and anchored in six fathom water, where, to our great joy, we found the Resolution.

We saluted the garrison with 13 guns, and were answered by the same number: Captain Cook, with the principal officers and gentlemen belonging to the ship, came on board to bid us welcome. By them we learnt that they had been at the Cape near three weeks; that they had stopt at Vera Cruz only three days, and had taken on board some wine, of which they

very

very kindly offered us a part, and that they made no ftay at Port Praya except to purchafe fome goats as prefents to the Chiefs of the Southern Ifles.

On our landing, our Captain was met by the officers of the garrifon, and the gentlemen belonging to the Dutch Eaft-India Company, who received him very politely, and gave him a general invitation to fhare with them the entertainments of the place.

The fubordinate officers on board, were met by another clafs of inferior gentry, belonging to the fame Company, with a like invitation, but on different terms. Almoft every officer in the pay of the Dutch Company entertain ftrangers, who lodge and board with them on moderate terms, from two fhillings a-day to five.

Nothing in nature can make a more horrid appearance than the rugged mountains that form the Bay. One would almoft be tempted to think that the Dutch had made choice of the barreneft fpot upon earth, to fhew what may be effected by flow induftry and continued perfeverance; for befides the craggy cliffs that render the open country almoft inacceffible, the foil is fo fandy and poor, that, except fome vineyards, there is fcarce a fhrub or a tree to be feen within any walking diftance from the place; infomuch that the vaft profufion of all forts of provifions of beef, mutton, poultry, flour, butter, cheefe and every other neceffary, is

brought

brought from four to five and twenty days journey from Cape-town, where the Governor and
Company have their residence.

This town has already been so fully described
by Captain Cook in his former voyage, and by
other writers before him, that little remains to
be added. The town is neatly built, and according to the natural character of the Dutch,
as neatly kept in order. It has the advantage
of a small rivulet, by means of which there are
canals in all the principal streets of the town;
on both sides of which are planted rows of state-
ly oaks. The town is situated below the mountains, and when seen from their summits, appears, with the gardens and plantations that
run along the shore, exceedingly picturesque:
nothing can be more Romantic, nor any prospect more pleasing to the eye.

The ship was no sooner moored, than all
hands were employed to strip off the rigging,
and to unload the stores; places proper for
repairing the one, and for airing and examining the other, being prepared before-hand by
Captain Cook; and the utmost dispatch was
made to shorten our stay, as the time for navigating the high latitudes through which we
were to pass, was advancing a pace, and the
Resolution was already in a state fit to undertake the voyage.

What remained for Captain Cook to do when
we arrived, was chiefly to purchase live cattle

for prefents to Arees in the South Sea; likewife live ftock for the fhips ufe; thefe are always the laft things provided, becaufe it is found necef-fary to fhorten, as much as poffible, their con-tinuance on board. He had already laid in fuffi-cient ftore of beef, mutton poultry and greens for prefent ufe, and had contracted for a good quantity of falted beef, to fave what we had brought from England, as that is found to keep better than the beef falted at the Cape, though this laft is preferred for prefent ufe.

Among the cattle purchafed, were four horfes and mares of a delicate breed, for Omai; feveral bulls and cows of the buffaloe kind, as more fuitable to the tropical climates than any brought from Europe; likewife fome Afri-can rams and ewes; dogs of the fhe kind, fome with and fome without puppies; cats we had plenty on board, and goats Captain Cook had purchafed at St. Jago.

Stored with thefe, the Refolution refembled the Ark, in which all the animals that were to ftock the earth were collected; and with their provender, they occupied no fmall part of the fhip's ftowage.

While the riggers, fail-makers, carpenters, caulkers, fmiths, coopers, and ftore keepers, were bufily employed in their feveral ftations, the aftronomers were not idle, nor the furgeons; the former were engaged in making obferva-tions; the latter in attending the fick, of whom
there

there were not many, and those, on being carried on shore, very soon recovered. The dry
soft air of the African mountains proved a re-
storative superior to all the physic in the world.
Of the efficacy of this salubrious air, the Dutch
East-Indiamen have experience every voyage,
both in going to and returning from their settle-
ments in India.

While we remained at the Cape, two of their
ships arrived full of sick soldiers, who had been
enlisted in Holland, and who were in a miserable condition both as to health and want of
common necessaries. They had been near five
months on their voyage from Amsterdam, and
had lost on the passage, more men than the
compliments of both our ships amounted to,
owing to nastiness and close confinement. It is
remarkable, that no ships have the appearance
of being neater kept than those of the Dutch ;
nor any more slovenly where they are not exposed to open view.

A very uncommon incident happened while we
were at the Cape, which might have embroiled us
with the government there, had not the delinquent been found out and punished. It was difcovered that a number of counterfeit schellings
and double keys had been circulated, and several
of our people had taken them in exchange for
gold. Complaint was made by our officers
against the inhabitants, for taking the advantage of the ignorance of strangers to impose
counter-

counterfeit money upon them, as it was not to be supposed that they could be judges of the goodness of their country coin. On the other hand, the inhabitants charged the bad money as proceeding from us. Each were warm in their representations, and each were positive in their opinions. It was not thought possible that any of our people could be prepared to counterfeit Dutch money, and yet there had been no instance of counterfeit money having ever been seen at the Cape before the arrival of our ships at that port. Thus the matter rested for while, till one of the ships cooks, having obtained leave one day to go ashore, made himself drunk, and offered base money in payment for his liquor. Being detained, and notice given to his commanding officer, he caused him to be searched, when several other pieces of a base coin were found upon him; and on examining his chest, the implements were found artfully concealed, by which he had been enabled to carry on the fraud. He was instantly delivered up to the Dutch Governor, to be tried by the laws of the country where the offence was committed; but it not being clear, whether the crime of coining was committed on shore, or on board his Britannic Majesty's ship, the Magistracy very politely returned him, to be dealt with as the Commander in Chief should think proper; who not being vested with the power of life and death in civil cases, ordered him to

receive

receive the discipline of the ship, and to be sent home in the Hampshire Indiaman. Thus ended a very critical affair, of which there is no instance upon record.

On the 27th of November orders were given to prepare for sailing. And,

On the 28th of the same month, the Governor and principal Officers belonging to the Company, were entertained on board the Resolution, where they came to take leave of our Captains before their departure, as we were expected to sail in a few days, the repairs of the ships being fully compleated. The stores had all been ordered on board some days before, and a large quantity of beer purchased for the ship's company at the only brewery that is publicly tolerated within the jurisdiction of the town. In short, there is not one necessary article relating to the repairing, providing, and victualling of shipping, that is not to be purchased at the Cape of Good Hope, and that too at very reasonable prices. The wine at the Cape has been thought dear; because that of the choicest vintage is scarce, and, like the styre in England, confined to a very small spot. Of the real Constantia, which is the wine so much prized in Europe, the whole plantation does not perhaps produce more than forty pipes annually, though there may be two or three hundred disposed of under that name. The wine commonly taken on board the shipping for the officer's use, is of

a kind

a kind not unlike Madeira, but of an improved flavour, the vines here being highly fublimed by the warmth of the fun and the drynefs of the foil.

On the 29th our live ftock were all got on board, and properly provided for and fecured; and having difpatched our letters to our friends, and left nothing to do but to weigh and fail.

On the 30th, having quitted our moorings, we next day came to an anchor in 18 fathom water, Penguin Ifland bearing N. by W. five or fix miles.

On the 1ft of December, at three in the morning, we took our departure, after faluting the Fort with 11 guns, which they returned with the fame number. At this time we obferved that luminous appearance about our fhips, which different Voyagers have attributed to different caufes; but which Dr. Franklin has endeavoured to account for on the principles of Electricity. About five in the afternoon, we met with one of thofe terrible gufts fo frequently experienced by Voyagers in doubling the Cape of Good Hope, in which our main-fail was fplit, but fortunately we received no other damage; the foutihernmoft land then bearing S. by E. diftance nine or ten leagues, both fhips in company.

On the 24th in the morning it blew a hurricane, and fplit the jib. About two in the afternoon, unbent and bent another.

On

On the 7th, the weather that had been cloudy and boisterous ever since leaving the Cape, became clear and moderate. In latitude 39 deg. 57 min. S. the Resolution's boat, with Mr. King, the second Mate, and Omai on board, came to compare the time-pieces, and found no material variation.

On the 10th, in lat. 43 deg. 56 S a dreadful storm came on, which obliged both ships to lay to that and the following night under bare poles.

On the 12th, in lat. 46° 18′ S. it began to snow and hail, and the weather became intolerably cold; insomuch, that from a scorching heat which we felt at the Cape, the change was so great in the space of thirteen days, that we were obliged to line the hatchways with canvas, to defend the men below as much as possible from the effects of the frost. Here the Albatrosses and other sea fowl, began to make their appearance; and here seals and porpoises were seen to sport about the ship, which gave us hopes of soon approaching land.

On the 13th, at six in the morning, we came in sight of land, having the appearance of two islands, the Eastermost bearing S S E ½ E; the Westernmost S by W ½ W. At ten in the forenoon, passed between the islands through a very narrow channel. Piercing cold, with sleet and snow, with which the islands were lightly covered, but neither tree nor shrub to be seen, nor any living thing, except penguins and shags,

the

the former fo numerous that the rocks feemed covered with them as with a cruft. Thefe were the Marion Ifles already noticed.

M. de Marion, when he difcovered thefe iflands, had two fhips under his command, one the Mafcarin, Captain Crozet, the other the Caftrie, Captain du Clefmure. They proceed- ed to the Southern extremity of New Holland, and from thence to the Bay of Iflands in New Zealand, where M. de Marion was killed with twenty-eight of his men by the natives. He was obliged, having loft his mafts, to look out for new ones in the woods of this country; but when he had found trees fit for his purpofe, neceffity obliged him to cut a road three miles long through the thickets, to bring them to the water-fide. While one party of his people were employed in this fervice, another party was placed on an ifland in the bay, to cleanfe the cafks, and fill them with water; and a third was occafionally fent on fhore to cut wood for the fhip's ufe. Thus employed, they had been here thirty-three days upon the beft terms with the natives, who freely offered their women to the failors, when M. de Marion, not fufpecting any treachery, went one morning as was his cuftom to vifit the different parties that were at work, without leaving word that he intended to come back to the fhips the fame day. Having called to fee the waterers, he went next to the Hippah, a fortification of the natives, where he com-

monly

monly used to stop in his way to the carpenters,
encamped in the woods, with M. Crozet at
their head, to direct their operations. Here he
was suddenly set upon; and with his few attendants, barbarously butchered; as were the
boat's crew that carried him on shore. Next
morning, the Lieutenant who commanded on
board, not knowing what had happened, sent
a party to cut wood, and when every one was
at work, the natives watched the opportunity
to fall upon them likewise, and murdered every
one except a single sailor, who ran for his life,
and threw himself, wounded, into the sea. Being seen from the ships, he was speedily
taken on board, and gave the general alarm.
M. Crozet's situation in the woods, with his
small party, was now become most critical. A
corporal and four marines was immediately difpatched to acquaint him of his danger, while
several boats attended to receive his people, at
a place where the sick had been lodged in tents,
for the recovery of their health. He disposed
every thing as well as the time would admit,
and effected his retreat to the sea-side. Here he
found multitudes of the natives assembled, dreft
in their habits of war, with several chiefs at their
head. M. Crozet ordered the marines who attended him, to direct their fire, in case he found
it necessary to give the word, against such persons as he should point out. He then commanded the carpenters and convalescents to
strike

strike the tents, and the sick to embark first, with their whole apparatus, while he with the soldiers, should talk with the chief. This man immediately told them, that M. Marion was killed by another chief, upon which M. Crozet seized a stake, and forcing it into the ground, made signs that he should advance no farther. The countenance with which this action was attended, startled the savage, whose trepidity M. Crozet observing, insisted on his commanding the crowd to sit down, which was accordingly complied with. He now paraded in front of the enemy till all his people were embarked, his soldiers were then ordered to follow, and himself was the last who entered the boat. He had scarce put off when the whole body of natives began their song of defiance, and discharged their vollies of stones; however, a shot from the ship soon dispersed them, and the company got all safe on board. From this time, the natives became troublesome, and made several attempts to attack his people by surprize. They formed an attack against the watering party in the night, which, but for the vigilance of the guard, would have been fatal to them; they afterwards openly attacked the ships in more than a hundred large canoes, full of men, who had cause sorely to repent their audacity, and severely felt the effect of European arms. At length M. Crozet finding it impossible to supply the ships with masts, un-

less

lefs he could drive the natives from his neighbourhood, made an attack upon their Hippah,
which they vainly boafted was beyond his power
to approach. He placed the carpenters in the
front, who in an inftant levelled their palli-
fadoes with the ground; then cut a breach
through the mound, and levelled the ditch,
behind which their warriors ftood in great numbers on their fighting ftages.

Into this breach a chief inftantly threw himfelf, with his fpear in his hand. He was fhot
dead by M. Crozet's markfmen, and prefently
another occupied his place, ftepping on the
dead body. He likewife fell a victim to his
intrepid courage, and in the fame manner eight
chiefs fucceffively defended it, and bravely fell
in this poft of honour. The reft feeing their
leaders dead, took flight, and the French
purfued and killed numbers of them.—
M. Crozet offered fifty dollars to any perfon
who fhould take a New Zealander alive, but
this was found impracticable. A foldier feized
an old man, and began to drag him towards
his Captain, but the favage, being difarmed,
bit into the flefhy part of his enemy's hand,
the exquifite pain of which, fo enraged the
foldier, that he ran the fellow through with his
bayonet. M. Crozet found great quantities of
arms, tools and clothing, in this Hippah, together with ftore of dried fifh and roots, which
feemed to be intended for winter provifion.

He

He now compleated the repairs of his ships without interruption, and profecuted his voyage, after a ftay of fixty-four days in this Bay of Iflands. From whence, after pafling through the Weftern part of the South Sea, he returned by the Philippinas, to the Ifle of France.

There appears fome inconfiftency in the above relation, which we cannot help remarking. It feems improbable, if M. Marion was mudered in the Hippah, fituated on the prominence of an inacceffible rock, that the boatmen below, who landed him, fhould not make their efcape, and much more improbable, that neither the leader nor his followers fhould be miffed, till the woodmen were maffacred by the favages the next day. Upon the whole, we are rather inclined to think, confidering the ftrength of the place, that the lofs might be fuftained in fair combat. M. Marion might find it neceffary for the fafety of his people, to endeavour to drive the favages from their Hippah or Fort, which is one of the ftrongeft in New Zealand. Captain Cook, after defcribing it, adds, that it muft be confidered as a place of great ftrength, in which a fmall number of refolute men may defend themfelves againft all the force, which a people with no other arms than thofe that are there in ufe, could bring againft it. M. Crozet, therefore, might think it lefs difhonourable to attribute the lofs of his General and fo many men, to the treachery, rather than the valour

F 4

of

of the favages. It is acknowledged that they defended the place bravely. But to proceed,

On the 14th, the weather began to clear up, and thefe iflands promifing no refrefhment, both fhips purfued their courfe to the S E; wind W S W; a brifk gale, but piercing cold. The Captain ordered the jackets and troufers to be delivered out, which, with the blankets and other warm clothing provided by the Lords of the Admiralty againft the feverity of the frozen climates, were found of infinite ufe in preferving the men in health, who were moft expofed to the action of the froft.

On the 17th, in lat. 48° 27′ S. the fogs came on fo thick that we could but juft difcern the largeft objects at the diftance of the fhip's length. This being forefeen, fog-fignals were appointed, and repeated every half-hour.

Nothing remarkable till

The 20th, when we loft fight of the Refolution. Signal guns were fired, falfe fires lighted, and lights hung at the maft-head; but no anfwer received.

On the 21ft, in the morning, the fog ftill continuing, a very heavy ftorm came on, attended with fleet, and frequent gufts with hail. All this day we continued firing fignal guns, and at night burning falfe fires, and carrying lights at the maft-head; but all to no purpofe.

On the 22d, the gale ftill increafing, we
                                        carried

carried away our jib-sheet, and split the jib; but in the evening it cleared up, and fortunately for both ships, the Resolution came in sight, which revived the drooping spirits of the crew, who were now visibly affected in finding themselves alone in a wide tempestuous ocean, where they could expect no succour in an adverse moment, if any such should happen; and where, from the continual failure of one part or other of the rigging, such a moment was much to be dreaded.

We were now accompanied with a great variety of sea fowl, among which were, pintadoes, sheerwaters, fulmers, and grey peterels, which last seldom appear at any considerable distance from land.

On the 23d, (answering to the middle of June in the Northern Hemisphere) the weather cleared up, and we were proceeding at a great rate, all reefs out, when on a sudden the weather coming on hazey, increased to a fog, and we again lost sight of the Resolution; but on ringing the fog bell, and firing a gun, we were answered by our consort, to our inexpressible joy.

About 12 at noon, the fog began to disperse, a clear sun-shine brightened the horizon, and shewed that we were at no great distance from land. This, as it was unexpected, was the more welcome. The man at the mast-head anounced it; but as it seemed at a great distance, very lofty, with the summits of its hills involved in mist, some of our officers who had

accom-

accompanied Captain Cook in his former voyage, and had experienced many difappointments from the fallacious refemblance of ice iflands to thofe of land, expreffed their doubts. However, the nearer we approached it, the more convinced we were of its reality. But what feemed to us very fingular, the fea began to change its complexion, and from a dark green colour, to look white like milk; we had indeed obferved the like phœnomenon before, on croffing the Tropic in the Northern Hemifphere; but do not recollect any fuch appearance noticed by former voyagers in thefe high Southern latitudes.

On the 29th, we obferved great quantities of fea-weed floating on the furface, and the feabirds to encreafe; and before noon were fo near the land as to difcover rocks towering one upon another, as we imagined, to an immenfe height; but could difcern no plantations or other indications of its being inhabited. As the coaft appeared bold and rocky, it was judged proper to proceed with caution. When we firft difcovered land, it bore South, but on advancing flowly, we came in fight of a feparate ifland, bearing S E by S; which in the direction we firft beheld it, feemed to be part of one and the fame ifland.

On the 25th, at fix in the morning, wore fhips, and flood in for the land; we paffed the tremendous rock, which firft came in view, and
which

which rose to an astonishing height in form of
a sugar loaf, and bore away to the Lee Island,
where we found a bay with good anchorage in
24 fathom water, oozy bottom; but the surf
rather rough and inconvenient for landing and
watering.

On the 25th, at four in the morning, the
boats were sent out to reconnoitre the coast,
and, if possible, to discover a more convenient
harbour for taking in water. About seven they
returned, having found a bottle with a letter
inclosed, importing that in January 1772, this
island was discovered by M. de Kerguelen; that
it contained plenty of water, but no wood;
that it was barren and without inhabitants; but
that the shores abounded with fish, and the land
with seals, sea-lions and penguins. The harbour where this bottle was deposited, being
more commodious than that where the ships
were anchored; and Capt. Cook intending to
keep Christmas here, and refresh his men, gave
orders to weigh, and the ships to change their
station; which orders were instantly obeyed.

The contents of the letter inclosed in the
bottle were in every respect found to be true;
a short account therefore of the voyager who
left it, will be necessary to render our account
of the discoveries in the South Seas compleat.

" M. de Kerguelen, a Lieutenant in the
French service, had the command of two ships
given him, the La Fortune, and Le Gros Ventre.
He

He failed from the Mauritius about the latter end of 1771, and on the 13th of January following, difcovered the two ifles of which we are now fpeaking, and to which he gave the names of the Ifles of Fortune. Soon after M. de Kerguelen faw land, as it is faid, of a confiderable extent and height, upon which he fent one of the officers of his own fhip a-head in the cutter, to found. But the wind blowing frefh, the Captain of the other fhip, (M. de St. Allouarn) in the Gros Ventre, fhot a-head, and finding a bay to which he gave his fhip's name, ordered his yawl to take poffeffion. In the mean time, M. de Kerguelen being driven to leeward, and unable again to recover his ftation, both boats returned on board the Gros Ventre, and the cutter was cut a-drift on account of the bad weather. M. Kerguelen returned to the Mauritius, and M. de St. Allouarn continued for three days to take the bearings of this land, and doubled its Northern extremity, beyond which it trended to the South-eaftward. He coafted it for the fpace of twenty leagues, but finding it high and inacceffible, and deftitute of trees, he fhaped his courfe to New Holland, and from thence returned by way of Timor and Batavia, to the Ifle of France, where he died. M. de Kerguelen was afterwards promoted to the command of a 64 gun fhip, called the Rolland, with the frigate l'Oifeau, in order to perfect the difcovery of this pretended land; but returned

with

with difgrace, pretending again to have juft feen it."

That the iflands we now fell in with are the fame difcovered by Kerguelen, there cannot remain a doubt; but that M. de Kerguelen ever faw a great country, fuch as he pretends, in or near thofe iflands is very problematical. There are indeed numberlefs iflands thinly fcattered in this almoft boundlefs ocean, as every day's experience evinces; but that there are none fo fuperior to thofe already difcovered in riches and cultivation, as to be worth the fearch, will fcarcely admit of a queftion.

We were now bufied on board in repairing our rigging, which had fuffered much in the frequent fqualls with which we had been harraffed ever fince our departure from the Cape; at the fame time, thofe who were on fhore were no lefs ufefully employed in fupplying the fhips with water, and the crews with frefh provifions; which laft, though not of the moft delicate kind, yet to ftomachs cloyed almoft to loathing with falt provifions, even feals, penguins, and fea-fowl were not unfavory meat.

On the 27th, our repairs being nearly completed, and a great part of our water on board, Chriftmas was proclaimed; a double quantity of grog ferved out to each common man; and a certain proportion of wine and fpirits to every petty officer: leave was likewife given to fuch as were ailing, to go afhore for the benefit of

the

the land air; and the officers of both ships reciprocally met in compliment to each other;
paſt dangers were forgotten, and the day was
ſpent by the common ſailors with as much mirth
and unconcern as if ſafely moored in. Portſ-
mouth harbour.

On the 28th, parties were ſent out to procure
what vegetables the iſland produced, by way of
refreſhment; but none were found for culinary
purpoſes, except a kind of wild cabbage, and
that in ſmall quantities, and gathered with much
labour among the cliffs of the rocks. Mr. Nelſon, a gentleman whom Mr. Banks ſent out to
collect ſuch varieties as he ſhould find indigenous to the iſlands and climates through which
he ſhould paſs, found growing among thoſe
cliffs, a kind of yellow moſs of a ſilky ſoftneſs,
which he had not yet diſcovered in any of his
former reſearches.

On the 29th, the Reſolution weighed, with
orders to ſurround the iſland, in order to explore the oppoſite ſide, which, however, upon
examination, was found equally barren, craggy,
ſteep, and deſolate, with that we had juſt left.
Penguins and ſea-lions, were its chief inhabitants, among which our people made great
havock; of the former for the ſake of provi-
ſion, penguins having been found tolerable eating
when freſh, or juſt ſalted; and of the latter, for
blubber, which was afterwards boiled and converted into oil on our arrival at New Zealand.

On the 30th, at nine in the morning, we
weighed,

weighed, and took leave of this Ifland, which we found by obfervation to lie in lat. 49° 30' S. 78° 10' long. At 12 the fouthernmoft part of the land bore S S W ¼ S. diftant about five leagues. We now purfued our courfe for Van Dieman's land, and having no difcoveries in view, took every advantage of the weather to carry fail.

On the 1ft of January, 1777, we obferved great quantities of fea-weed paffing to leeward in a direction contrary to that we had feen in approaching the ifland, which gave reafon to fuppofe there were other lands at no great diftance, and affords fome ground for believing that M. de Kerguelen might have feen other lands in this latitude. Nothing more remarkable prefented till

The 14th, when a hurricane arofe, accompanied with fo thick a fog, that our fhips were every moment in danger of falling foul one of the other. We kept the fog-bell conftantly ringing and guns firing, which were anfwered by the Refolution. The wind blew with fuch violence that we were obliged to take in all our fails, to ftrike our top-gallant-mafts, and to fcud under our bare poles. This ftorm continued with more or lefs violence till the 19th, during which time the Refolution had carried away her main-top-maft, and fore-top-gallant-maft and yard; and the Adventure had loft her top-gallant-fails, fplit her middle ftay-fails, and had fcarce half a yard remaining of her jib.

On

On the 20th in the morning, we lay by to repair our rigging; and the weather brightening up with a brisk but moderate gale in the afternoon, we set all the sails we could, unreefed our top-sails, and run at the rate of seven and eight miles an hour by the log, both ships in company.

On the 22d, the weather continuing clear and moderate, Mr. King, the second Mate of the Resolution came on board to compare the time-pieces. He brought word that the ship's crew were in perfect health, those only excepted who had been hurt at the Cape, and even they were fit to do duty; and that the damage they had received during the blowing weather, was not so considerable as might have been expected.

On the 24th in the morning, the man at the mast-head called out, Land, distance about 5 leagues, the Mewstone, so called by Capt. Furneaux, in 1773, bearing N E ½ E. Made the signal for seeing it, which was answered by the Resolution.

On the 25th, sounded and found ground at 55 fathom, sandy and shelly bottom.

On the 26th, stood off and on to find the bay, called by Tasman, Frederic Henry's Bay.

On the 27th came too, and moored in 14 fathom water, and was presently joined by the Resolution. No sooner were the ships properly secured than the pinnace was ordered to be launched, the boats to be manned, and all hands

hands set to work in wooding, watering, over-
hauling the rigging, and getting every thing in
readiness to continue our course.

The officers, astronomers and gentlemen on
board both ships eagerly embraced the opportunity of going ashore to take a view of this
delightful country, with the appearance of
which all on board were charmed. The first
thing that attracted our notice were the trees,
that by their magnitude and loftiness exceeded
every thing we had ever seen of the kind: but
what was remarkable we found many of them
burnt near the ground, and not a few lying in
a horizontal position, which being much scorch-
ed had been thrown down by the violence of
the wind.

On the 28th, Capt. Cook, accompanied by
officers and gentlemen from both ships, and
guarded by a party of marines, made a second
excursion into the country in order to make
discoveries, and to procure, if possible, an in-
terview with some of the inhabitants; they
penetrated several miles through paths that
seemed to have been frequented, before they
could get sight of any human being, till at
length passing by the edge of an almost impenetrable thicket they heard a rustling which at
first they mistook for the rousing of some wild
beast; but searching closely they found it to be
a girl quite naked and alone. At first she seemed much frightened; but being kindly treated,
and her apprehensions of death removed, she

G   became

became docile, and ready to anſwer every thing we could render intelligible to her underſtanding. We queſtioned her concerning her reſidence, which we did by pointing to every beaten path, walking a little way in it, and then returning and taking another, making motions to her at the ſame time to lead us along and we would follow her. To make her quite eaſy, one of our company pulled off his handkerchief and put it about her neck by way of ornament, and another covered her head with his cap, and then diſmiſſed her. She ran among the buſhes, and in leſs than an hour nine men of the middle ſtature made their appearance, naked but armed according to the faſhion of their country; theſe were kindly treated by the company, one gentleman giving to one a part of his cloathing, another putting ſomething upon a ſecond, and ſo on till each had received ſome trifling ornament for his perſon, when all took their flight at once as if by ſignal, and vaniſhed in an inſtant.

It was not long, however, before the girl we had firſt ſeen returned, and with her ſeveral women, ſome with children on their backs, tied by a kind of hempen ſtrings, and ſome without children. Theſe were likewiſe kindly received, and led to the place where the wooders were at work, with whom it was not long before they became acquainted. They were however moſt miſerable looking objects, and Omai, though led by natural impulſe to an inordinate

desire

defire for women, was fo difgufted with them that he fired his piece in the air to frighten them from his fight, which for that time had the defired effect. Night coming on, we all returned to our refpective fhips.

On the 28th, we extended our excurfions ftill farther into the country, and found it beautifully diverfified with hills and vallies, ftately groves of trees, rivers, meadows and lawns of vaft extent, with thickets full of birds of the moft beautiful plumage, parrots and paraquets, and birds of various notes whofe melody was truly enchanting; befides thefe we found fome lagoons full of ducks, teal, and other wild fowl; of which we fhot great numbers, while our Naturalifts were loading themfelves with the fpontaneous productions of the foil; a foil, we may venture to fay, the richeft and moft fertile of any in the habitable Globe, the trees growing to an aftonifhing height and fize, and not more beautiful to the eye, than they are grateful to the fmell. We found fome that rofe ninety feet high without a knot, and of a girt that, were we to report it, would render the credit of the reporter doubtful. It was now the time when Nature pours forth her luxuriant exuberance to cloath this country with every variety; but what appeared ftrange to us, the few natives we faw were wholly infenfible of thofe bleffings, and feemed to live like the beafts of the foreft in roving parties, without arts of any kind,

fleeping

sleeping in summer, like dogs, under the hollow sides of the trees, or in wattled huts made with the low branches of ever-green shrubs stuck in the ground at small distances from each other, and meeting in a point like sheaves of corn in a field here after harvest.

Our fishermen were no less successful in fishing during our stay than our fowlers in shooting wild fowl; insomuch that nothing was wanting to make our living here delicious.

On the 30th, the poor wretches of natives being now divested of their fears, issued from the thickets like herds of deer from a forest, and drew themselves up in ranks on the beech, making signs for our people to come on shore, probably with a view to partake of our bounty, certainly not with any design to do us any hurt. They were indeed armed with lances about two feet long, terminated by a shark's tooth or piece of bone sharpened to a point, which they threw to a great distance, and to a great nicety ; but these lances were the whole of their armour.

There were among them, as among all the inhabitants of the countries in the Southern Ocean, some to whom the multitude seemed to pay obedience, though even these were here without any marks of distinction, other than Nature had bestowed upon their persons. This indelible dignity, through all the classes of animal nature, has marked some to rule, while others, destitute of that advantage, willingly submit,

mit, and are contented to obey. To thefe chiefs, as no quadrupeds of any kind were feen in the country, Capt. Cook gave a boar and a fow, and made figns to turn them loofe in the woods where it is poffible they may have a better chance to breed than among the more ferocious inhabitants of New Zealand, where feveral of them had formerly been turned loofe. He alfo offered them nails, knives, beads, and other trifles, to which they paid little or no attention, but were greedy after fhreds of red cloth.

It does not appear that the natives here are canibals, or indeed that they feed at all upon flefh, as no appearance of any fuch food could be traced among them. Fifh, fruit, and the natural productions of the earth, were the only articles of food that were obfervable about their fire-places; but what was ftill more ftrange, there was neither canoe nor boat to be feen, though the country abounded fo much in timber. It may therefore be reafonably concluded, that thefe natives are a fort of fugitives who have been driven out from fome more powerful community, and fubfift here in a ftate of banifhment, as it is hardly poffible otherwife to conceive fo fine a country poffeffed by a people wholly deftitute of all the arts of civil life.

Capt. Cook prefented their chiefs with Medals (great quantities of which he carried out with him to be diftributed among the chiefs wherever he went) infcribed with the names of

the

the fhips and the Commanders; with the date of the year and that of his Majefty's reign; in order to perpetuate the memory of this Voyage, provided any future European adventurer, prompted by unprofitable curiofity, fhould think fit to revifit the remote parts of the Southern Hemifphere.

On the 31ft, having been here and on the coaft near feven days, and having got plenty of wood and water on board, and whatever elfe the country afforded, the fignal was made for unmooring. By ten in the morning the fhips were under fail, and at twelve Cape Frederic Henry bore N by W. We fet out with an eafy gale; but, before night, fqualls came on, which made it neceffary to double reef our top fails, and fo to continue till break of day.

On the 1ft of February we fet our top-gallant fails, both fhips in company, fteering a direct courfe for New Zealand, and in nine days came in fight of Adventurer's Ifland, diftant about nine or ten leagues from Charlotte Sound.

On the 10th we were off Charlotte's Bay, our deftined place of rendezvous.

On the 12th, in ftanding for the Sound, the Difcovery had the misfortune to ftrike upon a rock; but by the affiftance of the Refolution was warped off without receiving any confiderable damage; and about two in the afternoon both fhips moored in 9 fathom water.

Not

Not a man on board who did not now think himself at home, so much like Great-Britain is the Island of New Zealand. It is between six and seven hundred miles in length, but varying in breadth, being broadest towards the middle, and narrowing at the extremities. In this it seems to differ from the regular course of nature in the formation of Islands and even of Continents, where, like insects, they seem to be divided in the middle, and only connected together by an inconsiderable space. Almost every island of any extent in the Southern Ocean is divided in this manner. The Continent of Europe, Asia and Africa is held together by a thread in comparison at the Isthmus of Suez, and North and South America in like manner as that of Darien.

We were no sooner securely moored in Charlotte Sound, together with the Resolution, than the natives came in droves to welcome our arrival; to bring us fish; and to offer to trade; but every hand being then employed, little or no notice was taken of their overtures; some of our people were busy in carrying out the tents, others in erecting them on shore; some in forming intrenchments for the security of the stores, and some in unshipping stores; in short, not an idle person being to be found to attend to them, the savages, thinking themselves neglected, departed, seemingly very much discontented.

G 4   On

On the 13th, we had hard fqualls with heavy rain. During the intervals of fun-fhine, we obferved feveral water-fpouts, but none near us. Mr. Fofter, who accompanied Capt. Cook in his former voyage, in his paffage from Dufky Bay to this Sound, had frequent opportunities of obferving thefe phænomena, and has given the following defcription of them. Their bafes, he fays, where the water of the fea was violently agitated, and rofe in a fpiral form in vapours, was a broad fpot, which looked bright and yellowifh, when illuminated by the fun. Directly over this fpot, a cloud gradually tapered into a long flender tube, which feemed to defcend to meet the rifing fpiral, and foon united with it into a ftrait column of a cylindrical form. We could diftinctly obferve the water hurled upwards with the greateft violence; and it appeared, that it left a hollow fpace in the centre. He adds, that thefe water-fpouts made the oldeft mariners uneafy; all, without exception, had heard dreadful accounts of their pernicious effects, when they happen to break over a fhip, but none had ever been fo befet with them.

On the 14th, at feven in the morning, the pinnaces of both fhips were ordered to be manned, and both Captains went on fhore with other gentlemen to reconnoitre the country, without venturing too far at firft, for fear of a furprize. Before they landed they were obferved by an old man, who approached the fhore, holding a green bough in his hand, and

waving

waving it in sign of peace, which was instantly answered by hoisting a white flag. Friendship being thus established we all landed, and the old man began an oration, accompanied by very significant gestures, and a theatrical display of the passions by various modulations of his voice, till at length he concluded in a plaintive tone, which we interpreted to mean submission. This done, he saluted the Company, according to the custom of the southern islanders, by joining noses, a mode, though not the most agreeable, yet necessary to be complied with for the sake of peace. Capt. Cooke, more earnest to examine the state of the plantations, which he had caused to be laid out, and sewed with garden seeds in his former voyage, than to pursue the sports of fishing and fowling, which chiefly engaged the attention of other gentlemen while on shore, went with Captain Clarke to visit the inclosures on Long Island, and found many of the plants and roots in a flourishing condition, though it did not appear that any care had been taken to dress, or even to weed them, by the natives. Indeed it should seem that this part of the country, like that of Dusky Bay, is but thinly inhabited, and probably occasionally only, as none of their towns were found within any reasonable distance of the shore. Some straggling huts indeed, in which single families were found to reside, were now and then discovered in the recesses of the woods, but no regular plantations, the effects of indus-

try,

try, were obfervable in any part of this found. Their canoes, and their cloathing were works of great labour, but where the former was performed could never be known, though it appeared that the latter was the fole employment of their women.

During our refidence here, though nothing was to be found but vegetables and fifh, fuch was the plenty of both, that loads of the former were to be procured for the labour of cutting and carrying away, and of the latter as much as was fufficient for the fuftenance of one perfon a whole day for a fingle nail.

It had been obferved by former voyagers, that the women in this ifland were chafter, when firft vifited by our people, than thofe in the warmer climates, probably owing to the phyfical effects of their colder conftitutions; not to the reftriction of any law, or the force of cuftom; nor to that delicacy of fentiment that naturally excites thofe fympathetic fenfations that in a more advanced ftate of refinement, ferve to bind the fexes in the indelible bonds of mutual fidelity. But, to whatever caufe it might be owing before the loofer paffions, by their commerce with the European failors, took root among them, they have been found to thrive fo well, that they now exceed all others in indulging them. Even the men are now become fo abandoned, as to proftitute their very wives for a nail, and lay no reftraint

on

on their daughters, of whom the men make little account.

It was no sooner known that our ships were moored in Charlotte Sound, than the natives flocked from the remotest corners of the island to traffic for nails, broken glass, beads, or other European trumpery, for which they would sell their arms, clothes, and whatever else they were possessed of, not even reserving their working implements, which they could not replace without infinite labour.

The women, who accompanied these commercial emigrants, were no less saleable, than the wares they brought, and the favours of many were purchased by the seamen, who, tho' the first price was trifling, cost them dear in the end. This traffic was carried to a shameless height, and Omai, who, from natural inclination and the licentious habits of his country, felt no restraint, indulged his almost insatiable appetite with more than savage indecorum.

Before our present arrival, it had been questioned, even by Capt. Cook, whether these islanders would sell their children to strangers; but experience has now taught us, that there is nothing they will not sell for iron, so great is their desire for that metal. The love of gold is not more prevalent in Europe, than the love of iron in New Zealand. The story which Capt. Cooke relates, in proof of the irresistable force of Nature in the retentive care of their chil-

children only shews, that he himself had erred in the conclusions he had drawn from it.

" One of them, says Capt. Cook, agreed to go with us; but afterwards changed his mind. It was even said that some of them offered their children to sale. I however found this to be a mistake. The report first took its rise on board the Adventure, where they were utter strangers to their language and customs. It was very common for these people to bring their children with them, and present them to us, in expectation that we would make them presents, this happened to me. A man brought his son, a boy about nine or ten years of age, and presented him to me. As the report of selling their children was then prevalent, I thought, at first, that he wanted me to buy the boy. But at last I found, that he wanted me to give him a white shirt, which accordingly I did. The boy was so fond of his new dress that he went all over the ship, presenting himself before every one who came in his way. This freedom, used by him, offended old *Will*, the ram goat, who gave him a butt with his horns, and knocked him backward on the deck. *Will* would have repeated his blow, had not some of the people come to the boy's assistance. The misfortune, however, seemed to him irreparable. The shirt was dirted, and he was afraid to appear in the cabin before his father, until brought in by Mr. Foster; when he was told a lamentable

able

able ſtory againſt *Goury*, the great dog (for ſo
they called all the quadrupedes on board) nor
could he be reconciled, till his ſhirt was waſhed
and dried." This ſtory, adds the Captain, tho'
trifling, will ſhew how liable we are to miſtake
thoſe people's meaning, and to aſcribe to them
cuſtoms they never knew, even in thought"—
This reflection recoiled upon himſelf; for Capt.
Cook lived to ſee the truth of the report confirmed, and that the favourable opinion he had
conceived, of the natural affection of theſe ſavages for their children, was not well founded.

On the 16th in the morning ſeveral natives
came along ſide the Reſolution to trade as uſual.
Then Omai, who was plentifully furniſhed with
every kind of iron ware, diſplayed his merchandize to the greateſt advantage. The ſavages, inflamed with the richneſs of the exhibition, perfectly trembled as they ſtood, and
were ready to board the ſhip, at the peril of
their lives, to make themſelves maſters of what
appeared to them ſo vaſt a treaſure. This, to
an European, to whom nails, broken glaſs, and
ſhreds of red cloth, are of little or no value,
may ſeem exaggerated; but to thoſe who have
traverſed the globe, and marked the impetuoſity
of the ſavage's paſſions when excited to a certain pitch, will rather wonder how they could
be reſtrained, than that they ſhould be ready to
commit any deſperate action to poſſeſs themſelves of thoſe things which appeared of ſo much
value

value in their eyes. Omai, though but one degree above the savage whom he despised, yet had cunning enough to take advantage of the desires which he had excited, and after purchasing from them every article that suited him, he artfully asked one party of them, if they would sell their boat? to which they readily consented. Observing two promising youths on board with another party, he asked the father if he would not part with his boys. The youths looked with eagerness at their father, as if they wished to follow the man that was so rich, and the father, seemingly as willing to part with the lads as they were to go, replied in the affirmative, and the bargain was instantly struck. Thus for two hatchets and a few nails he purchased two fine boys, the eldest named Tibura, about 15 years old, and the youngest called Gowah, about ten.

On the 17th the Captains of both ships, with other officers and gentlemen, embarked on board the Pinnace, attended by a party of marines, well armed, and directed their course to the north-west, round Canibal bay for Long Island, and Grafs Cove; there they visited the spot where the boat's crew belonging to the Adventure was murdered about four years before; but did not find any trace of that horrid massacre remaining, nor any native from whom they might learn the cause.

Oma

Omai, who could scarce make himself understood, nor indeed could he understand the natives so well as many of the common men who had been frequently here before; yet being a favourite with Capt. Cook, was always preferred when in company, to confer with the natives, and was desired by him, when he met any of them alone, to question them concerning the fray that had happened some years before, and from what cause it had taken its rise; and he was the more desirous to come at the truth, as the natives in general were friendly and ready to furnish the ships with what ever their country afforded. But from what Omai was able to learn, Capt. Cook received no satisfaction. It should seem, that in Otaheite there are two dialects spoken, as in almost every other part of the world; one by the priests and chiefs, and another by the common people. This was apparent here; for Tupia, who accompanied Mr. Banks to this place, in Capt. Cook's second voyage round the world, could converse with the natives fluently; and was in such esteem with them, that his memory is held in veneration from one end of the island to the other at this day; Obedee likewise, who was of the class of Areoes, or gentlemen, and who accompanied Capt. Cook in his last voyage from Otaheite to the Thrum Isles, the Hebrides, New Zealand, Easter Island, and the Marquisses, could converse with the New Zealanders though Omai

could

could not, a proof that he was of the inferior
clafs in his own country. While we continued
here, he found frequent opportunities to difcover his real character,—when from under the
watchful eye of his protector and friend.—
He had grog always at his command, and was
fometimes entrufted to give it out, efpecially
when any extra quantity was to be delivered by
the Captain's orders for hard fervice, or on days
of feftivity.   At thofe times he was clofely
watched, and was never known to exceed; but
now when the Captain was abroad for whole
days and nights, and he left in charge of liquors,
he fet no bounds to his excefs, and would drink
till he wallowed like a fwine in his own filth.
At thofe times he out-acted the favage in every
kind of fenfuality; and when he could no longer act the brute, he would often act the drunk-
en man; ftorming, roaring, brandifhing his
arms, and by the contortions of his mouth
and face, fetting at defiance, after the manner
of his country, the whole hoft of his enemies,
who were reprefented by the common failors,
with whom, upon thefe occafions, he was generally furrounded; and who knew how to
practice upon him, as he endeavoured to do
upon the poor Zealanders.   He was indeed far
from being ill-natured, vindictive, or morofe,
but he was fometimes fulky.   He was naturally
humble, but had grown proud by habit; and
it fo ill became him, that he was always glad
                                                when

when he could put it off, and would appear among the petty officers with his natural eafe. This was the true character of Omai, who might be faid, perhaps, by accident, to have been raifed to the higheft pitch of human happinefs, only to fuffer the oppofite extreme by being again reduced to the loweft order of rational beings.

In the excurfion of the two Captains among the Ifles, plentiful provifion was made for the live ftock on board, and the long boats of both fhips came heavily laden home with grafs for the cattle and vegetables for the fhip's companies from the gardens of Motuara and Long Ifland, which were found to remain in a flourifhing though flovenly condition. To the quadrupeds, which the Captains Cook and Furneaux had left to breed in the ifland in their former voyages, our Captains added two yews and a ram, thofe that had been left before of this fpecies having died almoft as foon as fent on fhore.

Wooding, watering, airing the ftores, drying and new packing the powder, examining and new baking the damaged bread, forging bolts and new pintles for the rudders, with other neceffary bufinefs for repairs of the fhip, went on without intermiffion on fhore. By the abfence of fo many ufeful hands; fmiths, armourers, gunners carpenters, rope and fail makers, with their attendants; very few peo-

ple were left on board to take charge of
the ships, nothing being apprehended from the
attempts of the natives, who had hitherto
behaved with unexampled honesty, hardly any
complaints having been preferred against any
of them for misbehaviour of any kind.

In this situation, with scarce men enough on
board to hand the sails, a storm arose in the
morning of the 19th, which before ten o'clock
drove the Discovery from her moorings, and it
was owing to Providence that having run foul
of the Resolution, we did not perish, the surge
carrying her off instantaneously with little
damage to either ship. All hands on board
were thrown into the utmost consternation. No
sooner was she clear than we dropped the
best bower anchor, got down the top-gallant
yards, struck the top-gallant masts, and lowered the yards, got in the cables, and moored
with best bower and sheet anchors; and thus
fortunately rode out the storm. Mr. Blythe,
master of the Resolution, and Mr. Bentham
our Captain's clerk, seeing the danger the ships
were in, and at the hazard of their lives attempting to get on board in a canoe, were overset,
but providentially recovered by the boats from
the ships. The gale continuing the whole day,
no Indians came to trade.

It should have been remembered that, from
the time of landing, our brewers began brew-
ing; and the woods affording plenty of spruce

the

the crews of both ſhips were ſupplied with this wholeſome beverage during our continuance at New Zealand, and for ſeveral weeks after we were at ſea. This liquor was found ſo ſalutary, that it ſeemed to ſtrike at the very root of the ſcurvy, and left not the leaſt ſymptom of it remaining about any man in the ſhip.

Indeed great care was taken to ſupply the crew daily with plenty of ſcurvy-graſs and wild celery to boil with their portable ſoup; and ſalt meat was witheld, and fiſh ſubſtituted in its room. This laſt the Indians abundantly provided at a trifling expence, and what is not a little ſurprizing, when our fiſhers could catch the leaſt, they generally caught the moſt, tho' their implements ſhewed infinitely leſs ingenuity in the conſtruction, than thoſe with which our people were furniſhed. It is not eaſy to ſay by what arts they allured the fiſh; but certainly ſome means were uſed by them, to which we are ſtrangers, nor would they ever be prevailed upon to diſcover their ſecret.

During our ſtay in Charlotte Sound, an adventure happened which, though the parties were not of the higheſt claſs, may, notwithſtanding, be worth relating.

Belonging to the Diſcovery there was a youth, with whom a young Zealander girl, about fourteen years of age, fell deſperately in love, nor was ſhe wholly indifferent to our adventurer. What time he could ſpare, he

generally

retired with her, and they spent the day, but
oftener the night, in a kind of silent conversation, in which, though words were wanting,
their meaning was perfectly understood. Mo-
ments fly rapidly on that are spent in mutual
endeavours to please. She, on her part, had no
will but his; and he, in return, was no less attentive to hers. Minds so disposed naturally
incline to render themselves agreeable. A conformity in manners and dress become significant signs between lovers. Though he appeared amiable in her eyes in the dress of a
stranger, yet he wished to render himself still
more so, by ornamenting his person after the
fashion of her country; accordingly he sub-
mitted to be tattowed from head to foot; nor
was she less sollicitous to set herself off to the
best advantage. She had fine hair, and her
chief pride was in the dress of her head. The
pains she took, and the decorations she used,
would have done honour to an European beauty,
had not one thing been wanting to render it
still more pleasing. Ghowannahe (that was
her name,) though young, was not so delicate,
but that the traits of her country might be
traced in her locks. To remedy this misfortune, and to render it less offensive, she was
furnished with combs, and taught by her lover
how to use them. After being properly prepared, he would by the hour amuse himself
with forming her hair into ringlets, which flow-

ing

ing carelesly round her neck, with a kind of
coronet rifing from her temples, gave her an
air of dignity that added frefh charms to the
brilliancy of her eyes. The diftafte arifing from
colour gradually wore off, and the ardent defire of rendering their fentiments more and
more intelligible to each other, gave rife to a
new language, confifting of words, looks, gef-
tures, and inarticulate tones, by which pleafure and pain were more forcibly exprefled
than by the moft refined fpeech. Having at
firft acquired the art of imparting their paffions,
they very foon improved it to the ftory of their
lives. Love and jealoufy directed her enquiries
concerning the women in the world from whence
he came, wifhing, at the fame time, that he
would ftay with her, and be a *Kakikoo* or chief.
He made her to underftand, that the women
in his world were all *tatoo* (man-killers) and if
he ftayed with her fhe would kill him. She
anfwered no ; fhe would *eh-na-row*, love him.
He faid, her people would kill him. She replied no, if HE did not fhoot *them*. He made
her to underftand, that nine or ten of the men
of his world, had been killed and eaten by
her people, though they did not fhoot them.
Her anfwer was, that was a great while ago,
and the people came from the hills *roä roä*,
meaning a great way off. This excited his
curiofity to know, if any of her relations were
among the murderers : fhe fighed, and appeared

H 3   much

much affected when he asked her that question.
He asked her if she was at the feast, when they
broiled and eat the men? she wept and looking
wishfully at him, hung down her head. He
became still more pressing as she grew more
reserved. He tried every winning way that
love and curiosity suggested, to learn from her
what he found she knew, and what she seemed
so determined to conceal. But she artfully e-
vaded all his questions. He asked her, why
she was so secret? She pretended not to understand him. He repeated the same question,
and why she kept him in the dark, at the same
time closing his eyes and keeping them shut. She
continued to weep, but made him no answer.
Finding all his persuasions ineffectual, he turned from her, seemingly in anger, and threatened to leave her. She caught him round the
neck in violent agitation. He asked her what
she meant, and why she wept? She said they
would kill her if she told. He said, they
should not know it. Then He would hate her,
she said. He answered no, but love her more
and more, pressing her to his bosom at the
same time. She grew more composed, and
said she would tell him all she knew. She
then made him understand, that one Gooboa,
a bad man, who had been often at the ship,
and had stolen many things; when he came
to know that it was preparing to depart, went
up into the hill country, to the hippah, and
invited

invited the warriors to come down and kill the
ftrangers. They at firft refufed, faying the
ftrangers were ftronger than they, and would
kill them with their *pow pow*, or fire-arms;
he told them, they need not fear, for he knew
where they muft come before they departed,
in order to get grafs for their *goury* or cattle,
and that on fuch occafions they left their *pow
pow* behind them in the fhip, or careleffly a-
bout the ground, while they were at work.
They faid they were no enemies but friends,
and they muft not kill men with whom they
were in friendfhip. Gooboa faid they were
vile enemies and wicked men, and complained
of their chaining him and beating him, and
fhewed them the marks and bruifes he had received at the fhip; and told them befides how
they might filence their *pow pow*, by only throwing water over them, and then they could not
hurt them. Gooboa undertook to conduct
them in fafety to the place where the ftrangers
were to come, and fhewed them where they
might conceal themfelves, till he fhould come
and give them notice, which he did. And
when the men were bufy about getting grafs,
and not thinking any harm, the warriors rufhed
out upon them, and killed them with their
patapatows, and then divided their bodies a-
mong them. She added, that there were women as well as men concerned, and that the
women made the fires, while the warriors cut the

H 4   dead

dead men in pieces; that they did not eat them all at once, but only their hearts and livers; that the warriors had the heads, which were esteemed the best, and the rest of the flesh was distributed among the croud. Having, by various questions in the course of several days, extorted this relation, of which, he said, he had no reason to doubt the truth, he forbore to ask her, what part her relations and herself bore in this tragedy, as there was reason to believe, they were all equally concerned. He was, however, very sollicitous to learn, if any such plot was now in agitation against the people that might be sent, upon the same service, to Grafs Cove or any other convenient place. Her answer was, no; the warriors were afraid, at first, that the ships were come to revenge the death of· their friends, and that was the reason why she was forbidden to speak of killing the strangers, or to own any knowledge of it, if she were asked about any such thing. She said she was but a child, not ten years old; but she remembered the talk of it, as a gallant action or great atchievement; and that they made songs in praise of it.

In the course of his conversation with this girl, who seemed rather of the better sort, he learned many things concerning the natural temper of the natives, that had escaped the penetration of former voyagers, and likewise with respect to their domestic policy. She said, the

the people of T'Avi-Poenammoo, or the
fouthern divifion of the ifland, were a fierce
bloody people, and had a natural hatred to
the people of Ea-hei-no-mauwe, and killed
them when they found them at any time in their
country; but that the people of Ea-hei-no-
mauwe were a good people, and were friendly
to one another, but never fuffered any of the
people of T'Avi-Poenammoo to fettle among
them, becaufe they were enemies; that thefe
two nations, the people on the north part of
the Sound, and thofe of the fouth were ever
at war, and eat one another; but that the
people of either country, when they fought,
never eat one another; [fo that it fhould feem, that
habitual antipathy has a great fhare in the ten-
dency of thefe favages to devour one another.]
With refpect to their domeftic policy, fhe faid,
the fathers had the fole care of the boys as foon
as they could walk, and that the girls were left
wholly at their mother's difpofal. She faid, it
was a crime for a mother to correct her fon,
after he was once taken under the protection
of the father; and that it was always refented
by the mother if the father interfered with
the management of the daughters. She faid,
the boys, from their infancy, were trained to
war, and both boys and girls were taught the
art of fifhing, to weave their nets, and make
their hooks and lines; that their canoes came
from a far country, and they got them in exchange for cloth, which was chiefly manufaCtured

factured by the women; that their arms and
working tools descended from father to son,
and, that those that were taken in battle supplied the rising generation; that they had no
kings among them, but that they had men
who conversed with the dead, who were held
in great veneration, and consulted before the
people went to the wars; that they were the
men, who addressed strangers that came upon
the coast, first in the language of peace, at
the same time denouncing vengeance against
them, if they came with any hostile design;
that the persons of these men were held sacred,
and never killed in the wars which ever side
prevailed; that when the warriors of either
nation made prisoners, they were never of the
meaner sort, but of some chief, whom they
afterwards killed and eat, but that to the common sort they never gave quarter; that they
sometimes tortured an enemy, if they found
him singly lurking in the woods, looking upon
him as one who came upon no good design; but
never otherwise; that they lived chiefly upon
fish, which were caught in the Sound in abundance, during the summer, but that in the
winter they retired to the north, where they
subsisted on the fruits of the earth, with which
they were supplied for their labour, working
in the plantations, or assisting the builders in
fabricating their boats.

The

The intelligence thus obtained from this young Zealander appears to be authentic from many circumstances ; but chiefly from observing, that the large vessels that came from the north to trade, several of them having 90 or 100 persons on board, had never any fish to sell, but were laden with the various manufactures of cloth, wood and green stones formed into implements of use, or consisting of raw materials ready prepared for fabrication. Their crews appeared to be of a superior class to those who constantly plied in the Sound, and were under proper discipline ; whereas the fishing boats seemed to be the sole property of the occupiers, no other person claiming any superiority over them.

On the 23d, in the morning, the old Indian who had harangued the Captains, when they approached the shore, came on board the Discovery, and presented the Captain with a compleat stand of their arms, and some very fine fish, which were kindly received ; and, in return, the Captain gave him a brass pata-patow, made exactly in their manner, on which were engraven his Majesty's name and arms, the names of the ships, the date of their departure from England, and the business they were sent upon ; he gave him likewise a hatchet, a few nails, a knife, and some glass ornaments, which he highly prized, though of small value. This day the wood-cutters lost a wood-ax, which

one

one of the natives dexterously carried off, without being discovered. In the evening they brought a man bound, whom they offered to sell; but their offer being rejected, they carried him back, and in the night, a most horrid yelling was heard in the woods, which excited the curiosity of the gentlemen on board, to examine into the cause. The cutter was ordered to be manned, a party of marines well armed to be put on board, and the Captains, with proper attendants, directed their course to the west side of the bay, where they saw several fires just lighted, and where they hoped to have surprized the natives, before they had put their poor captive to death, whom they had just before consigned to slavery; but, in this hope they were disappointed. The savages in an instant disappeared, and left no trace behind them of any slaughter having been committed.

About four in the morning, the tents were struck, and orders delivered out for sailing.

Next day, Feb. 24th, the Indians flocked in great numbers about the ship, bringing with them a plentiful supply of fish, and whatever else they thought marketable among the sailors.

Though the natives appeared friendly during our stay, it was judged proper to keep the time of our departure secret till all things were on board, and we were in readiness to sail. This precaution Capt. Cook thought the more necessary,

from

from what he had juſt heard of the treachery of the ſavages, By not allowing them to concert any new plot, he effectually ſecured our forageing parties from the danger of a ſurprize, and by thus ſuddenly giving orders to ſail he prevented our own men from rambling after the women when their buſineſs was done, which they never failed to do whenever it was in their power. The foraging parties here meant are thoſe who were ſent to the coves, at the diſtance, perhaps, of ſix or ſeven leagues from the ſhips, to cut graſs for the live ſtock, and to gather herbs to boil with the portable ſoup for the men; and thoſe alſo who were ſtationed in the woods to get ſpruce to brew into beer for their preſervation from the ſcurvy, againſt which that liquor, as has already been obſerved, was found a moſt powerful antidote. Of graſs and herbs an immenſe quantity was brought on board, and of ſpruce as much as ſerved the crews for drink near thirty days, during which time no grog was delivered out. The parties ordered upon theſe ſervices went always well armed and guarded by marines, though Capt. Cook himſelf entertained very high notions of the honour as well as bravery of the New Zealanders.

On the 25th, previous to the ſhips ſailing, the crews of both ſhips were ordered upon deck, as uſual, to anſwer to their names, when one was miſſing, who, upon enquiry, was found ill a-bed. This was our adventurer, who pretended

tended ficknefs in order to facilitate his efcape; for this purpofe, as foon as he had paffed the furgeon's examination, and the coaft was clear, he dreffed himfelf in the habit of a New Zealander; and being tattowed all over, to fay the truth, the copy was not eafily to be diftinguifhed from the original. Ghowannahe, who was in the fecret, had affembled her friends together, and fent them on board in order to increafe the croud, which upon fuch occafions, when the fhips are ready to fail, are generally pretty numerous. Among this party he feized a favourable opportunity to mix, and haftening to their canoe, when the decks were ordered to be cleared, they were not long in paddling to fhore. The pleafure which Ghowannahe expreffed, on feeing the fhip fet fail without him, may more eafily be conceived than expreffed; but her joy was of fhort continuance.

It was about feven in the morning, when the fhips cleared the bay, and about eleven, when they entered the mouth of Cook's Streights, where they caft anchor; and Capt. Clarke, and Mr. Burney, his firft Lieutenant, went on board the Refolution, to dine with Capt. Cook. Here the friends of the two Zealander youths, whom Omai had purchafed, came to take their laft leave of them, and expreffed, very affectingly, their grief at parting, though the boys were as yet in pretty good fpirits. Some prefents were

made

made by Omai to the parents, and they departed, seemingly with great reluctance.

In the afternoon, our adventurer's mess-mate went down to enquire after his health, and was not a little surprized when no answer was made. He at first thought he might have retired ; but on searching every where below to no effect, he gave the alarm throughout the ship, when it was discovered, that he had eloped, bag and baggage ; and that the chest he had left in his birth was empty. A messenger was instantly dispatched on board the Resolution, to know how to proceed ; and, when the message was delivered, the Captains and officers were joyous over their bottle. At first it only furnished a subject for harmless pleasantry ; but it came to be seriously debated, at last, whether the man should be sent for back, or totally deserted. Some were in doubt, whether an accident might not have happened to him, such as had happened to the corporal of marines, formerly mentioned, but that doubt was soon cleared up, when it was known, that his effects were missing as well as the man. Most of the officers present were for leaving him to follow his own humour ; but Capt. Cook thinking it would be a bad precedent and an encouregement to other enamoratoes, when they came to the happier climates, to follow his example, was for sending an armed force, and bringing the man back at all hazards. Of this opinion was his own Captain,

with

with whom he was a favourite, who gave orders for the cutter to be properly manned, a ferjeant's guard of marines to be put on board, and his mefs-mate as a guide to direct them to the place where he was to be found. Thefe orders were inftantly carried into execution. It was midnight before the cutter could reach the landing-place, and near two in the morning before the marines could find the fpot where the lovers ufed to meet. They furprized him in a profound fleep, when he was dreaming of nothing but kingdoms and diadems; of living with his Ghowannahe in royal ftate; of being father of a numerous progeny of princes to govern the kingdomsEa-keinommauwe andT'Avi-Poenam-moo; and of being the firft founder of a great empire! But what a fudden tranfition! to be waked from this vifionary fcene of royal grandeur, and to find himfelf a poor prifoner, to be dragged to punifhment for, as he thought, a well-laid plan to arrive at monarchy; and what was worfe, his final feparation from his faithful Ghowannahe, was a tafk he had ftill to undergo. Their parting was tender, and for a Britifh failor and Savage Zealander was not unaffecting. The fcene, however, was fhort. The marines paid no regard to the copious tears, the cries, and lamentations of the poor deferted girl, nor did they think it fafe to tarry in a place fo defolate, where lamentations in the night were not unufual to bring numbers together, for the

purpofe

purpofes of flaughter. He was hurried to the
fhore, followed by Ghowannahe, who could
hardly be torn from him, when ready to embark. Love, like this, is only to be found in
the regions of romance, in thofe enlightened
countries, where the boafted refinements of
fentiment have circumfcribed the purity of affection and narrowed it away to mere conjugal
fidelity. He was fcarce on board the cutter,
when he recollected that he had left his baggage behind ; all that he had provided for laying the foundation of his future grandeur. It
was therefore neceffary, that he fhould return
with the marines to the magazine where all
his ftores were depofited, which were not a few.
Befides his working implements, he had a pocket compafs, of which he had thought on fome
future occafion to make the proper ufe. He
had alfo a fowling piece, which had been fecretly
conveyed away by Ghowannahe, as foon as
the plan of empire was formed between thefe
two unfortunate lovers. It would be tedious
to recount the numerous articles that he had
provided. Let it fuffice, that the marines and
himfelf were pretty heavily laden in bringing
them on board the cutter.

It was noon, the next day, before he arrived
at the fhips, and the Captains began to be in
fome fear for the party of marines, who were
fent to bring him back. Before he came in
fight, it had been concerted to try him for a

I   deferter;

deserter; and instead of being received in his own ship, he was ordered on board the Resolution, where he underwent a long examination, and where he made a full confession of all his views, and of the pains he had taken to bring them to perfection.

He said, the first idea of desertion struck him when, in the excursion round the bay, in which he attended in the suite of Capt. Clarke, he was charmed with the beauty of the country, and the fertility of the soil; that seeing the gardens that had been planted on Long Island, at Motuara, and at sundry other places, in so flourishing a condition; and that there were European sheep and hogs, and goats, and fowls, sufficient to stock a large plantation, if collected together from the different places where they had been turned loose, it came into his head, that if he could meet with a girl that was to his liking, he could be happy in introducing the arts of European culture into so fine a country, and in laying the foundation of civil government among its inhabitants. This idea improved upon him hourly, and when he happened to meet with the girl before mentioned, who had seen him in his tour, and who had followed him to the tents; and had learnt from herself that love had brought her there, it inflamed his desire beyond all bounds. And moreover finding her intreaties to meet the wishes of his heart, he no longer hesitated, but became firmly resolved,

folved, at all events, to yield to the force of inclination. He had revolved in his mind, he faid, the hazard and the reward; and had concerted with his Ghowannahe the plan for his efcape.

When Capt. Cook heard his ftory, his refentment was converted into laughter at the wild extravagance of his romantic plan, and inftead of trying him for defertion, ordered him on board his own fhip, to be punifhed as Capt. Clarke fhould think proper, who fent him to the gun, to receive twelve lafhes; and thus terminated all his hopes of being a mighty emperor.

The diftrefs of Ghowannahe is fcarce to be conceived. She was left a woeful fpectacle, to lament her fate. She expreffed her grief, by the punctures fhe made in her face, arms, and whereever defpair prompted her to direct the bloody inftrument. It is wifhed, for her fake, that thofe favage people, whofe bodies are expofed to the feverities of the feafons, are not fo fufceptible of pain as thofe of a finer texture; otherwife her perfonal feelings muft have been exquifite, independent of thofe of her mind. But to take leave of her, now, for ever.

On the 27th, both fhips came to fail, and on the 28th, cleared the land.

On the 1ft of March, a ftorm came on, but as the wind was fair, we got down the top gallant-yards, clofe-reefed the top-fails, and pur-

fued

fued our courfe E. by N. About four in the afternoon it cleared up, we fpoke with the Refolution, and all well, except the two New Zealanders, who, notwithftanding their conftant refidence on the margin of the main ocean, and their employment of fifhing near the fhores from their infancy, yet, when they came to leave the land, and to fee nothing but foaming billows all round them, their hearts failed them; they now began to pine and refufed to eat.

On the 3d, the wind continuing fair, and the breeze moderate, Capt. Clarke, with Mr. Burney, went on board the Refolution, to dine with Capt. Cook. When the New Zealanders were told there was a boat come on board, whatever their apprehenfions then were, it was not eafy to difcover; but they ran and hid themfelves, and feemed to be in a great panic. It did not appear that their fear took its rife from the thoughts of being carried back, becaufe when the gentlemen were coming away, they wanted to come with them. It fhould rather feem, therefore, that they were apprehenfive of fome defign upon their lives, as in their country a confultation among the chiefs always precedes a determined murder. This was in part confirmed by their behaviour afterwards. Nothing remarkable till

The 7th, when a great fwell from the fouthward gave notice of an approaching ftorm. Albatroffes,

batroffes, men of war birds, flying fish, dolphins and sharks had played about the ships for several days, and some of our gentlemen had shot albatroffes that measured eleven feet from tip to tip, and this day a large shark was caught, most of which was eaten by the ship's company; tho' they had not yet lost the relish of the New Zealand fish, nor were they quite exhausted, most of the sailors having purchased quantities to salt, which were esteemed excellent.

On the 8th the storm that was foreseen came on, accompanied with thunder, lightening and rain. The sea rose mountain's high, and the wind increased to such a degree, as made it necessary to take in almost all our sails with the utmost expedition; and to scud it under double reefed top-sails. We still kept our course, steering N. E. by E. The gale continued all night and part of next day, when about four in the afternoon the wind abated, and fine weather succeeded till

The 11th, when it began to blow very hard in the morning, and before we could hand the top-gallant sails, it carried away the main top-gallant yard; about two in the afternoon it became fine, but attended with a great swell from the southward.

On the 14th a fine breeze, and still in the latitude of 39. We were now going briskly on at the rate of 7 and 8 knots an hour, when all on a sudden the wind shifted to the south-east.

On

On the 15th it blew a hurricane, attended with rain and a high sea, which breaking over our bows, cleared the decks of every thing that was not firmly secured. It carried away our main top-gallant yard in the slings, and split our fore-top-mast stay-sail in a thousand shivers. At night we shifted our course, and stood N by E ½ E. There were some on board who disapproved of the course we steered from the beginning, foreseeing, that by going so fast to the northward, we should fall too suddenly into the trade winds, especially if we should be met by an easterly wind before we approached the Tropic. Among the seamen on board a king's ship, there are always some expert navigators, whose judgment, ripened by experience, is much to be depended upon; but the misfortune is, that these men are never consulted, nor do they even dare so much as to whisper their opinion to their superior officer. Like gamesters standing by, they can see the errors of the game, but must not point them out till the game is over. This was the real case on board the Discovery, some of whose people did not scruple to foretel what would happen the moment we left the 39th degree of southern latitude, while we were yet only in the 190th degree of eastern longitude. They did not scruple to say among themselves, that instead of 22 degrees short of the longitude of Otaheite, (which lies in 212° E. nearly) before we altered our latitude to the north,

we

we ought to have ftretched at leaft 12 degrees
farther eaftward, being then certain, that how
far foever we might be to the eaftward of our
intended port, when we came to crofs the Tropic we fhould be fure of a fair wind to carry
us to it.

On the 18th having continued our courfe
N N E for the laft 24 hours, we found ourfelves in lat. 33 deg. 8 min. by obfervation, and
in long. 200 E. that is, more than 12 degrees
to the weftward of Otaheite.   Here we faw fea-
weed in abundance, and by a large tree floating
by us, we judged we could not be far from land ;
but found none.   The tree appeared to be about
30 feet long, and of a confiderable girt, and by
its frefhnefs feemed not to have been long in the
water.   Clear weather till

The 22d, when the heavieft rain began
to pour down that any man on board had ever
experienced.   It fell in fheets, and as the wind
increafed, the men in handing the fails, were
in the utmoft danger of being wafhed off the
yards.   It continued for fix hours inceffantly.
It came, however, moft feafonably for the Refolution, where the number of live ftock, horfes,
cows, goats and fheep had exhaufted a large
proportion of their frefh water, and we were
yet at a great diftance from our deftined port.
Here the wind began to veer to the E, as we approached the Tropic.   This was apprehended
by many, who finding our longitude not to in-

I 4   creafe

creafe in proportion as our latitude decreafed, began to fufpect that we fhould not be able to make Otaheite this run.

On the 24th, our latitude was decreafed, to 24 deg. 24 min. and our longitude only increafed one fingle degree. The wind E. by S. and our courfe ftill N by E, we confequently made but little way. But the weather continuing fair, Capt. Clarke, and Mr. Burney went on board the Refolution, to dine with Capt. Cook, and when they returned, brought the forrowful news of the alarming fituation of the Refolution, for want of provifions and water for the live ftock; that they were obliged to kill a great part of their fheep, hogs and goats for the ufe of the crew; not having a fufficient quantity of water to keep them alive; that the horfes and cows were mere fkeletons: being reduced to the fcanty portion of four pounds of hay, and fix quarts of water for 24 hours; and the men put to the allowance of 2 quarts of water, for the fame fpace of time: that the wind ftill continuing foul, all thoughts of reaching Otaheite were laid afide, and that the ifles of Amfterdam and Rotterdam were now our only refource. Nothing remarkable till

The 19th, when, in the latitude of 26 deg. fouth, we faw a large whale, at a little diftance; a fight feldom feen in fo low a latitude in the northern hemifphere. This day our beer, which having been periodically brewed from the fpruce

brought

brought from New Zealand, had lasted us till the present day, was all exhausted, and grog served out in its stead. Hitherto not a man was ill on board the Discovery, nor any other alteration made in their allowance. It was the number of live stock on board the Resolution, that occasioned the distress for water, from which the Discovery was in a manner exempt, having few or none on board, more than were necessary for the ship's use.

On the 23d, the weather continuing, we began to be accompanied by our tropical companions, many of which surrounded the ship, and one man of war bird had the audacity to settle on mast-head.

On the 27th, the weather, which for two or three days had been squally, attended with thunder and lightning, increased to a storm, so that it became necessary to hand our sails, one after another, till our double reefed top-sails were all that were abroad. We now saw sea-weed in abundance, and some land fowl began to make their appearance, which were indications of land at no great distance.

On the 28th, the tempestuous weather still continuing, we altered our course to the north. The wind for the last 24 hours, blowing mostly from the S E. We, this day, crossed the southern tropic; when the weather cleared up, and we were saluted with a fine breeze, and attended by numerous shoals of flying fish, bonitos,

nitos, dolphins, sharks; and whole flocks of tropical sea-fowl, which abound near the islands in the low latitudes, but are seldom seen in the deep Pacific sea.

On the 29th, about ten in the morning, the sky being clear, and the weather moderate, the man at the mast-head, called out LAND, bearing N E. distant about 7 or 8 leagues. We made the signal, which was soon answered by the Resolution. About 12, the weather began to alter, and to blow in gusts from the land. At four in the afternoon tacked ship, and stood in for the land. Saw no sign of inhabitants, while day-light remained, but in the night observed several fires.

On the 30th, saw several canoes approaching the ships, and many inhabitants on the beach, seemingly in arms to oppose our landing. About ten, the boats were hoisted out and manned, in order to reconnoitre the shore, and found for anchorage, who, to our great disappointment, returned without having succeeded.

Two of the canoes came within call, having three persons in each canoe; but none of them could be prevailed upon to come on board. Our Captain shewed many articles of European manufacture to excite their curiosity, but they seemed to set little value on any thing except the new Zealand cloth; of which he threw a piece over-board, and they came and dived for it; but they had no sooner recovered it, than

they

they paddled off as faft as they could, without offering any thing in return. In the mean time the boats were furrounded by multitudes from the fhore, who came, fome in canoes, and fome fwimming; they even attempted to board the boats by force, and feveral faftened round them with their teeth. Thus circumftanced, and in danger of being funk, they chofe rather to return to the fhips, than hazard their own fafety: or, to fecure themfelves, deprive any of the innocent people of life; an injunction that was frequently repeated by Capt. Cook, during the voyage, and which was the more neceffary, as the common failors were very apt to forget, that the life of an Indian was of any account. About noon, the Refolution, being in much diftrefs for water, though fomewhat relieved by the rains which had fallen, Captain Cook ordered the cutter to be manned, and went in it himfelf, to talk with the natives, and to examine the coaft; but after a fruitlefs fearch, was forced to return, the furf being fuch as rendered the watering of the fhips from the fhore an abfolute impoffibility. While he lay too, he had fome friendly converfation with the natives, and fome prefents paffed between them; but nothing that anfwered the purpofes of fupplying the fhips, or refrefhing the crews.

This ifland, which we fuppofed to be in length, from S S W. to N N E. about eight leagues, and in breadth about four leagues, made a moft

delightful

delightful appearance, and, as Capt. Cook was
made to underſtand, abounded in every thing of
which the ſhips were in want; it may therefore
eaſily be conceived, with what reluctance we
left it.   Some peculiarities were obſerved by
thoſe who attended Capt. Cook, particularly
in the dreſs both of the men and women, who
wore a kind of ſandals, made of bark, upon
their feet; and on their heads caps, probably
of their own manufacture, richly ornamented,
and encircled with party-coloured plumage.
They were rather above the middle ſtature,
well-made, tattowed, and like thoſe of the friendly
iſles, were without cloathes, except a kind of
apron which encircled their waſtes, reaching
little more than half way down their thighs.
Both men and women were armed with ſpears
thirteen or fourteen feet long; and the men had
maſſy clubs beſides, about three feet long, of
a hard wood and very heavy.   Armed with
theſe weapons, 5 or 600 people were drawn
up upon the beach, who eagerly gazed at the
ſhips, having probably never ſeen an European
veſſel before. Though this, with the iſlands
adjoining, were diſcovered in Capt. Cook's
former voyage, at the diſtance of ſeven or eight
leagues, and being firſt ſeen by Mr. Harvey,
firſt mate of the Endeavour, was from him
named Harvey's iſles, and are laid down in
lat. 19° 18′ S. and long 158° 54′ W. from Greenwich.

On

On the 31ft, before ten in the morning, the man at the maft-head called out land a-head, diftance feven or eight leagues. Here 12 canoes were feen approaching the fhips at once, waving green branches, which we underftood were enfigns of peace; thefe we anfwered, and one, who appeared to be a chief, came on board the Difcovery, with a bough in his hand, and another was feen to afcend the fide of the Refolution. After the ufual ceremonies, and fome prefents of little value had paffed, while Capt. Clarke was endeavouring to make his wants known to the Indian,—Omai came on board by Capt. Cook's direction, who now could make himfelf perfectly underftood. The chief addreffed him in an elaborate fpeech, which, tho' Omai pretended to interpret, very little of it could be underftood by any one elfe. He then was directed by Omai to the Captain, to whom he prefented his green bough, at the fame time inviting him afhore, and promifing to furnifh him with whatever refrefhments the ifland produced. This invitation was accepted, the boats were ordered out, and the Captain, with Omai and fuitable attendants, were inftantly landed. It was no fooner known that peace was eftablifhed, than fwarms of canoes were feen paddling to the fhip, laden with cocoa-nuts, yams, bread-fruit, and plaintains, which they exchanged with the failors for bits of broken glafs, beads, or any baubles that were offered them.

them.   Here the natives appeared in aftonifhment with every thing they faw, and more particularly at the carpenters who were at work
upon the boats, with whofe tools they were no
lefs captivated than thofe of the nimble finger'd
inhabitants of the other ifles ; nor were they lefs
fuccefsful in carrying fome of them off, notwithftanding the ftricteft eye was kept over
them by thofe whofe bufinefs it was to watch
them.

About two in the afternoon, the Captain returned with the chief to dinner, bringing with
him a fmall hog, with a whole load of the
fruits of the ifland, which were chiefly diftributed among the fhip's company.

On this ifland all kinds of tropical fruits were
found in plenty, and even fifh were furnifhed in
abundance, and thofe of the moft delicious
kinds; but the article moft wanted, namely water,
was the fcarceft.   Scurvy grafs and celery were
every where to be gathered, and great quantities were brought on board ; and no people
upon earth could fhew greater civility to
ftrangers than the natives of this happy ifland,
who feemed moft delighted, when they could
beft gratify the wifhes of their guefts.   They
even took pleafure in diverting them, and made
mock fights among themfelves to fhew their
dexterity in the ufe of arms.   While they were
thus employed, one of our gentlemen fired a
great gun, which in an inftant cleared the fhip

of

of the poor affrighted warriors ; for which, as he well deferved, he afterwards received a fevere reprimand.

Parties from both fhips having been fent out to fearch the ifland for water, and being returned without being able to meet with any within watering diftance, as foon as dinner was over, orders were given to make fail. About four we left the ifland, fteering N. by W. with a fine breeze.

On the 1ft. of April, being in lat. 20° 22′, and long. 202° 26′ eaft of Greenwich, we continued our courfe to the S W. and

On the 3d. in the morning, the man at the maft called out LAND, which was foon anfwered by the Refolution ; and about three in the afternoon fell in with a fmall ifland, but tho' water was here equally unattainable as in the other iflands of this group, the night was fpent in ftanding on and off, on the following occafion :

One of the chiefs who came on board in the evening gave Omai to underftand, that three of his countrymen were in that ifland, and that if he chofe to fee them, he would be his guide. Omai's curiofity was raifed to know how they came there. On their meeting, they were all equally furprifed, and equally impatient ; they to hear Omai's adventures, and Omai to know theirs. Omai took them on board, and entertain'd them with a pleafing relation of all that had happened to him ; and

they

they in return acquainted Omai with what had
befallen them.   Their story was truly pityable,
they said, that of near 50 Uliteans, they were the
only survivors; that about twelve years ago,
they with their families and friends going from
Ulitea to settle at Otaheite, were overtaken in
a dreadful tempest, by which they were driven
into the main ocean ; that the storm continuing
to increase, and the sea to run mountains high,
the women and children were washed over
board, and perished before they experienced any
further distress ; that after three days, when the
storm abated, those who remained, found themselves in an unknown ocean with little more
provisions than was sufficient to serve them
another day ; that having no pilot to direct
their course, they continued to go before the
wind day after day, till famine had reduced
their number to less than twenty ; that those
who survived, had nothing but the sea-weed
which they found floating in the sea, and the water which they saved when it rained to keep them
alive ; that, ten days having elapsed, and no
land in prospect, despair took place of hope,
and several unable to support the pangs of
hunger, jumped over board in their phrenzy,
and perished by an easier death ; the groans and
lamentations of the dying, and the terrible agonies with which some were affected before
death came to their relief, exceeded all description.   In this melancholy situation they had
                                    existed

exifted for thirteen days, and how much longer
they could have no recollection, for they were
taken up infenfible of pain, and hardly
to be diftinguifhed from the emaciated bodies
of the dead among whom they were found,
feemingly without life or motion, till by the
friendly care of their deliverers, they were reftored.   When they recovered, they faid, it was
like waking from a dream : they knew not
where they were, nor how they came upon
land ;   but being told that they were taken up
at fea, and in what condition, as their fenfes
gradually returned, they by degrees recollected
all the circumftances already related ; they
added, that ever fince they were brought to life,
they had remained with their deliverers, and
were now quite reconciled to their condition,
and happy in the fituation in which the Etoa or
good fpirit had placed them.   Omai, after hearing their relation, with which he was apparently
much affected, told them, they might now take
the opportunity of returning home with him ;
that he would intercede for them, and that he
was fure if they chofe it, the chiefs of the Expedition would grant his requeft.   They
thanked Omai for his kindnefs ; nor had they
any reafon to fuppofe, that fuch an offer would
ever be made them again : but they were now
determined to end their days with the people
who had reftored them to fecond life, and as their
deareft relations and friends were of the number

K   of

of thofe who perifhed, the return to their own country would only renew their grief, and inftead of affording them pleafure, would increafe their melancholy.

Capt. Cook being told the manner in which Omai was engaged, and that he was much delighted with the company of his countrymen, ordered the fhips to lie too that he might not be interrupted; and Mr. Burney, Mr. Law the furgeon, and feveral more of us went only with our fide arms about us to divert ourfelves on fhore, and to take a view of the country. We had not proceeded many miles before we were furrounded by a multitude of armed inhabitants, who without ceremony began to examine us, as we thought a little too roughly. We at firft fuppofed it matter of curiofity that had occafioned this familiarity; but we foon found that, like the gentlemen of the road in our own country, tho' they did not offer any violence to our perfons, they were determined to make free with the contents of our pockets; they accordingly ftript us of every thing but our cloaths, and then they all difperfed, leaving us to purfue our journey; but Mr. Burney having loft his note-book, which was of greater confequence to him than all we had loft befides, determined to find the friendly chief, and to apply to him for redrefs. This, to us who were ftrangers, was matter of no fmall difficulty; thofe of whom we enquired, pretended not to underftand

our

our meaning, and probably did not, as none but women and children were now to be seen; we therefore thought it the shortest way to return to the ship, and get Omai and his three friends to assist us in this enquiry. In this we succeeded, and it is hardly to be conceived, how speedily our losses were restored, not an article being omitted, no, not so much as an iron cork-screw, which to them was a valuable acquisition.

On the 4th in the morning we set sail; and on the 6th came in sight of another island.

On the 7th tacked and stood in for land. For the last 24 hours the storms of thunder, lightning, and rain, were almost incessant, insomuch, that it was found necessary to cover the scuttles of the magazine to secure the powder. The people in both ships were now employed in catching water, which though none of the best, because of its tarry taste, was yet richly priz'd, and he who could save but a gallon a day when the rains began, thought his labour amply rewarded; but this proving the rainy season, we in a few days filled all our empty casks, and every man had liberty to use what he pleased. Before these heavy rains fell and furnished them with a supply, the people on board the Resolution had been greatly distressed for water, as we have already remarked; but now it was determined to direct our course to Anomocoa or Rotterdam Island, and accordingly that

　island

island was appointed our place of rendezvous in case of separation. The weather continued variable, and tho' plenty of rain fell almost every day, yet it was found adviseable to make use of the machine on board the Resolution, and to use water obtained by distillation for every purpose for which it was fit. It was apt to discolour the meat that was boiled with it, and to tincture every thing with a disagreeable blackness: but it was rather preferred to rain water because of the tarry taste communicated by the latter. Nothing remarkable till

The 18th, when at day-break, we discovered land bearing S W. by W. distance about six or seven leagues; but, being then under double reef top-sails and a hard gale, it was thought dangerous to approach it. In the evening we hove too, and so continued during the night. In the morning the boats were ordered out, and about noon returned, having found good anchorage in 12 and 15 fathom water, fine sandy bottom near the shore. The boats came back laden with the fruits of the island, which they made free with tho' they saw no inhabitants; we had no sooner cast anchor, than parties from both ships were sent out to reconnoitre the country. The weather now began to alter. The rainy season, which generally continues from six to eight weeks in this climate, was as we hoped, nearly expired when we fell in with this delightful island, which tho' it was found desti-

tute

tute of inhabitants, was notwithstanding full of fruit-trees of all the various sorts that are in-digenous to the tropical climates. In our rambles throughout we found plenty of scurvy-grass and other wholesome esculents, of which the sailors laid in a good store; but it was unfortunate, that after the strictest search no water could be discovered. It must doubtless surprise the greatest part of our readers, and perhaps stagger their belief when they are told of so many islands abounding with inhabitants, who subsist with little or no water. Yet true it is, that few or none of the little low islands between the tropics have any water on the surface of the ground, except perhaps in a lagoon, the water of which is generally brackish nor is it easy to find water by digging. The fact is, the fruits of the earth are their chief food, and the milk of the cocoa nut serves them for drink. They want no water to boil any part of their food, for they knew not the art of boiling till the Europeans taught them, nor had they a vessel fitted for the purpose: neither have they any occasion for washing their cloaths, the materials of which they are made being of the paper kind, will not bear washing. Salt water therefore answers their purpose with very little fresh, and adds a relish to their fish, in which, when it is broiled, they dip almost every mouthful they eat. This in a great measure accounts for their subsisting without water,

tho'

tho' in the climate of England it would not be easy to subsist without it a single week. And now having supplied the ships with the produce of this island, and not being able to find anchorage near any of those adjoining, we set sail

On the 17th, steering N W. tho' W. S. ½ W. seemed to be our course for Rotterdam. The islands we had just left were the Palmerston Isles, in lat. 18 deg. 11 min. S. and long. 164 deg. 14 min. W.

On the 20th, we varied our course, steering N W.

On the 22d, clear weather, but a great swell from the south, a sure presage of an approaching storm. This day we altered our course to S. S. W. with the wind variable.

On the 25th, the expected storm came on, which increased to such an alarming heighth before night, attended with thunder, lightning, and rain, with a tremendous sea, that with all our sails handed, our top-gallant yards struck, we were obliged to lie too under bare poles till morning appeared.

On the 26th, the storm being somewhat abated, the Resolution of which we had lost sight, bore down to us, and at five in the afternoon we made sail under close reefed topsails. About eleven at night we narrowly escaped running on shore on Savage Island, the man at the mast-head calling out LAND, when, dark as it was, we soon got sight of it close

on

on our lee-bow, steering directly for it. We instantly put about, and fired a gun as a signal for the Resolution, (then to windward about half a mile) to do the same. So narrow an escape made a strong impression on the ship's company, who, thoughtless as they are, could not help looking up to heaven with thankful hearts for so signal a deliverence. As soon as it was light next morning, we saw this execrated island, at the distance of about four leagues.

On the 29th, our carpenter's mate had the misfortune to fall down upon deck and break his leg. Happy that no other misfortunes had befallen us during a series of tempestuous weather, which few ships would have been able to resist. About nine in the morning, the storm still continuing, but the sky in part clear, the man at the mast-head called out LAND, which was presently known to be Anomocoa, or Rotterdam, so called by the Dutch who first discovered it, bearing S W. distance about four or five leagues. At ten saw two mountains, bearing S. S. W. distance about nine or ten leagues, and soon after a great smoak was seen to ascend from the lowermost island. The weather still continuing squally, we approached Anomocoa with great caution. About five in the afternoon, the signal was made from the Resolution to come too, which we obeyed, and about six cast anchor.

On

On the 30th, we weighed again, and in
the evening, worked into Anomocoa road.
About fix we moored, and was foon after joined
by the Refolution.   We had now been juft
fixty days in a paffage, which in a direct courfe
could not have exceeded ten, and had been expofed to the fevereft trials, owing to fome fa-
tality in purfuing a courfe which there was not
a feaman on board that did not difapprove.
It feemed to have no object of difcovery in
view, as we fell nearly into the fame track,
which our Commodore had formerly navigated,
nor did we meet with a fingle ifland, which one
or other of our late voyagers had not feen or
vifited in their different routs.   How it happened is not eafy to be accounted for, as it was
next to a miracle, that any creature on board
the Refolution remained alive to reach our prefent harbour.   Had not the copious rains that
fell almoft inceffantly from the time we paffed
the tropic till our arrival here, fupplied the
daily confumption of water on board our fhips,
not only the animals but the men muft have perifhed.   Happy, however, that we now found
ourfelves in fafety on a friendly coaft.   We
forgot the dangers we had efcaped, and thought
only of enjoying with double pleafure the fweets
of thefe happy iflands, whofe fpontaneous productions perfume the air to a confiderable diftance with a fragrance inconceivably reviving;
and whofe plantations exhibit a richnefs of profpect

pect as we approached them, owing to the beautiful intermixture of the various bloffoms, with
the vivid green leaves of the trees, of which
the moft animated defcription can communicate
but a faint idea. Add to thefe, the tufted
clumps that naturally adorn the little rifing hills
that appear every where delightfully interfperfed
among the verdant lawns, and rich low vallies
which furround them. Nothing in nature can
be more pleafing to the eye, or more grateful
to the fenfes.

We were no fooner moored in the harbour,
than we were furrounded with innumerable little
boats, or canoes, moft curioufly conftructed and
ornamented; the fides with a polifh that fur-
pafs'd the blackeft ebony, and the decks inlaid
with mother of pearl and tortoife-fhell, equal to
the beft cabinets of European manufacture. In
this kind of workmanfhip, thofe iflanders feem
to excel. Their weapons of war, their clubs,
the handles of their working tools, the paddles
of their boats, and even their fifh-hooks are
polifhed and inlaid with variegated fhells, by
an infinite accumulation of which their fhores
are margined, and among them our naturalifts found fome of fuperlative beauty. Thefe
boats held generally three perfons, and under
their decks, which take up two thirds of their
length, they brought the fruits of their plantations and the manufactures of their country,
which confifted, befides cloth of different fabrics,

brics, of a great variety of things ufeful, and others ornamental. Of the firft fort were combs, fifh-hooks, lines, nets made after the European fafhion, needles made of bone, with thread of different finenefs, purfes, calibafhes made of reeds fo clofely wrought as to be water-tight; with a variety of other utenfils. Among the latter, were bracelets, breaft-plates ornamented with feathers of a vivid glow; mafks, mantalets compofed of feathers, fo artfully and beautifully arranged, as even our Englifh ladies would not difdain to wear. Thefe were of immenfe value in the Society Ifles, where Omai faid a fine red feather would purchafe a hog, and of thefe, and red feathers, Omai laid in a ftore.

The people of thefe iflands have already been fo well defcribed by Capt. Cook, and Mr. Fofter, that what we have now to add, is rather to confirm their accounts than to advance any thing new. We found them of a friendly difpofition, generous, hofpitable, and ready to oblige. Some there were among them moft villainoufly given to thieving; but that propenfity did not appear to them fo much a vice in the light we are apt to confider it, as a craft fynonymous to *cunning*, according to our acceptation of the word. He who was detected and punifhed, was neither pitied nor defpifed by his neighbours; even the Arces, or great men among them thought it no crime to practice

that

that craft upon our commanders whenever they found an opportunity; and would only laugh when they were detected; juft as a cunning fellow in England would laugh when he had found an opportunity of out-witting an honefter man than himfelf.

As foon as the ufual ceremonies had paffed, and peace was eftablifhed, the commanders of both fhips gave orders that no perfon of whatever rank on board, fhould purchafe any thing of the natives till the fhips were fupplied with provifions. This order was iffued for two purpofes; one to regulate the prices, the other to oblige the natives to bring their provifions to market, when they found that nothing elfe was faleable; and it produced the defired effect. The number of hogs and fruit that were brought, were greater than the daily confumption; though the ordinary fhip-allowance was entirely ftopt, and the produce of the iflands ferved out in its ftead. We even falted for feveral days, from four to fix hogs a day.

The civility of the chiefs was not confined to their readinefs to fupply the fhips with provifions. They complemented the commanding officers with the ufe of a magnificent houfe, conveniently fituated upon the beach during their ftay: and at the fame time prefented them with breaft-plates moft beautifully decorated with feathers, being the richeft offering they had to make. In return, the commanders were

not

not wanting in generolity, loading them with hatchets, knives, linen cloth, glafs, and beads; with which they thought themfelves amply repaid. Tents were now carried on fhore; the aftronomers obfervatory erected; wooders and waterers appointed; and all the artificers on board employed in the reparations of the fhips; not a few being wanting after a voyage of two months, through a tempeftuous fea, during which the elements of fire, air, and water, might be faid to be in perpetual conflict.

While thefe things were about, the commanders and chiefs were every day contriving to vary the pleafures of their refpective guefts, and to entertain them with new diverfions. They were mutually engaged on board and on fhore to furprife each other with novelty. On board, the chiefs were entertained with mufic, dancing, and feafting, after the European manner; and with what feemed much more pleafing to them, as they paid more attention to it, with the various operations of the artificers who were at work on their refpective employments. The facility with which the boat-builders performed their work particularly attracted their notice; when they beheld the labour of a year with them, performed in a week by the fame number of hands on board, their aftonifhment was beyond conception; nor were they lefs in amazement to fee large timber cut through the middle and faw'd into plank, while they

were

were fpectators, which they had no means of effecting in their ifland in many days. On fhore, the chiefs, in return, endeavoured to entertain the commanders; they feafted them like tropical kings, with barbicued hogs, fowls, and with the moft delicious fruits; and, for wine, they offered them a liquor made before their faces, in a manner, not to be mentioned without difguft; but as the chiefs had refufed to drink wine on board, our commanders, and thofe who attended them, needed no other apology for refufing to partake of this liquor with them. They likewife, after dinner, introduced their mufic, and dancers, who were chiefly women of the theatrical caft, and excelled in agility and varied attitudes, many of the beft performers in Europe; a kind of pantomine fucceeded, in which fome prize-fighters difplayed their feats of arms; and this part of the drama concluded with a humorous reprefentation of fome laughable ftory, which produced among the chiefs, and their attendants, the moft immoderate mirth. The fongfters came laft, the melody of whofe voices was heightened by a kind of accompanyment, not unufual in the earlieft ages, among the politeft nations, as may be learnt from ancient paintings, where the fingers and dancers are reprefented with flat clams or fhells in their hands, fnapping them together, to harmonize their tunes, and regulate their movements. Though this farcical

exhibition

exhibition was otherwise infipid to us, it was not wholly without its ufe, in marking a fimilarity of manners among mankind, at the diftance of half the globe, and at a period, when the arts of civil life were in their infancy. Who knows, but that the feeds of the liberal arts, that have now been fown by European navigators in thefe happy climes, may, a thoufand years hence, be ripened into maturity; and that the people, who are now but emerging from ignorance into fcience, may, when the memory of thefe voyages are forgotten, be found in the zenith of their improvements by other adventurers, who may pride themfelves as the firft difcoverers of new countries, and an unknown people, infinitely fuperior to thofe who, at that time, may inhabit thefe regions, and who may have loft their boafted arts, as we, at this day fee, among the wretched inhabitants of Greece, and the ftill more miferable flaves of Ægyptian bondage.——Such are the viciffitudes to which the inhabitants of this little orb are fubject; and fuch, perhaps, are the viciffitudes which the globe itfelf muft undergo before its final diffolution. To a contemplative mind, thefe iflands prefent a mortifying fpectacle of the ruins of a broken and defolated portion of the earth; for it is impoffible to furvey fo many fragments of rocks, fome with inhabitants and fome without, and not conclude with the learned and ingenious Dr. Burnet, that

that they are the effects of some early convulsion of the earth, of which no memory remains. But to return;

During our stay here, we were nightly entertained with the fiery eruptions of the neighbouring volcanos, of which, notice has been taken by former voyagers. There are two mountains that occasionally emit fire and smoke; but the lowest is the most constant.

On the 19th day of our residence at Anomocoa, our wooders returned, almost blinded by the rains that fell from the manchionello trees, and with blotches all over their bodies, where the rains happened to have access. The poisonous quality of these trees has been noticed by other voyagers, but was more severely felt upon this occasion, than by any of our people in the like situation. Many capital thefts were committed during our stay, and some articles of considerable value carried off.

On the 4th of June, Capt. Clark's steel-yards were stoln out of his cabin, while he, with other gentlemen, were entertained by the chiefs with a Heiva, or dramatic force on shore: but was afterwards recovered. On the same day, as he was mingled with the croud, his scissars was taken out of his pocket, three different times, and as often replaced, when missed.

On the 7th, we unmoored, and shifted our station; but in so doing we parted our small bower anchor, with about 27 fathom of cable,

the

the anchor remaining among the rocks.   In the evening we moored again.   From this day till

The 12th, we were employed in recovering the anchor we had loft, which, after lofing the buoy-rope and grappling, was brought on board, and fecured.   One of the natives ftole an axe from the fhip, but was difcovered, and fired at. He efcaped by diving.   A party of them had unlafhed the ftream anchor, and was lowering it down into their canoe; but, being difco-vered in the act, paddled to fhore, and got clear off.

On the 13th, the live ftock, which had been landed the day after our arrival, on a fmall ifland, about half a mile from the fhore to graze, were brought on board amazingly re-covered; from perfect fkeletons, the horfes and cows were grown plump, and as playful as young colts.   This day orders were iffued for failing; the tents were ftruck, and Mr. Phillipfon, lieutenant of marines, loft all his bedding, by the careleffnefs of the centinel, who received 12 lafhes for neglect of duty.   In the morning, the long boat was found fwamped, and all the ftern fheets, and feveral other articles belonging to her, miffing, and never recovered, for which the marine, who had the care of the watch was feverely punifhed.

On the 14th, we made fail, by the advice and direction of a chief, named Tiooney, to an ifland about 40 leagues diftant, which abounded,

he

he said, in every thing we wanted ; wood, water, hogs, fowls, fruits, and grafs for our cattle. We failed with a fine breeze, wind N E. courfe W S W. and about eleven at night, paffed the burning mountains, bearing N N W. diftant about half a mile. The flames rifing from the lowermoft with a bellowing noife, louder than thunder, but hoarfer and more terrifying, illuminated the air in the night, and enabled us to work through the moft dangerous paffage, that could poffibly be navigated. We had more than 60 iflands within fight, all of them furrounded with reefs of rocks, with fo many windings and turnings, as truly might be faid to conftitute a labyrinth ; but by the affiftance of our Indian pilot, we paffed them all in fafety, and

On the 24th, moored in a fine bay, on the weft fide of Calafoy, in 22 fathom water, fhelly bottom. We had fcarcely moored, before we were furrounded with natives from all quarters, who had been apprized of our coming, and who had loaded their canoes with hogs, fowls, bread-fruit, yams, plantains, and every kind of fruit the ifland produced, which they exchanged for broken glafs, red and blue beeds, fhreds of fcarlet cloth, or indeed any thing we offered them.

On the 18th, the live-ftock were landed, and a proper guard appointed to look after them.

L   Here

Here our friend Tiooney assumed the same consequence, as at Anamocoa. He came on board with his canoe, laden with four large hogs, bread fruit, and shaddocks, a fine odoriferous fruit, in smell and taste, not unlike a lemon, but larger, and more round. He brought likewise yams of an enormous size, weighing from fifty to sixty pounds each.

He was followed by the Araké and chiefs of the Island who came laden in the same manner, with hogs, fowls, and every species of provisions the island afforded; these he introduced in form to the commanders and officers according to their rank. This ceremony over, the tents were landed, and all hands set to work, to finish the repairs of the ships. The chiefs were feasted on board, and the commanders and officers hospitably entertained on shore. On our part, fire-works were exhibited, the marines were drawn up, and went through their military manœuvres, surrounded by thousands of natives, who were frightened at first, and fled like herds of deer from the noise of the guns; but finding they did no harm, took courage, and rallied at a distance, but no persuasions could prevail upon them to come near. On the part of the natives, they were equally inclined to please; they gave heivas every day; and drew their warriors together, who went likewise through their military exercises, and beat one another severely in their mock-fights, which

which, in that respect, differed but little from our cudgel-players in England. In this manner, and in ranging the island, botanizing, examining the curiosities, natural and artificial, we employed our time, while the live stock were gathering strength, and recruiting their flesh, and the several artificers were compleating the repairs of the ships. It is not easy for people, who are totally unacquainted with the language of a country, to make themselves masters of the civil policy of the inhabitants. Indeed it is next to impossible in a short residence among them. As we observed no such medium as money, by which the value of property is ascertained, it was not easy to discover, what else they had substituted in its room, to facilitate the modes of traffic among themselves. That each had a property in the plantation he possessed, we could plainly discern; and the Araké and chiefs among them were ready enough to point out their possessions, the extent of which gave them consequence, as among other civilized nations; but no such thing as circulating property being discoverable, by the hoarding up of which, and laying it out occasionally to advantage, one might purchase another's landed or substantial property, we could not inform ourselves sufficiently, by what means the fisherman purchased his canoe, or the boat-builder his materials, yet there cannot remain a doubt, but that the boat-builder

had

had an interest in his boat, after it was built, as well as the chief in his plantation, after it was inclosed and cultivated.   With us, all was carried on by barter, and an imaginary value fixed on every article.   A hog was rated at a hatchet, and so many bread-fruit, cocoa-nuts and plaintains at a string of beeds: and so, in like manner, throughout; but among themselves, we saw no such value by way of barter.   We did not observe so much fruit given for so many fish; nor so many combs, needles, or useful materials, for a certain proportion of cloth; but doubtless, some mode of exchange there must be among them; for it is certain there was no such thing as money, at least none that we could discern: neither could we discover any distinct property, which one man claimed more than another in the forests or woods; but that every man, like us, cut what he wanted for use, and was under no limitation for fuel.   Salt, which is so necessary an article in European house-keeping, was wholly unknown to the tropical islanders.

On the 19th, an Araké came on board, and presented Capt. Clarke with a large and elegant head-dress, ornamented with pearls, shells and red feathers, wreathed with flowers of the most resplendent colours.   The Captain, in return, loaded him with many useful articles of European manufacture, knives, scissars, saws, and some showy strings of beads,
which

which were highly prized by the royal Cala-
foyan, who thought it no difgrace, to paddle
himfelf on fhore, with his rich acquifitions.

On the 20th, an affair happened on board
the Difcovery, that had nearly cancelled all
former obligations, and put an end to that friend-
fhip, which mutual acts of civility and generofity had apparently contributed to cement.
One of the chiefs, who had been frequently
on board, and who had been of the parties
cordially entertained, invited, perhaps, by the
familiarity of a young cat, and delighted by
its playfulnefs, watched his opportunity to carry it off; but unluckily for him was detected
before he could effect his purpofe. He was
immediately feized and clapt in irons, and an
exprefs fent on fhore, to acquaint the Araké,
or king, with the greatnefs of his crime, and
the nature of his punifhment. On this news,
the Araké himfelf, and feveral of his chiefs
haftened on board, when to their grief and
aftonifhment, they found the prifoner to be
the king's brother. This news foon circulated;
and the whole ifland was in commotion. Tioony
feafonably interpofed. He applied to Omai,
to know what was to be done, and upon what
terms his releafe might be procured. Omai
told him, his offence was of fuch a nature, as
not to be remitted without punifhment; he muft
fubmit to be tie'd up, and receive 100 lafhes; that
the higher he was in rank, the more neceffary it
was to punifh him, by way of example, to de-

ter others from practices of the like nature;
and that therefore it was in vain to plead for
his deliverance, upon any other terms than submission.   Tioony acquainted the Araké with
all that had passed, and presently a number of
chiefs entered into consultation upon the mea
sures that were to be pursued; some by their
gestures were for resenting the insult, and others
were for submitting.   Some, in great wrath,
were for instantly returning to shore, and assem-
bling the warriors in order to make reprizals,
and no less than seven attempted to leave the
ship, but found the way stopt, to prevent their
escape; two or three jumped over-board, but
were instantly followed, taken up, and brought
back.   Thus, finding themselves beset on all
sides, and the king himself, as well as the
chiefs in the power of our Commanders, they
again entered into consultation, and after half
an hour's deliberation, the result was, to make
a formal surrender of the prisoner, to the Araké
of the ship; to beseech him to mitigate the
rigour of his punishment; and at the same
time to put him in mind of the regard that
had been shewn to him and his people, not
only by the chiefs of the island in general, but
more particularly by the friends and relations
of the offender, who had it still in their power
to render them farther service.   This was what
was chiefly intended by the whole process.   The
prisoner was no sooner surrendered in form,
than

than he was tied to the shrouds, and received one lash, and dismissed. The joy of the multitude, who were assembled on the shore, waiting with anxious suspence to learn what was to become of their unfortunate chief, is hardly to be conceived when they saw him at large; they received him on his landing with open arms, and instead of resenting the indignity that had been offered to the second person of the state, was ready to load his prosecutors with gifts, and to prostrate themselves in gratitude. Nothing can be more characteristic of the pacific disposition of these friendly islanders, than their behaviour on this occasion. They seem to be the only people upon earth who, in principle and practice, are true christians. They may be truly said to love their enemies, though they never heard the precept that enjoins it.

Early on the 31st, the king came on board, with four large hogs, and as much bread-fruit, yams, and shaddocks as his boat would hold, as a present to the Captain, for which he would take no return; but a hatchet and some beads were put into his boat, with which he returned, much gratified.

On the 22d, their warriors were all drawn up in battle array, and performed a mock-fight, but lest any stratagem should be intended, the marines were ordered to attend the engagement: nothing, however, that indicated treachery appeared. The battle was followed by a heiva,

in

in which the two young princesses, neices to the chief who stole the cat, were the principal performers, and the evening concluded with every mark of perfect reconciliation.

On the 23d, orders were given to prepare for sailing. The live stock, that had been grazing, possibly, on the lands of him who received the lash, were got on board, wood and water were brought in plenty, the former of the best quality, and the latter excellent. In short, nothing could exceed the accommodations of every kind, with which we were furnished in this delightful island.

On the 25th, we unmoored, and

On the 27th, made sail in company with the Resolution, but in the night, heavy squalls, with thunder, lightning and rain, to which these islands are much expos'd. Many of the natives accompanied us as passengers to A-namocoa.

On the 30th, we were employed beating to windward, and about 12 at night, the Resolution fired a gun, as a signal of distress. She had run a ground on a reef, but before we could come to her assistance, she rolled off.

On the 1st of June, we came in sight of the burning mountains, distance about 4 leagues. And, about 11 in the forenoon, moored in a fine bay. Here the Indians came to us with hogs in abundance, some of which we killed and cured, but the pork soon contracted a disagreeable

greeable taint, which was much complained of by the ships companies. While eaten fresh, the meat was of an exquisite flavour.

Nothing remarkable till the 5th, when we made sail, and about 5 in the afternoon, the Resolution reached Anamocoa, and moored in her old birth; but the Discovery not being able to beat up against the storm, did not arrive till seven in the evening. When, casting anchor, she drove, and in less than an hour, was three leagues to leeward of the Resolution, and in the utmost danger of being wrecked. All hands were now employed in weighing up the anchor, and a number of hands came seasonably from the Resolution to our assistance. The night was tempestuous, with a heavy rain and a high sea. Our labour, till four in the morning was incessant. We made but little way to windward, notwithstanding the utmost exertion of our whole strength. Providentially the gale subsided; we swayed the anchor, and before daylight was safely moored by the side of the Resolution.

On the 8th, Tioony came on board, and gave an account of the loss of several of his people, in attempting to accompany us in their canoes from Calafoy and Appy, the island on which the burning mountains are situated; that he himself was in the utmost danger; that being overset in his canoe, he was obliged to swim

swim more than two leagues; and that at last, he was miraculously discovered and taken up, by a fishing canoe on the coast of Appy, when he was almost spent. We expressed great joy on his deliverance; and he no less, to find the ships safe in their former station, as he thought it almost impossible, he said, that they could weather the storm. Being now provided with every necessary this island could afford,

On the 9th, we set sail for Tongataboo, or Amsterdam Island; but in our passage, both the Resolution and Discovery fell foul of the same rock: the Resolution only touched upon it slightly; but the Discovery stuck fast, and hung upon it, gunnel too; happy it was, that we had day-light, and fine weather, and that the Resolution was within call. By clapping the sails to the mast, and lightening the ship abaft, we swayed her off with little damage. We were then within two leagues of Amsterdam; off which, in the evening, we cast anchor in six fathom water. We were instantly surrounded with natives, who came to welcome us, and seemed overjoyed at our arrival. It is not uncommon with voyagers, to stigmatize these islanders with the name of SAVAGES, than which no appellation can be worse applied, for a more civilized people does not exist under the sun. During our long stay with them, we did not see one instance of disorder among themselves, nor one person punished for any

mis-

misdemeanor, by their own chiefs; we saw but few quarrels among individuals. On the contrary, much mirth and seeming harmony was observable. Highly delighted with their shows and heivas, they spend their time in a kind of luxurious indolence, where all labour a little, but none to excess. The Araké or king paddles himself in his canoe, though he must have a tow tow to help him to eat. This seems strange to an European, as it reduces the man to the condition of a child, and yet it is but one remove from what we see daily practiced before our eyes. The gentleman has his table spread, his food of various sorts set before him; has all his apparatus made ready, his bread cut, his meat carved, and his plate furnished; he has his drink handed to him, and in short, every thing which the tropical king has, except only conveying all those matters to his mouth, which the Araké thinks may as well be done by his tow tow. Yet the omission of this single act of handing his meat and drink to his mouth, brings a term of reproach upon the Araké, tho', by the handiness of his servants in the services of the table, the European gains the character of the polite gentleman. Such and so slender are the distinctions in the refinements of nations; the barriers that divide sloth from sumptuousness; and the simplicity of the Araké from the magnificence of the prince.

On

On the 11th we weighed and failed in company with the Refolution, and moored again in Maria's Bay, one of the fineft harbours in the South Seas. Here we were furrounded by more than 150 canoes at once, all laden with provifions, or the manufactures of the country. Tiooney, who feemed to be the emperor of the iflands ftill accompanied us. And about fix leagues from this harbour had his chief refidence. Plenty of hogs, and fowls without number, were brought us, and were purchafed at fo cheap a rate as a hog for a hatchet; and a fowl for a nail, or two red beads. Our live ftock were put afhore upon a moft delightful lawn, where they ranged at pleafure, and where their paftures were bounded by refrefhing fhades. On the little ifland on which they were placed to graze, a plafh of water was found, which by digging was enlarged to a pond, that not only fupplied drink for the cattle, but water in plenty for the ufe of the fhips. In this harbour too were found every neceffary for repairing the damages the fhips had received in ftriking againft the rocks; and here too every attention was paid us that our Commander in Chief had experienced in his former vifits, of which the inhabitants had not yet loft the remembrance. But an accident happened that put the whole ifland in motion. While our people were engaged in preparing fire-works to entertain the chiefs, two turkies, a fhe-goat, and a peacock

were

were stolen from the Discovery, and craftily carried off. They were no sooner missed than complaint was made to Tiooney of this breach of hospitality, and a peremptory demand made to have the creatures purloined, restored. Whether he was privy to the theft, and was willing to connive at it; or, what was more probable, knew not by whom it was committed, nor how readily to recover creatures of so much curiosity, which he knew would be artfully concealed, he seemed to make light of it, and to offer hogs and fowls in return; but this offer was rejected, and Capt. Cook being applied to, ordered all the canoes to be seized, two chiefs that were in the ship to be detained, and an order issued for carrying fire and sword through the island, if they were not, in four and twenty hours, restored. This order being known abroad, the inhabitants assembled from all quarters, and in less than half a day, more than 1500 appeared in arms, upon the beach; in the mean time, our two Captains had ordered their pinnaces out, their boats to be manned and armed, parties of marines to be put on board, and every preparation to be made, as if to carry their threats into execution. Upon their first landing, a native issued from the woods, out of breath, as if just come from a long journey, and acquainted the Captains that he had seen the strange creatures, that had been taken away, at the house of a chief, on the oppofite

oppofite fide of the ifland, whither he was ready to conduct them, if they chofe to follow him. The Captains thinking this a proper opportunity to furvey the ifland, accepted the offer; and accordingly fet out, in company with Mr. Blythe, mafter of the Refolution, Mr. Williamfon, 3d Lieutenant, with feveral other gentlemen, attended with a party of marines, directing their courfe as the Indian led the way.

They had hardly been gone an hour, before ftrong parties of Indians poured down from the hills, to ftrengthen thofe that were already affembled upon the beach. The Captain of marines, who had charge of the boats, having drawn up his men on feeing the numbers of the enemy begin to appear formidable, ordered them to fire over their heads. This they difregarded, and were beginning their war-fong, which always precedes their coming to action, when the Captain gave Tioony to underftand, that he would inftantly deftroy them, if they did not that moment difperfe. Tiooney terrified by the countenance with which this threat was accompanied, rufhed among the foremoft ranks of the warriors, feized the fpears of the chiefs, broke feveral of them, and returning, laid them at the Captain's feet. This had in part the defired effect; the Indians retreated in a body, but feemingly unwilling to difperfe.

The

The Captain difliking the appearance of the
enemy, made figns from the fhore for the fhips
to bring their broadfides to bear, and at the
fame time drew up his men under their guns.
The commanding officers on board improved
the hint, and inftantly fired fome round fhot directly over the heads of the thickeft of the enemy. This compleated what Tioony had begun; a panic feized the chiefs, and the reft fled
like fo many fheep without a purfuer. Capt.
Cook, ignorant of what had happened, but
not out of hearing of the great guns, was at
a lofs to determine whether to go on or to return; but the great guns ceafing after the firft
difcharge, he rightly concluded that, whatever
might be the original caufe of their firing, it
did not require a fecond difcharge to remove
it; he therefore refolved to proceed. In his
progrefs, the heat became almoft intolerable,
which was rendered ftill more infupportable
by the want of water, there being none to be
met with, except in lagoons, that were brackifh.
After a journey of more than 12 miles, through
a country interfected with numerous plantations,
and where there was hardly any beaten path, he at
length arrived at the refidence of the chief, whom
he found feafting on a barbicued pig, a ftewed
yam, and fome bread-fruit, of which he had
plenty. Surprized at the fight of the Captain
and his attendants, and confcious of their errand, he went out immediately, and produced
the

the turkey, goat, and peacock, which he readily returned, but made no apology for the
theft, nor for the trouble he had given the
Araké of the ſhips, in coming ſo far to recover
the loſs.

On their return to the tents, they found
Tiooney ſtill there, who welcomed them with
much ſeeming ſincerity, and began with apo-
logizing for the conduct of his people, owing,
he ſaid, to the miſapprehenſion of the orders
from the ſhips, which were, as they thought,
to burn and deſtroy all without exception, men,
women, and children, and to lay waſte the
iſland. He then invited Capt. Cook to accompany him a little way into an adjoining wood,
with which invitation he very readily complied,
and found two cocoa-nut trees, with the branches ſtript of their leaves and fruits, hung with
yams, bread-fruit, and ſhaddocks ranged in
ſpirals curiouſly interſected, and terminated
each with two hogs, one ready barbicued, and
one alive, which he had ordered to be prepared
as preſents to the two Commanders, for which
he would receive no return. The barbicued hog
was an acceptable preſent to the people who had
travelled four and twenty miles, with no other
refreſhment than what they carried with them,
except ſome fruit, which they gathered on the
road. A party of Indians were planted in readineſs to diſmantle the trees, and the boats
were employed to carry their contents on board
the ſhips; and thus ended this memorable day,
which,

which, probably, will be commemorated as a day of deliverance, by their lateſt poſterity.

During our ſtay here, more capital thefts were committed, and more Indians puniſhed than in all the friendly iſlands beſides; one was puniſhed with 72 laſhes, for only ſtealing a knife, another with 36, for endeavouring to carry off two or three drinking glaſſes; three were puniſhed with 36 laſhes each, for heaving ſtones at the wooders; but what was ſtill more cruel, a man for attempting to carry off an axe, was ordered to have his arm cut to the bone, which he bore without complaining.

It is not to be wondered, that after ſuch wanton acts of cruelty, the inhabitants ſhould grow outrageous; and, though they did not break out into open acts of hoſtility, yet they watched every opportunity to be vexatious.

On the 19th, Mr. Williamſon and Mr. Blythe, who were fond of ſhooting, and conſequently of ranging the woods and thickets, were ſet upon by ten or twelve of the natives, who took from them their fowling-pieces and ſhot-bags, the former of which they carried off, but dropped the ſhot-bags on being purſued.

Recourſe was had to the former expedient, of ſeizing the canoes, and threatning the iſland, as before, and one of the fowling-pieces was, by that means, recovered; but the other was never returned

M

On the 25th, orders were given to prepare for sailing, the live stock were taken on board, so altered, that they could not have been known for the same poor skeletons which, two months before, had been landed on these fertile shores. Capt. Cook made Tiooney a present of a horse and a mare, a bull and a cow, a ram and a ewe, for the many services he had rendered him and his people, during their residence in the friendly isles, by which he gratified him beyond his utmost wishes. These valuable presents were immediately driven to his palace, at Tonga-ta-boo, distant about four leagues. The ships being now compleatly stowed; having wood and water as much as they could make room for, with hogs and bread-fruit, cocoa-nuts, yams and other roots, greens in abundance, and, in short, every thing that the ships could contain, or the crews desire, the boats were sent out to seek a passage to the south-east-ward, in order to visit the celebrated little Island of Middleburgh, of which, former voyagers have given a most flattering description.

On the 29th, the boats returned, having discovered a narrow gut, not half a cable's length in breadth, and from $3\frac{1}{2}$ to 5 fathom water, loomy bottom.

This day, Mr. Nelson, of whom mention has already been made, being alone on the hills and rocks, collecting plants and herbs, indigenous to the island, and at a considerable distance

tance from the ships, was attacked by five or six Indians, who first began by throwing stones, at which they are very dextrous; and then, finding he had no fire-arms, closed in with him, stript him of his cloaths and his bag, which were all that he had about him.

On the 1st of July, the boats were manned, and the Captains of both ships went on shore, to prefer their complaints to the Araké; but the offenders, upon enquiry, being found to be boys, and the cloaths and bag of plants of small value, Mr. Nelson, unwilling to embroil the inhabitants in any more disputes, interceded with Capt. Cook, as we were just upon our departure, not to make his loss an object of contention, but to take leave of the chiefs, in the most friendly manner, who upon the whole had behaved with uncommon kindness and generosity,

On the 3d, while we were getting things in readiness to depart, we had an opportunity of discovering the reason of a very singular mark, which was observed by former navigators a little above the temples of many of the chiefs. We perceived that this day was kept sacred throughout the whole island; that nothing was suffered to be sold, neither did the people touch any food, and besides that several of our new acquaintance were missing. Enquiring into the cause, we were told that Tiooney's mother was dead, and that the chiefs, who were

her

her defcendants, ftayed at home to have their
temples burnt. This cuftom is not confined
to this ifland only, but is likewife common to
feveral others, particularly to thofe of Ea-oo-
we, or Middleburgh, and Appee. This mark
is made on the left fide, on the death of a
mother, and on the right when the father dies;
and on the death of the high prieft, the firft
joint on the little finger is amputated. Thefe
people have therefore their religious rites, tho'
we were not able to difcover how, or when
they were performed.

On the 4th we unmoored, worked out of
the bay, and lay in readinefs to take the advantage of a wind to carry us through the gut,
in our way to Ea-oo-whe, or Middleburgh,
which,

On the 7th, we accomplifhed. Being now
clear of the reefs, we again caft anchor, at a-
bout three leagues diftance. We had fcarce
let fall our anchors, when there came along-fide
a large canoe, in which there were three men
and a woman, of fuperior dignity to any we had
yet feen; one of them, fuppofed by his venerable appearance, to be the high prieft, held a
long pole or fpear in his hand, to which he tied
a white flag, and began an oration which lafted
a confiderable time; and after it was ended, he
afcended the fide of the fhip, and fat down,
with great compofure, upon the quarter-deck,
till he was accofted by Capt. Clarke, who after

the

the ufual falutations, invited him, and thofe
who accompanied him into the great cabin; but
his attendants declined the invitation; and to
make known the dignity of the great perfonage,
in whofe prefence they were, they proftrated
themfelves before him, the women as well as
the men, and kifs'd the fole of his right foot.
This aged Indian brought with him, as a prefent to the Captain, four large hogs, fix fowls,
and a proportionable quantity of yams and
plantains. In return, the Captain gave him a
printed gown, a Chinefe looking-glafs, fome
earthen cups, and feveral other curiofities, which
he accepted with great courtefy, and with an
air of dignity, which remarkably diftinguifhed
him. The Captain and officers paid him great
attention, and fhewed him the different accommodations on board the fhip, at which he expreffed great aftonifhment. He was then invited to eat, which he declined. He was offered wine, of which the Captain drank firft;
he put it to his lips, tafted it, but returned the
glafs. After being on board little more than
an hour, he was defirous of taking leave, and
pointed to a little ifland, to which he gave the
Captain a very preffing invitation to accompany
him; but that could not be complied with, as
the fhips were every moment expected to fail.
This venerable perfon was about fix feet three
inches high, finely proportioned, and had a

com-

commanding air, that was both affable and graceful.

On the 8th, Tiooney came on board the Refolution, to take his final leave : he brought with him five hogs, with a large proportion of yams and fruit. He teftified his grief at parting, with all that appearance of fincerity that characterizes the people of thefe happy iflands.

On the 9th we weighed, and on the 12th caft anchor, on the S W. fide of the Ifland of Ea-oo-whe, or Middleburgh, where the people came on board with as little ceremony as if they had been acquainted with us for many years. They brought us the produce of the ifland; but being already fupplied with every neceffary of that kind, our chief traffic was for birds and feathers. Here the parrots and parroquets were of the moft beautiful plumage, far furpaffing thofe ufually imported into Europe from the Indies ; there were a great variety of other birds, on which many gentlemen in both fhips fet a great value, though they were purchafed for trifles. The feathers we purchafed were of divers colours for the northern market, but chiefly red from the Marquefas and Society Ifles. We alfo purchafed cloth, and many other articles of curious workmanfhip, the artifts of this ifland, for invention and ingenuity in the execution, exceeding thofe of all the other iflands in the South Seas. But what chiefly tended to pro-

long

long our stay here was the richness of the grass, which made into hay proved excellent food for our live stock. From the accounts circulated through the ship when we arrived, it was generally believed, that we might travel through this island with our pockets open, provided they were not lined with iron; but to this, the behaviour of a party of the inhabitants to William Collet, Captain's steward of the Discovery, was an exception. Being alone, diverting himself in surveying the country, he was set upon and stript of every thing he had about him, his shoes only excepted; and on preferring his complaint, his keys were all that he was able to recover.

On the 18th, orders were given to prepare for sailing: and Otaheite was appointed our place of rendezvous, in case of separation. We had now been near three months improving our live stock, wooding, watering, repairing our ships, and laying in fresh provisions in these friendly islands, when the above orders were issued out. The crews of both ships received these orders with alacrity; for, though they wanted for nothing, yet they longed to be at Otaheite, where many of them had formed connections that were dear to them, and where those, who had not yet been there, had conceived so high an idea of its superiority, as to make them look upon every other place they

M 4   touched

touch at as an uncultivated garden, in comparison with that little Eden.

At six in the morning we weighed, and were soon under sail, steering our course to the southward, to fetch a wind to carry us to our intended port.

On the 19th we were out of sight of land, when in lat. 22 deg. 24 min. S. the wind shifted fair W N W. with hard gales, which continuing for several days,

On the 23d we found our ship leaky, and no possibility of stopping her leaks till we could make land. All hands were employed in pumping out the water, and when we found it did not increase upon us, the leak gave us little or no concern.

Nothing remarkable till the 30th, when in lat. 28 deg. 7 min. the weather became tempestuous, and a sudden squall carried away our main-top and top-gallant mast, split our mainsail, and carried away the jeb. It is astonishing to see with what spirit and alacrity English sailors exert themselves on such occasions. Amidst a storm, when it is almost impossible for a landsman to trust himself upon deck, our sailors mounted aloft, and with incredible rapidity cleared away the wreck, by which they preserved the ship. Nothing equal to this disaster had happened to us in the course of the voyage. During the night we hoisted lights and fired guns of distress, but neither were seen or heard

by

by the Refolution,   The ftorm continuing with unabated fury during the night and all next day, we handed our fails, and fcudded under our fore-fail and mizzen ftay-fail at the rate of feven and eight knots an hour, and at length were obliged to lie too with our fhip's head to the weft, courfe E N E.

On the 30th we got fight of the Refolution, about four leagues to leeward. She had damaged her main-top maft head, but had fecured it, and was otherwife in perfect repair.

Auguft the 1ft we celebrated the anniverfary of our departure from England, having juft been one year abfent. The men were allowed a double allowance of grog, and they forgot in the jollity of their cups, the hardfhips to which they were expofed in the ftorm.

On the 2d our carpenters were employed in re-placing the old top-maft with a new one; but juft as they had got it in readinefs to point the bafe of the top-maft through the main-top, they difcovered, to our unfpeakable grief, that the main-maft head was fhattered four or five feet below the top. This put an end to our labour at this time. The top-maft was lowered till the main-maft could be fecured, which was a work of infinite difficulty in our fituation, and could not be accomplifhed without the affift-ance of the carpenters from the Refolution. The fignal of diftrefs was thrown out, but the fea ran fo high that no boat could live. In this

fituation

situation we continued till the storm abated, when the mast being lashed, a spare jeb-boom was got up for a main-top-mast, and a mizzen top-sail yard for a top-sail yard ; and thus e-quipped, we made what sail we could, the Re-solution shortening sail to keep us company.

In this crazy condition, with our leaks ra-ther increased, we met with a storm

On the 3d, which required the utmost exer-tion of our strength to encounter ; every hand in the ship was employed, some at the pumps, and others in handing the sails, which was a work of the greatest danger, yet happily accom-plished without an accident.

On the 4th at six in the morning the man at the mast-head called out land, which was joy-ful news to all on board, and about seven we stood in for it. About eleven we saw several canoes paddling towards the ships, in each of which were three naked Indians. We made signs for them to come on board, which they de-clined ; but made signs for us to land. Our boats were instantly hoisted out and sent to sound, but no anchorage being found, it was resolved to pursue our voyage without losing any more time. This island was a new disco-very. Its latitude by observation 27 deg. 31 min. longitude 208 deg. 26 min. E. The men appeared of the largest stature, and tattowed from head to foot ; the language different from any we were yet acquainted with, and their

dress

dress not unlike that of the Amsterdammers, their complexion darker, their heads ornamented with shells, feathers and flowers; and their canoes elegantly carved, and neatly constructed. Of their manners we could form little or no judgment. They appeared timid; but by their waving green boughs, and exhibiting other signs of peace, they gave us reason to believe that they were friendly. They exchanged some small fish and cocoa-nuts, for nails and Middleburgh cloth. The appearance of the island, as we approached it, was lofty, but small. Its greatest length about 4 leagues, and its breadth about 2 leagues.

We now proceeded with an easy breeze, till the 13th, when the man at the mast-head calling out Land, distance about seven or eight leagues, we soon perceived it to be the Island of Otaheite, of which we were in pursuit.

On the 14th, about six in the morning, we stood in for the land, and before night were safely moored in the harbour, called by the natives, Otaite Peha. Here we were surrounded by an incredible number of canoes filled with natives, besides men women and children, who swam to the ships, expressing their joy at our arrival. We were scarce moored, before the king, attended by most of the royal family, came on board the Resolution to welcome Capt. Cook; the shores every where resounded with the name of Cook; not a child,

that

that could, lifp Toote, was filent; their acclamations filled the air.   The king brought with
him fix large hogs, fome bread-fruit and plantains as a prefent; and Capt. Cook, after the
firft falutations had paffed, prefented the king
with two large hatchets, fome fhowy beads,
a looking-glafs, a knife, and fome nails.   He
alfo made prefents to his followers.

They were eager to enter into converfation
with Omai, and informed Capt. Cook, through
his means, of the arrival there of two Spanifh
fhips from Lima, about eight months before;
that at their departure they had taken, three of
the natives with them, and had left one of their
people in their room, who had been dead fome
time; that they had built a houfe on fhore,
and erected a crofs with an infcription, which
were ftill ftanding; that they had left fome
cattle, with goats, fheep, and geefe; but that
moft of them were dead; that they promifed to
return foon; and that they had been there more
than once, fince Capt. Cook's laft vifit.   Dinner was no fooner over, than both Captains,
accompanied by Omai, and conducted by the
royal family, went on fhore and vifited the
Spanifh erections; which feemed to indicate a
deeper defign than the natives were aware of;
they had taken poffeffion of the ifland, in the
name of his Catholic Majefty, and had infcribed
the crofs with the king's name, and date of
the year 1777, which Capt. Cook took the
liberty

liberty to pull down and carry away, telling them at the fame time to beware of their Spaniſh viſitors, and not to be over-fond of them. Moſt of the freſh proviſions, with which we were ſupplied at the friendly iſles, being expended in the voyage, orders were given to prohibit all trade with the natives, except for proviſions; and that only with ſuch perſons, as were appointed by the commanders as purveyors for the ſhips. By this neceſſary regulation, freſh proviſions were ſoon procured in plenty, and every man was allowed a pound and a half of pork every day.

On the 16th, Omai was put in poſſeſſion of the houſe the Spaniards had built; his bed put up after the Engliſh faſhion; and he was indulged to ſleep on ſhore during our ſhort ſtay at this part of the iſland. Capt. Cook likewiſe cauſed the Spaniſh inſcription to be eraſed, the croſs to be effaced, and a new inſcription to be cut, with the name of the Engliſh ſhips that had diſcovered the iſland, the date 1772 when firſt diſcovered, and the name of his Majeſty, King George, to take place of that of the Spaniſh King Carlos. Here alſo the live ſtock were landed, and put to graze in the meadows that bordered on the ſhore.

On the 17th, Capt. Cook, with Omai, took an airing on horſeback to the great aſtoniſhment of the inhabitants, many hundreds of whom

followed

followed them with loud acclamations. Omai, to excite their admiration the more, was dreffed cap-a-pee in a fuit of armour, which he carried with him, and was mounted and caparifoned with his fword and pike, like St. George going to kill the dragon, whom he exactly reprefented; only that Omai had piftols in his holfters, of which the poor faint knew not the ufe. Omai, however, made good ufe of his arms, and when the crowd became clamorous, and troublefome, he every now and then pulled out a piftol and fired it among them, which never failed to fend them fcampering away.

For thefe laft two or three days, the caulkers from both fhips were employed, in ftopping the leaks of the Difcovery; and the carpenters in fecuring the mafts, till we fhould arrive at the port of Mattavai, where the fhips were to undergo a thorough repair.

On the 18th and 19th it blew a hard gale, and we were obliged to vear out 20 fathom more of our beft bower cable, as we rode hard at our moorings.

On the 21ft, the fignal was made for unmooring,

Early on the 22d, in the morning, the live ftock were taken on board, and about nine we weighed and failed, accompanied with feveral canoes, though the wind blew a ftorm, and we failed under double-reefed top-fails. In the evening, the Refolution took her old ftation

in

in Mattavai Bay; but the wind suddenly shifting
and the breeze coming full from the land, we
were driven 3 leagues to leeward of the bay; by
which we were reduced to the necessity of working all night to windward, amidst thunder, lightning and rain, and among reefs of coral rocks,
on which we every moment expected to perish.
We burnt false fires, and fired several guns of
distress; but no answer from the Resolution,
nor could we see any object to direct us during
this perilous night.

In the morning of the 23d, the weather
cleared up, and we could see the Resolution
about three leagues to windward, when a shift
of wind happening in our favour, we took advantage of it, and by twelve at noon were
safely moored within a cable's length of
the Resolution. It is impossible to give an
adequate idea of the joy, which the natives expressed upon our arrival in this bay, because
their manner of expressing joy is so different
from our sensations, that were we to see persons
stabbing themselves with sharp instruments till
their bodies were besmeared with blood, we
should think they were pierced with the most
frantic despair, and that it would be almost
impossible to assuage their grief; whereas beating their breasts, tearing their hair, and prick-
ing their heads, their hands, their bodies, are
the most significant signs of their gladness to see
the friends they love best. At the same time
they

they are ready to overwhelm you with kindnefs, and would give you, for the moment, all they have in the world, but the very next hour crave all back again, and like children teize you for every thing you have got.

The fhips were no fooner fecured, than the failors began ftripping them of every yard of rigging they had left; for certainly no fhips were ever in a more fhattered condition. Our voyage from New Zealand, if not from the cape, might be faid to be one continued feries of tempeftuous weather, fufpended only by a few intervals of fun-fhine; and the employment of our artificers at fea and on fhore, a laborious exertion of their faculties to keep us above water. Here it was not only neceffary to ftrip the main-maft of the Difcovery; but to take it out and carry it on fhore, to be properly fecured. This was a work of no fmall difficulty. Here too it was found neceffary, to unfhip our ftores of every kind; to air and repack the powder; new bake that part of the bread that had contracted any dampnefs: to erect the forge on fhore; and in fhort, to fet all our artificers to work on board and on fhore, to refit the fhips for the further profecution of the voyage.

A meffenger was difpatched from Captain Cook to King Otoo, to acquaint him with our arrival, and to defire his permiffion to fend the cattle he had brought from Britain, to feed in the paftures of Oparree. The king expreffed
his

Dodd. del.   Royce sculp.

Omais Public Entry on his first landing at Otaheite.

his joy on the return of Capt. Cook, and readily gave his consent. He at the same time ordered one of his principal officers to accompany the messenger in his return, and to take with him presents of fresh provisions for the commanders of both ships, and to invite them on shore, to dine with him the next day. This invitation was accepted, and it was agreed between the Captains, that their visit should be made with as much state as their present circumstances would admit. The marines and music were therefore ordered to be in readiness at an appointed hour, and all the rowers to be clean dressed.

On the 25th, about noon, the commanders, with the principal officers and gentlemen, embarked on board the pinnaces, which, on this occasion, were decked in all the magnificence that silken streamers, embroidered ensigns, and other gorgeous decorations could display. Omai, to surprize the more, was cloathed in a Captain's uniform, and could hardly be distinguished from a British officer.

From Mattavai to Oparree, was about six leagues. They arrived at the landing-place, about one o'clock in the afternoon, and were received by the marines already under arms. As soon as the company were disembarked, the whole band of music struck up a grand military march, and the procession began. The road from the beach to the entrance of the palace

N   (about

(about half a mile) was lined on both sides with natives from all parts, expecting to see Omai on horseback, as the account of his appearance on his first landing on the other side of the island, as before related, had already reached the inhabitants on this. As he appeared to them in disguise, he was not known; they were not however wholly disappointed, as the grandeur of the procession exceeded every thing of the kind they had ever seen. The whole court were likewise assembled, and the king, with his sisters, on the approach of Capt. Cook, came forth to meet him. As he was perfectly known to them, their first salutations were frank and friendly, according to the known customs of the Otaheiteans, and when these were over, proper attention was paid to every gentleman in company; and that too with a politeness that, to those who had never been on this island before, was quite unexpected.

As soon as the company had entered the palace and were seated, and some discourse had passed between the king and Capt. Cook, Omai was presented to his Majesty. He had hitherto escaped unnoticed, with the other officers who were not particularly known. Omai paid his Majesty the usual homage of a subject to a sovereign in that country, which consists of little more than being uncovered before him, and then entered into familiar conversation, on the subject of his travels. The Earees, or kings

of

of this country, are not above discoursing with the meanest of their subjects, but Omai was now considered here as a person of rank, and a favourite of the Earees of the ships. The king, impatient to hear his story, asked him a hundred questions before he gave him time to answer one. He asked him concerning the Earee-da-hai, or Great King of Pretanne, his place of residence, his court, his attendants, his warriors, his ships of war, his morai, the extent of his possessions, &c. &c. Omai did not fail to magnify the grandeur of the Great King. He represented the splendour of his court by the brilliancy of the stars in the firmament; the extent of his dominions, by the vast expanse of heaven; the greatness of his power, by the thunder that shakes the earth. He said, the Great King of Pretanne had three hundred thousand warriors every day at his command, cloathed like those who now attended the Earees of the ships, and more than double that number of sailors, who traversed the globe, from the rising of the sun to his setting; that his ships of war exceeded those at Mattavai in magnitude, in the same proportion, as those exceeded the small canoes at Oparree.—His Majesty appeared all astonishment, and could not help interrupting him. He asked, if what he said was true, where the Great King could find people to navigate so many ships as covered the ocean from one extremity to the other? and if he could find men, where he could find provi-

sions

fions for fo great a multitude? Omai affured him, that he had fpoken nothing but truth; that in one city only on the banks of a river far removed from the Sea, there were more people than were contained in the whole group of iflands with which his Majefty was acquainted; that the country was full of large populous cities; notwithftanding which provifions were fo plentiful, that for a piece of a certain yellow metal, like that of which he had feen many [meaning the medals given by the Captain to the Earees] the great king could purchafe as much provifions as would maintain a failor on board a fhip a whole year; that in the country of the great king, there are more than 100 different kinds of four footed animals, from the fize of the fmalleft rat when it is firft brought forth, to the magnitude of a ftage erected on an ordinary canoe, on which fix men may ftand erect; that all thefe animals are fo numerous in their feveral kinds, and propagate fo faft, that were it not that fome were killed for food, and that others prey one upon the other, they would over-run the land. Omai, having by this relation obviated king Ottoo's doubts, adverted to his firft queftions. He faid, the fhips of war of Pretanne were furnifhed with poo-poos [guns] each of which would receive the largeft poo-poo his Majefty had yet feen, within it; that fome carried 200 and more of thofe poo-poos, with fuitable accommodations for a thoufand fighting men, and ftowage for all forts

of

of cordage and warlike ftores, befides provifions and water for the men and other animals, for 100 or 200 days; and that they were fometimes abroad as long warring with the enemies of the great king in the different parts of his dominions in the remoteft regions of the earth; that they frequently carried with them in thefe expeditions poo-poos, that would hold a fmall hog within them, and which throw hollow globes of iron, of a vaft bignefs, filled with fire and all manner of combuftibles, and implements of deftruction, to a great diftance; a few of which, were they to be thrown among the fleet of Otaheite, would fet them on fire, and deftroy the whole navy, were they ever fo numerous. The king feemed more aftonifhed than delighted with this narration, and fuddenly leftOmai, to join the company that were in converfation with Capt. Cook and the other officers. By this time dinner was nearly ready, and as foon as the company were properly feated, was brought in by as many tow-tows as there were perfons to dine; befides thefe, the king, the two commanders, and Omai, had each of them two perfons of fuperior rank to attend them. The dinner confifted of fifh and fowl of various kinds, dreffed after their manner; barbicued pigs, ftewed yams, and fruits of the moft delicious flavour, all ferved with an eafe and regularity that is feldom to be found at

N 3   European

European tables, when the ladies are excluded from making part of the company.

As foon as dinner was over, which admits of no ceremony, we were conducted to the theatre, where a company of players were in readinefs to perform a dramatical entertainment. The drama was regularly divided into three acts: the firft confifted of dancing and dumb fhew; the fecond of comedy; which to thofe who underftood the language was very laughable, as Omai and the natives appeared highly diverted the whole time; the laft was a mufical piece, in which the young princeffes were the fole performers. There were between the acts fome feats of arms exhibited. The combatants were armed with lances and clubs. One made the attack, the other ftood upon the defenfive. He who made the attack brandifhed his lance, and either threw, pufhed or ufed it in aid of his club. He who was upon the defenfive, ftuck the point of his lance in the ground, in an ob-lique direction, fo that the upper part rofe above his head, and by obferving the eye of his ene-my, parried his blows or his ftrokes by the motion of his lance. By his dexterity at this manœuvre he turned afide the lance, and it was rare that he was hurt by the club. If his anta-gonift ftruck at his legs, he fhewed his agility by jumping over the club; and if at his head, he was no lefs nimble in crouching under it. Their dexterity confifted chiefly in the defence,

other-

otherwise the combat might have been fatal, which always ended in good humour.

These entertainments, which generally last about four hours, are really diverting; their dancing has been much improved by copying the European manner. In the hornpipe they really excel their masters: they add contortions of the face and muscles to the nimbleness of the foot, that are inimitable, and must, in spite of our gravity, provoke laughter; their country dances too are well regulated; and they have dances of their own, that are equal to those at our best theatres; their comedy seems to consist of some simple story, made laughable by the manner of delivery, something in the style of the merry andrews formerly at Bartholomew fair; and their singing is very simple, and might be much improved. Had Omai been of a theatrical cast, he doubtless might have very much improved their stage; for their performers appear inferior to none in the powers of imitation.

The play being over, and night approaching, our commanders took their leave, after inviting the king and his attendants to dine on board the ships. We were conducted to the water-side in the same manner as we approached the palace, and were attended by the king and royal family.

On the 25th in the morning, Omai's mother, and several of his relations arrived. Their

meeting

meeting was too unnatural to be pleasing. We could not see a woman frantically striking her face and arms with sharks teeth, till she was all over besmeared with blood, without being hurt; as it conveyed no idea of joy to feeling minds, we could never be reconciled to this absurd custom. She brought with her several large hogs, with bread-fruit, bananos, and other productions of the Island of Ulitea, as presents to the Captains, and she and her friends received in return, a great variety of cutlery, such as knives, scissars, files, &c. besides some red feathers, which last were even more acceptable than iron. They continued to visit the ship occasionally till she quitted the island.

In the afternoon King Ottoo, with his chiefs and attendants, and two young princesses his sisters, performers in the interlude of the preceding night, came on board, bringing with them six large hogs, with a proportionable quantity of fruits of various kinds. They were entertained as usual, with a sight of all the curiosities on board the ships, and the young princesses, longing for almost every thing they saw, were gratified to their utmost wishes, with bracelets of beads, looking-glasses, bits of china, artificial nosegays, and a variety of other trinkets, of which, they had one of a sort each, while at the same time the king and his chiefs amused themselves with the carpenters, armourers and other artificers, employed in the repairs of the ships, casting

longing

longing eyes on the tools and implements with which they performed their work. In this manner they paſt the time till dinner was ready. King Ottoo, with his chiefs, dined with the Captains, the principal officers, and Omai in the great cabin, while the ladies were feaſted in an apartment ſeparated on purpoſe, and waited upon by their own ſervants. During dinner, the muſic, particularly the bag-pipes, with which the Indians ſeemed moſt delighted, continued to play, and the young ladies who were within hearing, though out of ſight, could hardly refrain from dancing the whole time. After dinner the king and his nobles were preſſed to drink wine; but moſt of them having felt its power before, declined taſting it ; one or two drank a glaſs, but refuſed to drink any more. When the tables were cleared, the ladies joined the company, and then horn-pipes and country dances after the Engliſh manner commenced, in which the young ladies joined with great good humour. Some jovial ſongs ſucceeded, and our Indian viſitors took leave in the evening in great good humour.

What contributed not a little to increaſe the pleaſure of the king, was a preſent made him by Capt. Cook, of a large quantity of the choiceſt red feathers that could be purchaſed in the iſlands of Amſterdam. Red feathers, as has already been obſerved, are held in the higheſt eſtimation in Otaheite, and in all the

society islands, but more particularly by the
chiefs of the former island, by whom they are
used as amulets, or rather as propitiations
to make their prayers acceptable to the good
spirit whom they invoke with tufts of those feathers in their hands, made up in a peculiar manner, and held in a certain position with much
seeming solemnity.   The ordinary sorts of red
feathers were collected by officers and men all
over the Friendly Islands; but those that were
now presented to king Ottoo were of a superior kind, and were in value as much above
the ordinary red feathers, as real pearls are in
value above French paste.   They were taken
from the heads of the paroquets of Tonga taboo and Ea-oo whe, which are of superlative
beauty, and precious in proportion to their
fineness and the vivid glow of their dazzling
colours.   Here we learnt that Capt. Cook, in
his former voyage, being in great distress for
want of fresh provisions, and being plentifully
supplied by king Ottoo, promised that if he
ever should return to Otahéite, he would make
him richer in *ouravine* (precious feathers)
than all the princes in the neighbouring isles.
This gave rise to an opinion, that it was to ful-
fil this promise that we were led so far out of
our way as has been already remarked.   But
there is much more reason to conclude, that
the strong easterly winds that prevailed when
we approached the southern tropic made our

direct

direct course to Otaheite impracticable.   Had
Capt. Cook regarded his promise to Ottoo as
inviolable, he would most certainly have shaped
his course from New Zealand to the Friendly
Islands the nearest way, which would have
shortened our voyage several months ; unless
we can suppose that he had forgotten his promise, and that when he came within a few days
sail of his destined port, he recollected himself,
and then changed his direction, to enable him to
keep his word.   To which of these causes it
was owing, some future publications may probably give light ; but to us who were not in
the secret, it appeared a mystery.   We were
advanced some degrees to the eastward of Her-
vey's Isles, which lie in 19 deg. 18 min. S. lat.
and 201 E. long. before we altered our course
to the westward to make for Amsterdam, which
lies in 21 deg. 15 min. S. and 185 deg. E. long.
whereas the island of Ulitea, of which Omai
was a native, lay in lat, 16 deg. 45 min. and
long. 208 deg. 35 min. E.   Why our course
to the former was preferred before the latter,
involves the mystery.

Though all public trade was prohibited, as was
usual, till the ships should be furnished with fresh
provisions ; it was not easy to restrain the men
on shore from trading with the women, who
were for ever enticing them to desert.   The
ladies of pleasure in London have not half the
winning ways that are practised by the Otahei-

tean

tean miffes to allure their gallants. With the feeming innocence of doves they mingle the wilynefs of ferpents. They have however one quality which is peculiar to themfelves, and that is conftancy. When once they have made their choice, it muft be owing to the failor himfelf if his miftrefs ever proves falfe to him. No women upon earth are more faithful. They will endeavour to make themfelves miftreffes of all their lovers poffefs, but they will fuffer no one elfe to invade their property, nor will they embezzle any part of it themfelves without having firft obtained confent; but that confent is not eafily witheld; for they are inceffant in their importunities, and will never ceafe afking while the failor has a rag or a nail to beftow.

During our four months ftay at this and the neighbouring iflands, there was hardly a failor on board that had not made a very near connection with one or other of the women of this ifland; nor indeed many officers that were proof againft the allurements of the better fort, who were no lefs amorous and artful, though more referved, than thofe of the inferior order.

The temperature of the climate, the plenty of frefh provifions, fifh, fowl, pork, bread-fruit, yams, (a kind of fweet potatoes, which they have the art of ftewing with their pork in a very favoury manner) added to the moft delicious fruits of the ifland, contributed not a little to make our ftay here not only tolerable, but

even

even defirable; nor did idlenefs get poffeffion even of thofe who were moft indolently inclined. We had not a vacant hour between bufinefs and pleafure that was unemployed. We wanted no coffee-houfes to kill time; nor Ranelaghs or Vauxhalls for our evening entertainments. Every nightly affembly in the plantations of this happy ifle is furnifhed by beneficent nature with a more luxurious feaft than all the dainties of the moft fumptuous champetre, though lavifhed with unlimited profufion, and emblazoned with the moft expenfive decorations of art. Ten thoufand lamps, combined and ranged in the moft advantageous order by the hands of the beft artift, appear faint, when compared with the brilliant ftars of heaven that unite their fplendor to illuminate the groves, the lawns, the ftreams of Oparree. In thefe elifian fields immortality alone is wanting to the enjoyment of all thofe pleafures which the poet's fancy has conferred on the fhades of departed heroes as the higheft rewards of heroic virtue.

But amidft fo many delights it was not for human nature to fubfift long without fatiety. Our feamen began to be licentious, and our officers to be punctilious. Several of the former were feverely punifhed for indecency in furpaffing the vice of the natives by their fhamelefs manner of indulging their fenfual appetites; and two of the latter went afhore to terminate an affair of honour by the decifion of their piftols,

l

It happened that neither of them were dextrous markfmen; they vented their rage by the fury with which they began the attack, and after difcharging three balls each, they returned on board without any hurt except fpoiling a hat, a ball having pierced it, and grazed upon the head of him who wore it. It was however remarked, that thefe gentlemen were better friends than ever during the remaining part of the voyage.

While thefe things went on by way of amufement to fome, others were more ufefully employed in the repairs of the fhip. The maft that was fhattered in the head, and carried afhore to be repaired, was in a fhort time rendered more firm than ever; the fails that had been fplit, and were otherwife rendered unfit for further fervice, were replaced: the cordage carefully examined, the mafts new rigged, and in fhort the whole repairs completed with more celerity and ftrength than could have been expected in a place where many conveniences were wanting to fit us out for that part of our voyage which ftill remained to be performed.

For this purpofe repairs were not more neceffary for our equipment than provifions. The purveyors, therefore, and butchers were inceffantly employed in purchafing and killing hogs for prefent ufe, and the falters in falting the overplus for future ftores, while the Captains and fuperior officers were devifing new amufements

ments to keep the king and his chiefs in good
humour, in order to encourage their people to
furnish us with ample supplies.

Not a day passed but some new exhibition
was contrived for their entertainment. Omai,
of whom little use had yet been made, contributed his share to vary the scenes of pleasure.
He one day rode out on horseback, in his armour, brandishing his glittering sword, to the
terror and amazement of the gaping multitude.
Another day he diverted them with playing off
fire-works, under the direction of the chief engineer. He was here made a principal in all
public shews, and was placed upon a footing
with king Ottoo himself. In a naval review,
which was exhibited by Towha, the great admiral, Omai had the command of one division
of the fleet, while king Ottoo commanded a-
nother division, and Towha the centre. The
great dexterity appeared in their arrangements
to land, where the military exercises were chiefly
carried on; one party endeavouring to supplant
the other, in order to get possession of the most
advantageous ground. In these manœuvres,
Omai acquitted himself with tolerable applause,
being well supported in all his exercises by
Capt. Cook, who played him off as a prodigy
of genius, in honour of Pretannie, where, it
was given out, his talents had been much improved.

During

During our ſtay, there was a rumour of actual war, and the forces of the iſland, both by ſea and land, were called forth in earneſt, to be in readineſs to embark on the firſt notice. All trade was now ſtopped; no cocoa-nuts to be had, the milk of which was the only liquor, except water, which the ſhip's company were allowed to drink, and the weather being exceſſive hot, there was great murmuring among the men both on board and on ſhore. Captain Cook was under the neceſſity of interceding with king Ottoo to renew trade. Whether peace was made, or only a truce for a ſhort time, is not certain, but in a few days the warriors diſperſed, and every thing went on again after the uſual manner.

On the above rumour, it was computed that near 300 war canoes were muſtered in Mattavai bay, with ſtages on each, on which ſat from three to ſix chiefs in their warlike dreſſes, which ſeemed calculated rather for ſhew than uſe in battle. On their heads were large turbans wound round in many folds, and over that a monſtrous helmet; and on their bodies, inſtead of the light airy dreſs worn in common, they were incumbered by many garments of their own cloth, which added indeed to their ſtature, but which muſt diſable them to exert their ſtrength in the day of battle. Men of fertile imagination, fond of tracing the analogy of antient cuſtoms, among the different nations

of

of the world, might possibly discover some similarity between these cumbrous dresses, and those of the knights of antient chivalry, who fought in armour. It is certain that the Otaheitean who fights on foot must feel the same encumbrance from his heavy war-dress, as the antient knight, who fought on horseback, must have done from his unweildy armour; and there is no doubt but the former will, one time or other, be laid aside in the tropical isles, as much as the latter is now in every other part of the world.

Before we left Mattavai, Oedidee, who made the voyage to the southward with Capt. Cook, in his former voyage for the discovery of a southern continent, came to pay his respects to his patron and friend. He brought with him a wife whom he had lately married, which discredits the notion that was universally believed by former voyagers, that those who belonged to the society of Areoys were sworn to celibacy. Either this man was an impostor or the fact just mentioned cannot be true. He appeared in a rich English dress, which had been sent him as a present from England, perhaps from the Admiralty. He was joyfully received by Capt. Cook, and had much respect paid him. Soon after his arrival, fire-works of a new device were played off, before many thousands of the natives; but it was easy to remark, that they were not all equally delighted with the exhibition.

O   The

The common people were thrown into the utmost confternation at the ftorm of thunder and lightening, which almoft inftantly fucceeded. Nor were they ever perfectly reconciled to us afterwards. They thought it prefumption in us to provoke the Etwas, by imitating their powers; and many of them retired to the woods, and never returned again to their houfes during our ftay.

Whether they really wifhed us to be gone, or dreaded our ftay, an alarm was foon after fpread, that four European fhips were arrived at Oaite Piha; that they had landed fome men there, and were taking in refrefhments to enable them to proceed. This report was every where circulated; and whether Capt. Cook believed it, or only made it a pretence to quicken our activity, he gave inftant orders to clear the decks, mount the guns, which lay as it were buried in the hold, and to get every thing in readinefs for action. In the mean time he fent Mr. Williamfon, 3d. Lieutenant, in the great cutter, manned and armed, to learn the truth of the report, by looking into the harbour of Oaite Piha, to fee if any foreign fhips were at anchor there, or whether the whole rumour was a fiction. That gentleman executed his commiffion with great celerity; and in little more than two days, twice doubled Point Venus, failed more than 300 miles, made the harbour he was fent to examine, and brought word that the

only

only grounds for the report were, that four large trading canoes from an adjacent isle, had been there a few days before his arrival, but that they sailed again immediately, having been totally disappointed of a market.

Though we were now relieved from the apprehensions of an attack, we were not suffered to relax in our preparations to depart. Wood and water had already been taken on board, and as much provisions as could be procured, and little remained to be done, except to reimbark our live-stock, to strike the tents, and bring off the baggage of the officers and men, who had been stationed on shore. Notice was therefore given to king Ottoo, of our intentions to sail with the first fair wind. He seemed to express great concern at our sudden resolution, and came on board, attended with Towha, his great admiral, and the principal officers of his court, who all brought with them presents of hogs and fruit, the only valuable productions of the island, except wood and water to European voyagers, and received in return axes, hatchets, spike-nails, and cutlery ware, &c. which were reserved to the last, in order to encourage the chiefs to use their utmost endeavours with their people, to bring in their hogs while it was yet in our power to receive them. No people on earth could express their gratitude with more seeming sincerity, than the king and his chiefs for the presents they had

received;

received; nor were our commanders and officers wanting in fuitable returns.

On the 28th, having now been juft 40 days on the ifland, king Ottoo came on board, to invite our commanders with their officers to Oparree, as he underftood it was to be the laft time that he fhould have the opportunity of paying us his acknowledgements on fhore.

On the 29th, the pinnaces were ordered out, and we proceeded to Oparree, in the fame ftate as on our ʃfirft vifit.   At the landing-place we were received with uncommon marks of friend-fhip.   Every chief in that part of the ifland of which Ottoo was the Earee-da-hai or Lord paramount, to the number of 500 and more, attended, and conducted us to the king's houfe or palace, where a fumptuous banquet was provided, and after dinner a more numerous and brilliant company of performers affembled at the theatre for our entertainment, than we had ever feen on any ftage in the tropical iflands before.

There is a famenefs in their drama, that admits of little or no variation, as perhaps to foreigners, who are unacquainted with the language and manners of a country, there may appear to be in every ftage-exhibition, wherever performed.   Be that as it may.   The dreffes on this occafion were entirely new, and by far more fhowy than formerly; the number of dancers were increafed; ten young ladies com-
                                                          pofed

Representation of the Hevva at Otaheite.

poſed the firſt group, with their heads moſt magnificently ornamented with beads, red feathers, ſhells of the moſt beautiful colours, and wreathed with flowers in ſo elegant a ſtyle, as hardly to be excelled; had their muſic been equal to their performance, this part of the exhibition would have been compleat.

A party of warriors were next introduced, dreſſed in their war-habits, conſiſting, as has already been obſerved, of different coloured cloth, of their own manufacture, ſo ingeniouſly faſhioned and blended together with ſo much art, as, with the helmets that cover their heads, to fill the ſtage with men, of whoſe majeſtic figure it is not eaſy to convey an idea. Theſe were armed with ſpears, lances, and battle-axes, and exhibited all the forms of attack and defence which are practiced in real action. The principal performers were the king's brother and a chief of gigantic ſtature, who diſplayed ſuch wonderful grimaces and diſtortions of face and countenance, by way of provocation and challenge, as were not only laughable in ſome attitudes, but terrible in others. After theſe diſappeared, the players were brought forward, and performed a more ſerious piece than we had yet ſeen, at which the natives ſat graver and more compoſed than uſual. And the whole performance concluded with a dance of ten boys, dreſt in every reſpect like the girls in the firſt ſcene, with their hair flowing in ringlets down their

O 3 ſhoulders,

shoulders, and their heads ornamented in a very theatrical style.

When the play was over we returned to our boats, attended by the whole assembly, who accompanied us to the water-side, where the king took a most affectionate leave.

On the 29th Capt. Cook ordered all the women to be put on shore, which was a task not easily effected, most of them being very loth to depart; nor was it of much consequence, as they found means afterwards to follow us to Hueheine, Ulitea, and the other society isles; nor did they leave us till our final departure on our northern discoveries, never more to return.

Several of the sailors being very desirous to stay at Otaheite, king Ottoo interested himself in their behalf, and endeavoured to prevail on Capt. Cook to grant their request; but he peremptorily rejected every application of that kind though often repeated; nor would he suffer any of the natives to enter on board though many would gladly have accompanied us whereever we intended to sail, and that too after they were assured that we never intended to visit their country any more. Some of the women too would have followed their Fhoonoas, or Pretanne husbands, could they have been permitted; but Capt. Cook was equally averse to the taking any of the natives away, as to the leaving any of his own people behind. He was sensible, that when once cloyed with enjoyment, they would

would reciprocally pine for home, to which it would not be in their power to return; and that for a little prefent gratification, they would rifque the happinefs of the remaining part of their lives.

King Ottoo, when he found he could not obtain his wifhes, in this refpect, applied to Capt. Cook for another favour, which was, to allow his carpenters to make him a cheft, or prefs, to fecure the treafures he had accumulated in prefents, and by way of traffic, from the European voyagers. He even begged a bed to be placed in it, where he intended to fleep. This Capt. Cook readily granted, and while the workmen were employed in this fervice they were plentifully fupplied with barbicued hogs, and fuch dainties as the country afforded, and were fo carefully attended and protected, that they did not lofe fo much as a fingle nail. It was fome of thefe workmen that Ottoo was fo defirous to retain; but thefe were of too much confequence on board to be parted with, had there been no other motive for bringing them away; nor was Ottoo much concerned about the departure of the reft.

While the carpenters were bufied in making this uncommon piece of furniture, king Ottoo was conftant in attending their operations, and Omai had frequent conferences with him on the fubject of his travels. He aftonifhed him more

by

by the relation he gave of the magnificence o
the Morais in *Pretanne*, than by all the wonders he had before surprized him. When he
told him that the king's morai was open to all
comers, and that the persons of the deceased
kings were to be seen as perfect to appearance
as when in the vigour of youth, he seemed to
lament that his date of existence was to be limi-
ted with his life; and that his remains were
to perish, while his Morai preserved no memory, that he had ever had a being. Omai endeavoured to impress him with an idea of the
magnificence of the tombs and memorials of
the dead that were to be seen in the Morais of
Pretanne; but having nothing to compare them
to, he was unable to make himself sufficiently
understood; nor was he more successful in de-
scribing the solemn grandeur of the places of
worship where the people assembled every se-
venth day and at other stated times, to offer
up their prayers to the good spirit. Of the
splendour of the theatres he could speak more
intelligibly, as some faint idea of them might
be gathered from what had been exhibited on
board the ships, and in the illuminations and
fire-works played off on shore. When Omai
told him of the magnitude of the palaces and
houses in Pretanne, of their decorations and
furniture; of the extent of their plantations,
and the multitude of living animals with
which they were stored, he listened to him with
                                        particular

particular attention, as not doubting the truth of his relation; but when he began to defcribe the roads and the rapidity with which the people travelled in carriages drawn by four footed animals, no child could ever exprefs greater furprize at Gulliver's travelling to the world of the moon on ganzas, than Ottoo, when Omai affured him, they could traverfe an extent of ground equal to the whole length of the ifland of Otaheite, in a fingle day.

The king, as appeared by his generofity to Omai, was highly entertained by the ftory of his travels; for when he went to take leave, his majefty prefented him with a double canoe, properly equipped and manned, in the room of that which he purchafed at New Zealand.

Every preparation for failing being already compleated, the live ftock all on board except two cows and a bull, two ewes and a ram, two fhe-goats and two geefe, which were left as prefents to king Ottoo,

On the 29th both fhips were under fail, directing their courfe to the weftward to Emoa and Hueheine, accompanied by Omai in his Otaheitean veffel, with his two New Zealand youths on board, who difcoveied no uneafinefs at their prefent fituation, nor any defire to return home.

The ifland of Otaheite has already been fo often and fo accurately defcribed, and the manners, cuftoms, and ways of living of the inhabitants,

bitants, fo amply enlarged upon by former voyagers, that little remains to be added. The writer was attentive only to two facts, one of which he found reafon to believe had been mifreprefented, and the other very unfairly related; the firft refpects the fociety of Arreoys, compofed, as it was faid, of a certain number of men and women, affociated in leudnefs, and fo abandoned to all fenfe of humanity, as to deftroy the iffue of their libidinous intercourfe; than which nothing could be more injurious to the characters of any people than this diabolical practice afcribed to this fociety.

There are in this and the adjoining iflands perfons of a middle rank between the Manahounas or Yeomen and the Earees, who having no concern in the government, nor any diftinct property in the iflands, affociate together for their own amufement, and the entertainment of the public. Thefe travel from place to place, and from ifland to ifland in companies, not unlike thofe of the ftrolling players in England, only that they perform without pay; but that they cohabit indifcriminately one with another, fo many men with fo many women in common, is no otherwife true, than the fame may be fufpected among the ftrolling companies juft mentioned; nor are they under any other reftraints from marrying, than that the fociety admits of no marriages among themfelves, nor of any married people to be of their fociety, it being

a rule

a rule with them, never to be encumbered with children; if therefore it fhould happen, that iffue fhould prove the confequence of a cafual amour, there is no alternative; the mother muft either quit the fociety, or fomehow or other difpofe of her child, which fome of them do there, as many unfortunate girls do here, by fecretly making away with them to avoid infamy, it being equally difgraceful there to be found with child while members of the fociety of Arreoys, as it is for women here to be fo found without hufbands.

The other fact, which the writer took pains to determine, was, whether the beaftly cuftom imputed to them, of gratifying their paffions without regard to places or perfons, was well founded? and he folemnly declares, that the groffeft indecencies he ever faw practiced while on the ifland were by the licentioufnefs of our own people, who, without regard to character, made no fcruple to attempt openly and by force what they were unable to effect with the free voluntary confent of the objects of their defire; for which feveral of them were feverely punifhed. To affert, therefore, that not the leaft trace of fhame is to be found among thefe people in doing that openly which all other people are naturally induced to hide, is an injurious calumny, not warranted by cuftom, nor fupported by the general practice even of the loweft clafs of individuals among them.

These

These people have one custom in common with the Neapolitans and Maltese, which ought not to be forgotten, and that is, their fishing in the night and reposing themselves in the day; like them too, they burn torches while they fish, which they make of the oil drawn from the cocoa-nut.

On the 29th we continued our course the whole day, under double-reefed top-sails; and in the evening came in sight of the little island of Emoa, where we anchored next day in a safe harbour, and were received by the people with every appearance of hospitality.

On the 30th, our live-stock was landed, our carpenters sent out to cut wood, and our purveyors to collect hogs. Here we found Omai, who had out-sailed us in his double-masted canoe, and who, on his arrival, had been diverting the natives with his feats of arms, and had raised their curiosity to a very high degree, by acquainting them with our intention of paying them a visit, as no European ship had ever anchored at their island before. The chiefs of the island came on board, with large hogs by way of presents; and were presented, in return, with axes, hatchets, looking-glasses, and red feathers: our purveyors were likewise much gratified, by the success they met with in marketing; purchasing the largest hogs for the meerest trifles; as for instance, a hog of 200

weight

weight for twelve red feathers, and so in proportion.

But this friendly intercourse was soon changed to a scene of desolation that no injury we could receive from the pilfering disposition of the inhabitants could justify. The people had brought us every thing their island afforded, and had left it to the generosity of the purchasers to give, in return, whatever they pleased; but unfortunately

On the 2d of October, a goat was missing from the live-stock. It had been secretly conveyed away in the night, from the pastures on which they were placed to feed, notwithstanding the vigilance of the guard appointed to look after them. With the loss of this animal, which no doubt was looked upon as a prize to the thief, the Earee of the island was made acquainted by Capt. Cook, and a preremptory requisition made to have it restored, on pain of having his country laid waste, his shipping destroyed, and himself personally punished for the crime of his subject. The king promised his assistance, and required time for enquiry, but as soon as he was at liberty he absconded, and was no more seen; and the goat being still missing, and no means used for recovering and restoring it, a party from both ships, with the marines in a body, were ordered out, to carry the threats of our commander into execution. For three days successively

The Ships approa

Royce Sc.

Island. A. Omai's Boat.

cessively they continued their devastations,
burning and destroying above 200 of the best
houses of the inhabitants, and as many of their
large war canoes; at the same time cutting
down their fruit-trees, and destroying their plantations.   The natives who lived at a distance,
hearing of the havock that was made near the
bay, filled their canoes with stones and sunk
them, in hopes of preserving them, but that
availed them nothing.   The Captain ordered
boats to be manned and armed, the canoes that
were sunk to be weighed up and destroyed;
and in short, a general desolation to be carried through the whole island, if the goat should
be still witheld.   Add to this, that two young
natives of quality, being found on board our
ship, were made prisoners, and told they were
to be put to death, if the goat should not be
restored within a certain time.   The youths
protested their own innocence, and disclaimed
all knowledge of the guilty persons; notwithstanding which, every preparation was apparently made for putting them both to death.
Large ropes were carried upon the main deck,
and made fast fore and aft; axes, chains, and
instruments of torture were placed upon the
quarter deck in the sight of the young men,
whose terrors were increased by the information
of Omai, who gave them to understand that,
by all these solemn preparations, their doom

was

was finally determined. Under thefe apprehenfions, the poor youths remained till

On the 9th, when about three in the afternoon a body of between 50 and 60 natives, were
feen from the fhip haftening to the harbour,
who, when they came near, held up the goat
in their arms, in raptures that they had found
it, and that it was ftill alive.

The joy of the imprifoned young men is not
to be expreffed; and when they were releafed,
inftead of fhewing any figns of refentment, they
were ready to fall down and worfhip their deliverers. It can fcarce be credited, when the de-
vaftation ceafed, how foon the injury they had
fuffered was forgotten, and provifions again
brought to market, as if no violences had ever
been committed by us; only the Earee of the
ifland never made his appearance.

All this while multitudes of the inhabitants of
Otaheite, who had ftolen off in the night in
their canoes (moftly women) were witneffes of
the feverity with which this theft was punifhed
at Emoa; but it feemed to make no unfavoura-
ble impreffion upon them. They continued their
good offices as long as we remained in the Society ifles.

Having procured a large quantity of wood,
of which Otaheite furnifhed but a fcanty fupply, and likewife a number of hogs for prefent
ufe and future ftores,

On

On the 12th in the morning we prepared to sail, and before noon were out at sea with a fine breeze, directing our course to Hueheine, to which island Omai had previously set sail before us.

In the night the weather being hazy, Omai lost sight of the ships, and fired his gun, which was answered by the Resolution. During the afternoon the breeze left us, and a dead calm ensuing, made our Otaheitean passengers immoderately sick by the working of the ship. They then began to repent their folly in following the fugitives whom they had no hopes of ever reclaiming, and to wish themselves safe home again on the shores of Mattavai.

On the 13th in the morning we came in sight of Hueheine, and about noon were close in with the land, when the natives came in multitudes, with hogs and provisions of all kinds, as presents to their friends. Omai, who had already reached the shore, and hauled his vessel upon the beach, was encircled by the natives, who crouded about him, some to gratify their curiosity, and others to express their joy at his return. In less than half an hour King Oreo was seen to go aboard the Resolution. He had with him two large hogs, as presents to Capt. Cook, with some bread-fruit ready roasted, and a large quantity of bananoes, plantains and other fruit. Capt. Cook received him with open arms, enquiring particularly after the good old venerable

rable

rable King Oree, for whom he entertained the most perfect friendship; and being told he was dead, he could not help shedding tears. We were soon after favoured with a visit from Oreo, who made a like present to Capt. Clarke, and received in return a breast-plate of red feathers, with which he seemed better pleased, than with any that had before been given him.

As soon as he returned on shore, he issued out orders, requiring all his people to behave with the strictest justice to his good friends from Pretanne, and he appointed proper officers to see his orders carried into execution, but without effect; for he had hardly reached his place of abode, before one fellow was detected on board the Resolution, in stealing iron from the armourer's forge, and had one side of his head and one of his eye-brows shaved, besides having an ear cut off, by way of example to deter others.

On the 19th, peace being established in the usual form, the live stock were landed, among which were two horses for Omai, with two cows and a bull for King Oree, if he had been alive, which were afterwards given to his successor.

As this was one of the most plentiful of all the Society Isles, it was proposed to make some stay here, in order to careen the ships, and to lay in provisions for future use. This was the more necessary, as we were about to sail to countries wholly unknown, where it was uncertain what accommodations we might meet with, or

P to

to what ftraits we might be reduced. The tents were therefore put afhore, the beds and furniture of every kind unladen, and every crevice of the fhips examined, fcraped, wafhed with vinegar, and fmoked, and while this laft operation was performing, the lower port-holes were left open, for the rats to make their efcape; in fhort, a thorough revifion was directed to be made of every thing on board, as well to cleanfe the furniture from the vermin, as to remove the danger of infection from putrid air, generated by a perpetual fucceffion of multitudes in clofe refort between decks ever fince our arrival at Otaheite. The fick were at the fame time landed for the benefit of the air, and every means ufed to recover, and to preferve them in health, when recovered.

Among the fick was Capt. Cook himfelf, for whofe recovery the crews of both fhips were under much concern, as the fuccefs of the voyage was thought in a great meafure to depend upon his care and conduct. By the doctor's advice, he was prevailed upon to fleep on fhore; where he was affiduoufly attended night and day by the furgeons of both fhips, who alternately watched with him, till he was out of danger. As foon as he was able, he rode out every day with Omai on horfeback, followed by multitudes of the natives, who, attracted by the novelty of the fight, flocked from the remoteft parts of the ifland, to be fpectators.

In

In the mean time, the ships were crouded with hogs, poured in upon us faster than the butchers and salters could difpatch them; for feveral days after our arrival, fome hundreds great and fmall were brought on board, and if any were refufed, they were thrown into the boats and left behind. Bread-fruit, bananoes, plantains, cocoa-nuts and yams were brought in the fame plentiful proportions, and purchafed for trifles. Red feathers were here, as at Otaheite, a very marketable commodity, with which the feamen made purchafes of cloth, and other manufactures of the ifland; thofe of them, who were followed by their miffes from Otaheite, kept feparate tables for them, at a fmall expence; the miffes catered and cooked for their mates, who feafted every day on barbiqued pigs, ftewed fowls, roafted bread-fruit, cocoa-nuts, and a variety of other delicacies, which were purchafed for them for the mereft trifles. Among the common men, there were many who laid in ftore of thefe good things for their future fnpport in cafe of being reduced to fhort allowance, and they had reafon afterwards to confole themfelves on their provident care.

The example made of the firft Indian thief, by expofing him to the ridicule of his countrymen, had a better effect than a thoufand lafhings, which were forgotten almoft as foon as inflicted; whereas the laughable figure the fellow

low

low made with one ear off, and half the hair of his head fhaved, was a perpetual punifhment, which it was not in his power to conceal. By this feafonable feverity and the vigilance of the officers, whom the king had appointed to fuperintend the police, we continued unmolefted for feveral days.

On our firft approaching the ifland we caft anchor till the ground for mooring fhould be examined, and in weighing, to change our ftation, our cable parted, and we were obliged to leave the anchor behind. This proved a troublefome bufinefs, in which we were affifted by the activity of the natives, who, at fervices of this kind, are very alert. By diving, and properly fixing ropes, they helped us to recover our anchor in a few hours, which we had laboured at, in vain, for feveral days.

The carpenters and caulkers had no fooner compleated their bufinefs on board, than they were ordered on fhore to erect a houfe for Omai, who had been enabled, by the generofity of Capt. Cook, and his other friends, to purchafe a fmall eftate for a plantation, in the cultivation of which he was to proceed after the Englifh manner, and to employ his two New-Zealanders as labourers in digging, and preparing the ground.

The erection of a houfe of pretty large dimenfions, with ftable and out-offices (appendages new, and hitherto unneceffary in this country) was

of

a work of no small labour, and could not be accomplished in any reasonable time, without the assistance of many hands ; the carpenters, and a number of labourers from both ships were therefore set to work, and though a watch was placed to look after their working-tools, the vigilance of Argos, with his hundred eyes, would have been insufficient to have guarded such a valuable treasure from so many crafty Jasons, as daily attended the workmen with a view to carry off some part of the golden prize. It happened, however, that a few chissels, gimblets, and other trifles were all that were missing ; for as no nails or iron were to be used in the construction of the buildings, the saws, axes, adzes, and larger tools were not so easy for them to conceal ; while therefore the chief attention of the centinels were fixed upon these, an Indian found means to carry off a quadrant from the astronomer's observatory ; and though it was almost instantly missed, and the thief discovered, and fired at while he was yet in sight, he found means to escape to the woods, where he concealed his booty, notwithstanding the most vigilant search. At the firing of the gun, and the bustle that succeeded among the Indians who were in crowds about the tents, the marines on board took the alarm, and putting themselves in arms hastened on shore, where they found all quiet, the thief having been found and brought in, by some of his companions, who

were

well rewarded for their fidelity. The fellow
was inftantly taken on board and put in irons,
where he remained all night. In the morning
it appeared he was of fome note, as a number
of hogs, and great quantities of fruit and cloth
were brought on board, to purchafe his releafe ;
but without effect. About noon he was brought
to trial, and fentenced to fuffer the lofs of both
his ears, befides having his head fhaved, and
his eye-brows fleed, than which, no punifhment could have fubjected him to greater difgrace. In this bleeding condition he was fent
on fhore, and expofed, as a fpectacle to intimidate the people from meddling with what
was not their own ; at the fame time they were
given to underftand that theft, among us, was
confidered as a capital crime. The Indians
look'd with horror upon the man, and it was
eafy to perceive, that this act gave them general difguft ; even Omai was affected, though
he endeavoured to juftify it to his Indian
friends, by telling them, that if fuch a crime
had been committed in the country where he
had been, the thief would have been condemned
to lofe his life. How well foever he might carry
the matter off, he dreaded the confequences to
himfelf, which, in part, appeared before we
left the ifland, and were probably more feverely
felt by him, foon after we were gone. However King Oreo and the chiefs about him ftill
continued to keep up appearances ; they paid
and

and received vifits as ufual, made prefents, and accepted returns, and fuffered trade to go on between the inhabitants of the ifland and the fhips companies, as if no offence had been given. At all their feafts and entertainments the Captains and Omai were invited to be guefts, and plays and fireworks fucceeded each other, by way of political finefse, to promote harmony. In the mean time, another theft was committed at the fame place. Mr. King, the aftronomer was robbed of his brandy-cafe, fome plates, and fome knives and forks, which he never recovered; but his quadrant was brought back in a few days after it was ftolen, though very much damaged.

On this occafion, trade was again interrupted, the Indians dreading to come to market when any of their people had been guilty of any fraud.

Capt. Cook, though he rode out every day, attended by Omai, ftill continued in a very weak condition; but was vifited, and had great attention paid him by the chiefs; he reafoned with Oreo on the abfurd cuftom of fufpending trade, whenever any of his people had done us an injury, reprefented the practice as equally hurtful to them as to us, and that, tho' the delinquent was liable to punifhment, no other perfon would ever be molefted, unlefs the courfe of juftice was interrupted, by refufing to deliver up the criminal, when detected. This

reafon-

reasoning had its weight with Oreo and his chiefs, who ordered the trade to be renewed as before. We had now been in harbour, in O-whar-re road, in Hueheine more than thirty days, when Omai's buildings were quite compleated, and he had got all his effects and furniture on fhore, the European feeds, with which Capt. Cook had furnifhed him, fown, and part of his grounds planted with the fruit and other trees of the country, in all which he was affifted with every fpare hand from both fhips.

One would have imagined that, feeing him-felf apparently the greateft man in the ifland, and poffeffed of much the fineft houfe, he would have been elated with his fituation, and overjoyed at being fo happily placed; but quite the reverfe; the nearer the time approached of our departure, the more dejected he grew, and when he made an entertainment at taking pof-feffion of his new fettlement, at which he was honoured with the company of the command-ers and officers from both fhips, and with the King and chiefs of the ifland, he could fcarce conceal his trouble, being apprehenfive, as he told Capt. Clarke fecretly, that as foon as we were failed, they would level his buildings with the ground, and make prize of all that he pof-feffed. Upon this occafion, however, Captain Cook, who had all along treated him more like a fon than a paffenger, and who was now pretty well recovered, being acquainted with the caufe

of

of his melancholy, embraced this opportunity of recommending him to the protection of the king and the chiefs prefent, intimating to them, at the fame time, that if any violence fhould be offered to Omai, or that he fhould be molefted in the free enjoyment of his property, he would, upon the return of the fhips, lay wafte the ifland, and deftroy every human being that had, in any manner, been inftrumental in doing him an injury. This threat made the deeper impreffion upon the chiefs, by what had happened at Emoa; for, notwithftanding all their profeffions, it was very evident they were more influenced by fear than affection. Omai, thus powerfully fupported, after having recovered his fpirits, went through the fatigues of the day better than could have been expected from the defpondency that appeared on his countenance when firft the company began to affemble. Perhaps his awkward fituation, between half Englifh, and half Indian preparations, might contribute not a little to embarrafs him; for having never before made an entertainment himfelf, tho' he had been a partaker at many both in England and in the iflands, he was yet at a lofs to conduct himfelf properly to fo many guefts, all of them fuperior to himfelf in point of rank, tho' he might be faid to be fuperior, in point of fortune, to moft of the chiefs prefent. Nothing, however, was wanting, to imprefs the inhabitants with an opinion of Omai's confequence.

sequence. The drums, trumpets, bagpipes, hautboys, flutes, violins, and, in short, the whole band of music attended, and took it by turns to play while dinner was getting ready; and when the company were seated, the whole band joined in full concert, to the admiration of crowds of the inhabitants, who were assembled round the house on this occasion. The dinner consisted, as usual, of barbicued hogs, fowls variously dressed, some after the manner of the country, and others after the English manner, with plenty of other provisions, and wine and other liquors, with which King Oreo made very free. Dinner over, heivas and fireworks succeeded, and when night approached, the multitudes that attended as spectators dispersed without the least disorder.

We now received orders to prepare for our departure. We had, in this island, procured more than 400 hogs, many of them large. Though it had been found in former voyages, that most of them that were carried to sea alive refused to eat, and consequently were soon killed, yet we resolved to make one experiment more, and by procuring large quantities of yams, and other roots, on which they were accustomed to feed on shore, we ventured to take a few in each ship. For this purpose our carpenters prepared styes for their reception in those parts where they might remain the coolest; and while

they

they were employed in that bufinefs, the live-stock that were ftill on fhore were taken on board, as were likewife every other article that remained.

Nothing remarkable happened till the 30th, when, early in the morning, we were furprized with an account, that Omai's plantation was rooted up and deftroyed, his fences broken down, and his horfes and cattle fet at large, without being able to difcover who were concerned in this malicious and deliberate act of premeditated mifchief. Capt. Cook, highly incenfed, offered confiderable rewards for difcovering and apprehending the offenders, when it was found that the fellow, who had his head fhaved, and his ears cut off, was the principal, and, being a native of Ulietea, an adjacent ifland, had fled there for refuge; but Capt. Cook offering fix large axes, for bringing him to juftice, and promifing to ftay feven days longer, to give time to apprehend him, fome defperadoes undertook the tafk, and on the 4th day brought him on board. He was charged as the fole perpetrator, but it was thought he muft have had accomplices, as he could not by himfelf, in one night, have plucked up fo many trees, deftroyed fo many plants, and dug and defaced the ground in fo many places, where the European feeds had been fown. However he refufed to make any confeffion, and when put in irons, remained fullen.

The

The preparations for our departure, which this event had fufpended, recommenced ; and, in the mean time, to fhew every attention poffible to Omai, the fpare hands from both fhips were fent afhore, in order to reftore his plantation to its former condition, and to rein-ftate him in the quiet poffeffion of it before the fhips fhould fail. And to recommend him the better to the chiefs, he was accompanied every day by Capt. Cook and fome of his offi-cers, who dined with him, and invited King Oreo, and the principal people of the ifland by turns, to be of the party. He alfo made entertainments for the young princeffes and their brothers, with mufic and dancing accor-ding to the Englifh fafhion, and to pleafe the public in general, Capt. Cook caufed fireworks to be played off almoft every other night, for their diverfion. But notwithftanding all thefe endeavours to reconcile Omai to his country-men, he could not help thinking himfelf the object of their envy, rather than of their ad-miration. They beheld him in the fame light as the gentlemen in every country fee a low-born citizen fuddenly rifing from indigence to wealth, giving themfelves airs, and affecting ftate ; at the fame time that they laugh at their folly, they encourage their profufion ; and while they partake of their entertainments, they take plea-fure in mortifying their pride. Such was the real cafe with Omai : while he was feafting

the

the chiefs, and had nails to give to one, red feathers to another, glaſs and china-ware to a third, and white ſhirts to the ladies ; Who but Omai? but, when he had expended in preſents moſt of what he had brought from abroad, and had but juſt enough left by the bounty of his friends, to buy him a plantation and to ſtock it, the chiefs, while they partook of his entertainments, paid him little or no reſpeƈt, and, had it not been for their deference to Captain Cook, would probably have treated him, amidſt the ſplendor of his banquets, with the utmoſt contempt——Such is the diſpoſition of mankind throughout the world. Men ſprung from the dregs of the people muſt have ſomething more than accidental riches to recommend them to the favour of their fellow citizens; they muſt have ſuperior ſenſe to direƈt their conduƈt, and ſuperior acquirements to render the virtue they poſſeſs conſpicuous. That this was not the caſe with Omai, every day's experience furniſhed ſufficient proofs. Not many nights had paſſed after the waſte made on his plantation, before lights were ſeen about his houſe, which, it was ſuppoſed, were intended to ſet it on fire, had not the precipitancy of the centinel, by firing his piece too ſuddenly, given the alarm, and furniſhed the incendiaries with notice to make their eſcape. The man too who had laid waſte his plantation, and who was in irons on board the

Refolution, the night before we intended to
fail, found means either to jump over-board, or
by fome invifible affiftance to unloofe his chains
and flip out of the fhip. He was to have been
punifhed, not by death, but by a banifhment,
worfe than death. He was to have been put on
fhore on fome defolate ifland, from whence it
would have been next to impoffible he could
ever have made his efcape to moleft Omai.
How he came to get from his confinement is
not publicly known, but the centinel who was
fet to guard him, was fentenced to be publicly
whipped, and to receive 24 lafhes every morning
for fix mornings fucceffively; and Mr. H— mate,
and Mr. M——, midfhipman, who command-
ed the watch were fentenced ; the firft, to be ex-
pelled the fhip, to which he never more returned during the voyage ; the other, to be turned
before the maft ; but on fubmiffion was forgiven,
as was likewife the centinel after fuffering the
firft day's punifhment. As foon as the mate
from the Refolution came on board the Difcovery, Mr. Martin, third lieutenant, was ordered to do duty on board the Refolution in his
room.

On the 2d of November being in readinefs
to fail, Capt. Cook took Omai afide, and gave
him leffons of inftruction how to act. At the
fame time directing him to fend his boat over to
Ulietea, his native ifland, to let him know how
the chiefs behaved to him in the abfence of the
fhips.

ships. If well, he was to send by the messenger three white beads; if they seized upon his stock, or broke in upon his plantation, three red beads; or if things remained just as we left them, he was to send three spotted beads.

In the morning of the 3d we unmoored, and the wind being fair, we made sail out of Oowburne road, and when we were under way, Omai came on board, either to prevail on Capt. Cook to let him return to England, or to take his final leave never to see him more. His parting was very affecting; if tears could have prevailed on Capt. Cook to let him return, Omai's eyes were never dry; and if the tenderest supplications of a dutiful son to an obdurate father could have made any impression, Omai hung round his neck in all the seeming agony of a child trying to melt the heart of a reluctant parent. He twined his arms round him with all the ardour of inviolable friendship, till Capt. Cook, unable any longer to contain himself, broke from him, and retired to his cabin, to indulge that natural sympathy which he could not resist, leaving Omai to dry up his tears, and compose himself on the quarter deck.

When he had vented his grief he returned and reasoned with Omai on the impropriety of his request, reminded him of his anxieties while in England, lest he should never more have been permitted to return home; and now that he had been restored to his country and friends

at

at an immenfe expence to his royal mafter, it
was childifh to entertain a notion of being carried back. Omai ftill renewed his tears; he had
wifhed, he faid, to fee his country and friends;
but having feen them, he was contented, and
would never long for home again. Capt. Cook
affured him of his beft wifhes, but his inftructions muft be obeyed, which were to leave him
with his friends. At parting, he added fix
large axes to the prefents he had before made
him, and fome chiffels and Sheffield ware,
which he knew would be ufeful to him.

Such was the parting of Omai from his beloved patron, who had contracted a real friend-
fhip for him. He faid, he fhould be the moft
miferable of all human beings when his protector was gone, for that the inhabitants would be
plotting his deftruction, and he fhould not have
a happy moment while he had any thing left to
live upon. His two New Zealand boys were
under little lefs concern to part from the fhips
than Omai himfelf. They had already learned
to fpeak Englifh fo as to be able to exprefs their
hopes and their fears. They hoped to have
gone along with the fhips, and they cried bit-
terly when they underftood that they were to be
left behind. Thence arofe a new fcene between
Omai and his boys, that, had not the officers
on the quarter-deck interpofed, might have ended unfortunately for Omai. They refufed to
quit the fhip, till they were compelled to it by
force

force, which was no eafy matter, the eldeft now
near fixteen, being of an athletic make, and of
prodigious ftrength, and the youngeft about
eleven, being likewife a giant for his age, were
not eafily managed.   They were both very trac-
table and obliging, till they found they were to
be left at Huakeine, but then they grew def-
perate till fubdued.   They difcovered difpo-
fitions the very reverfe of the iflanders, among
whom they were deftined to abide, during the
remainder of their lives; and, inftead of a
mean, timid fubmiffion, they fhewed a manly,
determined refolution not to be fubdued, tho'
overcome; and ready, if there had been a
poffibility to fucceed, to have made a fecond
or even a third attempt to have regained their
liberty.   We could never learn Capt. Cook's
real reafon, for refufing to take on board, fome
of thofe gallant youths from New Zealand,
who, no doubt, would have made ufeful hands
in the high latitudes we were about to explore,
and would befides have exhibited living pictures
of a people, whofe portraits have been imper-
fectly depicted even by our beft draughtfmen.
There is a dauntlefs fiercenefs in the eyes and
countenance of a New Zealand warrior, that
lofes all its force, under the feeble pencil of a
fribbling artift.   It is now, indeed, too late to
lament the non importation of a native from
every climate, where Nature had marked a vi-
fible diftinction in the characters of perfon and

Q   mind,

mind. As one in each climate might have been procured without force; when assembled together, they would have formed an academy for the study of the human figure, that would have attracted the notice of artists from every country, more than the celebrated statues of ＊＊＊＊＊＊.— We shall now take our leave of Omai, with just observing, that Capt. Cook having furnished him with the means of enriching his country and the adjacent isles with some of the most useful generæ of four-footed animals, (horses, cows, sheep and goats) besides a breed of geese, turkies and other domestic appendages that were strangers to the tropical islands, he may, with proper management, rise superior to all the Earees in the kingdoms round him, and in time make himself lord over all. But to proceed

In the evening of the 3d of November, the day we set out from Hueheine, we arrived at Ulietea and were suddenly surrounded with boats laden with provisions. Here, as usual, we landed our live-stock, carried the tents ashore, and erected the astronomer's observatory. One of our first exploits in this island was the act of a centinel who was set to watch the sheep and the goats, and who, being insulted by some of the natives, ran one of them through the body. The deceased was instantly carried off by his companions, and for a few nails, pro-

perly

perly difpofed of, fo that we never heard any
thing more of his murder. This happened

On the 6th, when the grind-ftone was ftolen
from the Difcovery, but the thief being detected and apprehended, it was brought back
the fame day, together with a large hog, by
way of ranfom for the pilferer.

On the 16th, about two in the morning, the
fentinel at the obfervatory fell afleep and fuffered his mufket to be carried away. He then
took it into his head to leave his poft and follow
after it, with a defign, however, never more
to return to the fhips. When this was known
on board, orders were immediately iffued for
fecuring the King and Royal family, till the man
fhould be taken and reftored, threatening at
the fame time to lay wafte the country, if he
was fuffered to efcape. It was fome days before
he was difcovered, and at length he was found
at the diftance of about ten miles, fitting in a
lone houfe, furrounded by Indians, chiefly
girls, who had ftripped him of his cloaths, and
difguifed him in an Indian drefs, with his head
curioufly ornamented with feathers, and his
mufket lying loaded by him. He made no re-
fiftance, but fubmitted to come back under
convoy of an officer and two marines, who had
orders to fhoot him, if he attempted to efcape. He was put in irons, tried, and fen
tenced to have 24 lafhes every day for a week;
but on fubmiffion was forgiven.

On the 23d, Mr. M———, midshipman, and the gunner's mate made their escape in a canoe, with two of their Otaheitean misses, and landed on an adjoining island, with a view to continue their course to Otaheite, as soon as they had furnished themselves with provisions for the voyage. They were no sooner missed and report made to Capt. Cook, than he ordered all the boats to be manned, and a pursuit to commence with all possible expedition; at the same time putting the King, his two sons, and two of the principal chiefs of the island under confinement, till the fugitives should be taken and restored. This he did, no doubt, to interest the people of the island in the pursuit, and to prevent their assisting the deserters in making their escape. He also promised a reward of large axes, looking glasses, and other articles of considerable value, to any of the natives, who should be instrumental in apprehending and bringing them back. To enforce his orders he caused all the shipping to be seized, and he threatened destruction to the country if his men should be witheld. He even threatened the King and the young princes with death, if they were not brought back within a certain time. This might seem hard usage, yet it had its effect, and without this steady resolute proceeding the deserters would never have been recovered. Our own boats went day after day, to all the adjoining islands, without being able to learn the least trace of
them,

them, and this they continued till having searched every island within the distance of two day's sail, they were at length obliged to give over any farther search, as fruitless.

On the 30th, after fourteen days absence, some Indians came on board, and acquainted Capt. Cook that the fugitives were found, and that in a few days they would be brought back, desiring at the same time the release of the prisoners, as a condition without which they would again be set at large. But Capt. Cook paid no regard to this information. On the contrary, he renewed his threatnings, which he said he would instantly order to be carried into execution, if the men were not delivered up.

Next day, [the 30th] about five in the evening, a number of canoes were seen at a distance, making towards the ships, and as they approached nearer, they were heard to sing and to rejoice as if they had succeeded in finding what they went in search of. About six they came so nigh, that we could discern, with our glasses, the deserters fastened together, but without their misses. They were no sooner brought on board, than the Royal prisoners were released, to the unspeakable joy of all but the two fugitives, who were under great apprehensions for their lives; their punishment however, was not so severe as might have been expected. S—— was sentenced to receive 24 lashes, and M—— turned before the mast,

Q 3　　　　　where

where he continued to do duty while there was little or nothing to do; but on asking forgiveness, was restored to his former station on the quarter-deck.

It appeared, that the Indians had traced them from island to island, from Ulietea to Otaha, from Otaha to Bolabola, from Bolabola to the little island Taboo, where they were found, but where they never would have been looked for by us, had not the Indians traced them out.

On the 1st of December the tents were struck, the live-stock taken on board, and we prepared to sail.—An account of our intercourse with the Earees and Chiefs of the island would only be a tedious repetition of what had passed before in the other islands; but one adventure which happened to Capt. Clarke, must not be omitted; sauntering about in the cool of the morning at a distance from the tents, he was observed by a party of the natives, who waylaid him, and in an instant surrounded him. Being incapable of resistance, they hurried him away, but without offering any violence to his person. It is probable they meant to keep him as an hostage in the room of their king, who at that time was in custody; but fortunately for him, they could not carry him off without coming in sight of the ships. In passing a rising ground, he found means to make a signal, which happened to be observed, and in an instant the boats were armed and manned, and the crews being

being joined by the marines on fhore, he was followed and brought back, not a little fatigued, and perhaps fomewhat frightened by the delicacy of his fituation. No other incident worth relating happened during our ftay on this plentiful ifland.

On the 2d, notice was given to the Otaheitean miffes that they muft all prepare to depart; that the fhips were in readinefs to leave the country, never to return to the Society Iflands any more. This news caufed great lamentation, and much buftle and confufion. They were now at a great diftance from home, and every one was eager to get what fhe could for herfelf before fhe could part from her beloved. Moft of them had already ftript their mates of almoft every thing they poffeffed, and thofe who had ftill fomething in referve led a fad life till they fhared it with them. But what is moft aftonifhing, notwithftanding what has been faid of the conftancy of thefe miffes, there was fcarce a man who had to do with them without being injured by them. When we took our departure from Ulietea, we had fcarce hands enough able to do duty on board, there being more than 30 under the furgeon's hands. In this fituation, thofe who were well were obliged to do duty for thofe who were hurt, which, to do them juftice, they very willingly performed.

It was not, however, till the 7th, that we could get the fhips clear of thefe troublefome gentry.

gentry. On that day we set sail with a brisk
wind to the westward, and, Capt. Cook having received advice that the King of Bolabola
had part of a large anchor to dispose of, we
directed our course to that island, where we arrived on the 8th. Here both Captains landed,
and were introduced to the old King He received them according to the tropical custom,
ordered mats to be spread for them, and plantains, bananoes, and cocoa-nuts to be brought
by way of refreshment. He then entered into
discourse with them, pressed them to bring
their ships into harbour, and treated them in
every respect with great apparent kindness, tho'
he had been represented by Tupia, to former
voyagers, as little better than a common rob-
ber. Being told that they were in haste to
sail, and that they could not stay to come into
harbour, he entered upon business; and after
walking with them to the place where the anchor lay, he told them, that one part of the purchase must be a ewe; that he had a ram, which
had been presented to him by some strangers,
who had lately visited his island, and who had
left him a ewe, but she was dead. Capt.
Cook instantly ordered a ewe to be brought from
the ship, for which, and four large axes, he
purchased the anchor, weighing about 1250 ℔.
weight. They then took leave, and having
brought the anchor on board, we set sail, steering N. by E.

The

The Ifland of Ulietea, which we juft left has nothing in it that differs effentially from what is to be met with in the other iflands, only that the women have more liberty here than at Otaheite, and are not reftrained from eating in company with the men. While here, we were vifited by the King and his chiefs; gave and received entertainments. We attended their plays, and, in return, amufed them with fireworks, illuminations, and other diverfions, in the fame manner as at the other iflands, and remarked very little difference in the characteriftics of the natives. As we were now taking our leave in earneft of thofe fertile ifles, we added to our live-ftock more than 200 hogs, which we found would eat after they had recovered the fea-ficknefs. In former voyages, it was not known that hogs would never eat while they were fick, it was therefore thought prudent to kill them, after fafting three or four days, from a belief that, having fafted fo long, they would never eat again, and, if they died of themfelves, none of the crew would eat carrion.

On the 9th in the morning we were by obfervation in lat. 15 deg. 15 min. S. and in long. 207 deg. 52 min. E. and it may not be improper to obferve, that the fpot on which the aftronomer's tent was erected in the ifland of Hueheine, was in lat. 16 deg. 41 min. S. and in long. 208 deg. 57 min. E. of Greenwich.

We

We now continued our direct courfe N. by E. as near as the winds would let us, with moftly fine weather till the 20th, when in lat. 4 deg. 54 min. S. we were furrounded with land and fea-weed and bodies of trees, which feemed to be but lately feparated from their refpective roots; but it was not till

The 23d that we difcovered land. On that day in lat. 2 deg. N. long. 203 deg. 55 min. E. after having croffed the line the day before, the man at the maft-head called out land, bearing N. E. diftance between fix and feven leagues. We inftantly wore fhip, and ftood in for a fine bay, on which we found good anchorage in 48 fathom water. On viewing the ifland from the fhips, there did not appear the leaft fign of an inhabitant; but near the fhore there were fhoals of fharks, and the fea feemed crufted over with fea fowls, fome of a very large fize. The boats that had been fent out to reconnoitre, returned in the evening with one large turtle each, and loaded with boobies and other tropical birds that by hungry mariners are generally efteemed good eating. They likewife brought feveral fharks, which they found in fuch fhoals, that they knocked them on the head with their oars.

On the 24th we changed our ftation, and anchored in 17 fathom water.

And on the 25th we kept Chriftmas in much mirth and feftivity, the crew having plenty of provifions, and the gentlemen plenty of turtle. The fhips being fafely moored, and the weather

ther fine, but almoſt inſupportably hot, the men were allowed the whole day to amuſe themſelves, and every one had a pint of brandy to drink health to their friends in Old England, though many thouſand miles diſtant.

In the evening, parties from both ſhips were invited to go a turtling, but none were preſſed to go on that ſervice; all were volunteers. On our landing all went different ways, and in order to know where to meet, fires were made in ſeparate directions, one fire for the Reſolution's party, and one for that of the Diſcovery's. Our party before morning had turned more than 20 turtles, and had carried them on board; and when the boats were unloaded, returned for more. In the mean time, a fiſhing party were likewiſe ſent out, and were no leſs ſucceſsful than the turtlers; but on this ſervice a ſeaman had a very narrow eſcape. As he was helping to draw the ſeine, a ſhark made a chop at his arm, but fortunately caught only a piece of his ſhirt's ſleeve, with which he made off.

The Reſolution's turtlers had made a trip to their ſhip to unlade; but on the return of their boats to the iſland, one of their men was miſſing, who, tired with carrying a turtle of more than 100 weight in the heat of the day, had laid it down on the beech, and retired to a thicket, to ſhelter himſelf from the ſun. Here he fell aſleep, and as ſoon as he awoke, he endeavoured to recover his turtle, but in vain; he

O
had

had entangled himself among the bushes, and in the evening, after a most painful search, he was found almost speechless through fatigue and for want of refreshment.

All this day our people continued their diversion on the S. E. side of the island; but

On the 26th about ten in the morning Mr. B——y, Mr. E——r, and Mr. P——k, with ten or twelve seamen in the cutter, having a good quantity of water on board, and each man a pint of brandy, directed their course to the N. E. quarter, and about noon arrived at a neck of land, over which they were to travel on foot to come at the place where the turtle were supposed to harbour, and where it was dangerous to attempt to approach them by sea, by reason of the surf. Here they safely secured their cutter, and near the shore they erected a kind of hut, to which they carried their provisions, and set down to rest and to refresh. This done, they agreed to divide, and to pursue their sport in separate parties. Accordingly they set out, and before the next morning they had sent in as many turtle as the cutter could well stow. This they did by placing them across a couple of oars in the nature of a brier, and keeping men employed in conveying them from the place where they were turned, to the cutter. As they grew tired of their diversion they repaired to the place of rendezvous; but it was some surprize to the rest, when at nine in the morning,

Mr.

Mr. B——y, Mr. P——k and Simeon Wood-roff, the gunner's mate, were miffing. It was then concluded, that they had gone too far within land, and that they had either loft their way, or fome accident had befallen them, per-haps from natives lurking fecretly in the woods, though none had openly appeared.

Under thefe apprehenfions two feamen, Bar-tholomew Loremer and Thomas Trecher were fent out in fearch of them, each carrying a gal-lon of water, with brandy and other refrefh-ments, in cafe they fhould meet with the gen-tlemen in the way. In a wild uncultivated country, over-run with bufhes and clofe cover, the reader, who has never been bewildered, can have no idea of men's being loft in the fhort fpace of a few miles. So, however it happen-ed. The gentlemen invited by the mixed me-lody of the birds in the woods, left their peo-ple as foon as they had properly ftationed them, and entered an adjoining thicket, with their guns. The fport they met with led them on till night began to clofe upon them. They were then at a great diftance from the turtlers, and in the midft of a tracklefs cover, with nothing but tall trees to direct their return ; but what was more alarming, the fun was no foorer fet, than a thick fog fucceeded, which involved the woods in darknefs, though the open beach re-mained clear. In vain they attempted to re-gain the fhore, for, inftead of being able to

discern

difcern the trees they had marked to fecure
their retreat, they could hardly fee one another at five yards diftance.   In this fituation, they foon began to lofe all knowledge
of their way; and leaft, inftead of proceeding in the right courfe, they fhould
purfue a contrary direction, they agreed to fit
down to reft, and for that purpofe chofe the
firft convenient fpot that chance threw in their
way.   Though their minds were troubled, they
had fcarce fet themfelves down, when fleep got
the better of their anxiety, and they all lay compofed, till attacked by fwarms of black ants (creatures more poifonous than bugs) with which they
were in a manner covered when they awoke,
and fo disfigured and tormented with their bites
and blifters, that it is hardly poffible to defcribe
their diftrefs.   Thus circumftanced, their firft
care was to clear themfelves from thefe vermin
by ftripping themfelves naked, and fweeping
them off with brufhes made of the wings of
the birds they had killed; this done, they
clothed themfelves again, in order to renew
their attempts to recover the fhore; but all in
vain.   The farther they walked, as it appeared
afterwards, the farther they went aftray.   At
length, fufpecting their error, they refolved to
remain ftationary, and each man, placing himfelf againft an adjoining tree, endeavoured to
confole himfelf as well as he could till morning, when the appearance of the fun enabled
                                                them

them to judge of the course they were to pursue; but in a trackless wilderness how were they
to make their way! The woods in many places were overgrown with thick grass and bram-
bles reaching to their middles, and in others
so thick intersected with boughs, and matted
with leaves, that it was hardly possible to keep
company, or to penetrate with their utmost
efforts, (when these obstructions happened) one
hundred yards in as many minutes. They were
now glad to abandon their game, happy if they
could regain the open country with the loss
of every thing they had about them. The
shirts and trowsers they had on were soon in rags,
their shoes could hardly be kept upon their feet,
and their linnen caps and handkerchiefs were
rendered unserviceable, by the frequent repetition of the uses to which they had been applied. In short, no degree of distress both of
body and mind could exceed that to which
these unfortunate gentlemen were now exposed.
To their minds it was some alleviation. when,
about ten in the morning, they heard the
feint sound of guns, fired from the ships on
purpose to lead them right, supposing them
to have lost their way. But this was poor comfort, when they reflected that their ships were
at an immense distance, and that, if they ventured to take them for their guide, they should
never live to see an end to their journey. Still
labouring to advance by the sun, they at length,

all

all at once, obferved an opening that led, as
they thought, to the long wifhed-for fhore.
The heart of man, dilated with the moft exquifite joy, can only be fenfible of the inexpreffible pleafure which the gentlemen felt on this
ray of hope. They forgot, for the moment,
the pains of their lafcerated bodies, though all
torn with briars and befmeared with blood, and
comforted themfelves with this dawn of deliverance ; but they had ftill much to fuffer.
When they rufhed with extacy from the cover
and came to furvey the open country, they difcovered, to their great mortification, that they
were yet at a great diftance from the neck of
land, over which their people had paffed ; that
this opening had brought them to another
creek or inlet of the fea, and that they had yet
to travel round a vaft circle of the thicket,
before they could come to the bay that was even
now fcarce within their knowledge. On this
difcovery, defpair had almoft taken place of
hope, when they heard, or thought they heard,
fomething like the found of a man's voice,
far within the thicket. This, in a fhort time,
was anfwered by a found not unlike the former,
but fainter. It was then rightly conjectured,
that thefe founds proceeded from men fent in
fearch of them ; and they all endeavoured to
raife a halloo in their turn ; but their throats
were fo parched, that with their utmoft efforts
they could fcarce rife above a whifper. They

now

now lamented the wafte of powder which they had fruitlefsly expended during the night, in making fignals of diftrefs, and rummaged their cafes to mufter up a fingle charge. This in fome meafure had the defired effect. The report was heard by one of the feamen who were in purfuit of them (as will be feen hereafter) both of whom had been ftruggling with equal difficulties, and toiling under greater encumbrances, without the leaft expectation of fucceeding in their fearch. Thefe men were now bewildered themfelves, and halloo'd to each other as well for the fake of keeping company as for fignals to the gentlemen, if they fhould be within hearing.

By this time the day was far advanced; and partly with fatigue and for want of refrefhment, the gentlemen were almoft fpent; they had been ever fince the morning's dawn engaged in the moft painful exertion of bodily ftrength, to extricate themfelves from the labyrinth in which they had been involved, that ever men experienced, and by confequence to an equal wafte of fpirits, without any thing to recruit them; and now, that they were lefs entangled, they were more expofed to the violent heat of the fun, which brought on an intolerable thirft that was no longer fupportable; they therefore, as the laft refource, repaired to the neareft beach, where, to their comfort, (for comfort it was to them)

R   they

they found a turtle, killed it and drank the
blood. They then took shelter in the hollow
of a rock till the heat of the sun abated, during which time a refreshing sleep gave them
some relief, and enabled them to perform a
journey of about seven or eight miles, which
otherwise they must have perished before they
could have accomplished. When they arrived
at the hut, to their great concern they found it
deserted, and destitute of every kind of provisions ; but, casting their eyes towards the ships
they perceived the boats hastening to their relief. The crew, and the officer who commanded,
had waited at the hut, till all their provisions
were expended, and, not knowing how to proceed, had repaired to the ship for a fresh supply, and for fresh orders ; and he was now returning fully furnished and instructed. On
his arrival he was struck with astonishment at
the sight of three such miserable beings as the
gentlemen and mate appeared to be, lascerated
all over, and besmeared with blood, and with
scarce a rag about them broader than a garter.
Their cry was for grog, which was dealt to
them sparingly, and they were instantly sent on
board to be properly taken care of. The first
enquiry they made, was, whether any of the
company had been sent after them, and being answered in the affirmative, and that they
were not yet returned, they could not help expressing their doubts whether they ever would

return ;

return ; adding their wishes at the same time that no means might be omitted to endeavour their recovery.—It is natural for men, who have just experienced any signal deliverance, to feel poignantly for the safety of others under the same critical circumstances. It was therefore no small satisfaction to the sufferers, when they were told, that every possible means would be tried for their relief; and to enable those who were to be sent on that errand the better to direct their search, the gentlemen described, as well as they could, the place where they were heard. The evening, however, was now too far advanced to undertake, with any probability of success, their deliverance. There were now twenty of the crew (seamen and marines) who had been dispatched from on board, for recovering the gentlemen. These had orders to traverse the thickets in a body, till they should find some of them either living or dead, for, till the gentlemen appeared, nothing could be concluded with certainty concerning them. The majority were of opinion that, if they had been alive, they most certainly would have returned as soon as it was dark, as they could have no motive to pursue their sport in the night; and it was by no means probable, that they should be bewildered, because they might surely have found the same way out of the cover, by which they went into it. This was very plausible ; but some on board, who had sailed with Commodore

R 2   Byron,

Byron, and who remembered the almoft impenetrable thickets in the Ifland of Tinian,
where men could not fee one another in the
open day, at the diftance of three yards, knew
well how the gentlemen might be entangled,
and how hard it would fare with them if it fhould
fo happen. But, as this inftance was known
only to few, it was regarded by none, and the
former opinion, that fome fatal accident had
happened to them, prevailed generally, till the
gentlemen appeared, when the tone changed,
and every one argued the improbality of it,
when the event had fhewn it to be ill-founded.

It was now the place for turtling, and, till
morning, nothing could be undertaken for the
relief of the poor men. Parties therefore went
out as before, and continued their fport, while
they had light, when many were turned, and
one found which had been killed by fomebody,
and brought in among the reft.

Early in the morning of the 29th, when the
whole company were affembled, the plan of
their proceeding was formed, By marching
in lines at fuch a diftance from each other, as
to be within hearing, it was thought impoffible to fail of finding the men, if living,
or of difcovering fome traces of them, if dead;
and they were to direct their line of march
towards the fpot where the found of the voices
was heard by the gentlemen.

After

After a diligent search of six hours, Bartholomew Loreman was discovered in a most miserable condition, almost blinded by the venomous bites of the vermin added to the scorching heat of the sun, and speechless for want of something to clear his throat. He made signs for water, and water was given him. He was moving about, but totally stupid, having no sense of danger, or of the miserable condition in which he was found. It fortunately happened, that the boats from both ships were previously sent round the point of land already mentioned, and planted along the coast, as the land trended, for the convenience of taking the gentlemen on board, in case they should have been found strayed to any considerable distance. If this precaution had not been taken, this man must have perished before he could have been conveyed by any other means to the place of rendezvous, and it was with the utmost difficulty that he was carried to the nearest boat. As soon as he could be brought to his speech, he said he had parted from his companion Trecher in the morning, not in anger, but not agreeing about the way back, nor ever expecting to see one another again; he said they had travelled the day before as long as they could in search of the gentlemen without success, and that when overcome with fatigue, they sat down to refresh, and he believed drank a little too freely of their grog, for they both fell asleep. They were

frightened

frightened when they waked to find it dark
night, and although they felt their faces and
hands covered with vermin, the thoughts of
having neglected their duty, and the dread of
the consequences so distracted their minds, that
they were hardly sensible of any other pain. As
rest was now no longer their object, they rose
and wandered, they neither knew nor cared
where, till day began to break upon them, and
then they endeavoured to recollect their way
with a view to rejoin their companions ; but after walking and winding about as they could
find a passage through the bushes, they at last
began to discover, that they were going from
the place of rendezvous instead of making towards it. Fatigued to the last degree with walking, and perplexed in their minds, they began
to grow careless about living or dying, and in
that humour sat down to lighten their burden,
by making an end of their provisions and grog.
This they had no sooner done, than sleep again
surprized them, and, notwithstanding the vermin, with which they found themselves covered
when they awoke, they found themselves again
in the dark, and again rose up to wander about
which they continued to do as before, lamenting
their melancholy situation, and consulting what
course to take. Several wild projects came into
their heads. They had heard of Robinson
Crusoe's living so many years upon an uninhabited island, with only his man Friday, and

why

why might not they live in this! But hitherto they had seen no four-footed animal, nor any thing on which they could subfist, but turtle and fowls, the latter of which they had no means to attain, and they were totally unprovided with every earthly thing but what they carried about them. That scheme therefore appeared too romantic; they next thought of climbing the highest tree, to try if they could discover any hill or eminence, from whence they might take a view of the country, in order to be certain whether it was inhabited or not. This was approved by both, and Trecher mounted the loftiest within his reach, from whence he said he could discern, towards the South-west, a mountain of confiderable height, and as that was the point that led to the ships, thither he proposed that they should go; but Loreman rather chose to depend upon Providence, and endeavour to regain the shore, as he judged by the report of a gun, which he thought he heard the day before, that it must lie in the direction from whence the sound proceeded, and thither he was endeavouring to make his way, till his eye-sight failed him, and he lost all sense of action. His companion, he said, who was at some distance farther in the thicket, and who did not hear the report of the gun, did not believe what he said; whereupon they agreed to part. What course Trecher

took

took he could not tell, but he believed to the South-weſt.

Loreman was judged in too dangerous a condition to admit of any delay ; he was therefore ſent off in the boat, and being put under the care of the Surgeon, ſoon recovered.

After this detail it was debated, whether to reſign Trecher to his fate, or to continue the ſearch. The humanity of the officer, who had the command of the party, prevailed. It was now about ten in the morning, of the 29th, when the whole party, after taking ſome refreſhment, ſet out to ſcour the thickets, and, by hallooing, ringing of bells, beating of drums, and purſuing different courſes, determined he ſhould hear them if he were alive. It was no eaſy taſk to penetrate a trackleſs cover, overgrown with underwood, and abounding with inſects, of which the muſkatoes were the leaſt troubleſome. But numbers make that eaſy, which to individuals would be impracticable. They went on chearfully at firſt ; but, before a few hours were elapſed, even the gentlemen, who were inſpirited by their ſucceſs in killing game, began to be tired, and it was thought adviſeable to reſt and refreſh during the middle of the day, and to renew the purſuit after they had dined. As yet they had not been able to diſcover any trace or track of the man they were ſeeking, though it had been agreed between Trecher and his companion, to cut boughs
from

from the trees, as they paffed along, by way of mark or guide to each other, in cafe of feparation.

This was no fmall difcouragement; and few had any relifh to renew a labour attended with fo much fatigue, and fo little profpect of fuccefs.

The officers were alone inflexibly bent on the purfuit. The men, though they were no lefs willing, were not all equally able to endure the fatigue, and fome of them were even ready to drop, before their dinner and their grog had revived their fpirits. The only expedient that now remained to be tried, was, that which Trecher himfelf had projected, namely, to climb the higheft tree that appeared in view, in order to look for the mountain which he pretended to have feen, and to which it was thought probable that he might direct his courfe. This was no fooner propofed than executed. In a moment a failor was perched at the top of every lofty tree in fight, and the high land defcried, feemingly at no great diftance from the place where the party had dined. It was now agreed, to make the beft of their way to the eminence, but this proved not fo eafy a tafk as it at firft appeared to be. When they thought themfelves juft ready to mount, they met with a lagoon that interrupted their progrefs; and coafting it along, they difcovered the fkeleton of a creature that, by its length, appeared to

be

be an allegator. In viewing this narrowly, something like the track of some large animal was obferved to have paffed it, and the high grafs on the margin of the lagoon to have been frefh trodden. This excited the curiofity of the whole party, who imagined that fome monfter inhabited the lagoon, againft which it was prudent for them to be upon their guard. The waters of the Lagoon were falt as brine, and every where fkirted with a kind of reed and fedge, that reached as high as a man's head, and could not be penetrated without danger from fcorpions or other venomous reptiles, feveral of which had been feen in the bufhes. All attempts therefore of fucceeding by this courfe appeared to be labour loft, and as no other were thought more probable, it was refolved to relinquifh the purfuit, and to return to the boats; but the day being already too far fpent to make their return practicable before the morning, it was agreed to coaft it along the lake, to endeavour to find accefs to the oppofite hills; and this was the more eafily effected, as between the fedgey border and the thicket there was an open fpace of unequal breadth, only fometimes interfected with brambley patches that joined the lake, but of no great extent. Through thefe they made their way with little oppofition till the lake appeared to deepen, when a moft ftubborn woody copfe feemed to bid defiance to their further progrefs.

This

This difficulty, however, was with much labour furmounted, and it was no fooner paffed, than the lake was found to terminate, and the ground to rife. The country now began to put on a new face. The profpect which had hitherto prefented nothing but a wild and almoft impenetrable thicket, as they afcended the rifing ground, became delightful. And when they had attained the fummit of the eminence, was exceedingly picturefque. Here they determined to pafs the night within a pleafant grove, which feemed to be defigned by nature for a place of reft. The whole party now affembled, and orders were given by the commanding officers to erect temporary tents to fhelter them from the evening damps. Thefe tents were only boughs and leaves of trees fet up tent fafhion. In this fervice fome were employed in cutting down and preparing the materials, while others were bufied in difpofing and putting them together; fome were ordered to collect fuel, and others to carry it to the fummit of an adjoining hill, in order to be kindled at the clofe of day, and kept burning during the night, by way of fignal, to let the boats know that the party were fafe, and that they had not yet relinquifhed the fearch. Add to thefe orders, that a fentinel was to attend the fire in the night, and a watch to be regularly fet and relieved to guard the tents. In the mean time the gentlemen amufed themfelves by taking a view of the lagoon from

the

the hills, and obferving its extent. They faw
it bounded on three fides by a ridge of hills,
and open only to the N. W. from which quarter
they had approached it. They alfo obferved an
open down to trend towards the fhore, by which
the low grounds were divided, and which gave
them hopes that their return in the morning
would be much fhortened. Before night fet in
the tents were compleated; and in due time
the orders that had been given were punctually
carried into execution; the fire was lighted,
the fentinel at his ftation, the watch fet, and
the party all retired to reft. It was about the
dead of night that the fentinel who attended
the fire was furprized by a four-footed monfter,
that had ftole upon him by a flow and filent
pace, and was juft ready to feize him, when
looking behind him he ftarted fuddenly from it,
and flew down to the tents to apprize the watch.
The man's fears had magnified the monfter to
twice the fize of an elephant, fo that the failor,
whofe turn it was to be upon the watch, was
equally alarmed and terrified. The officer on
duty was prefently made acquainted with the
danger, and confulted what was beft to be done.
The countenance of the fentinel, his known
courage, and the folemn manner in which he
attefted the truth of what he faid he faw, added
to the recollection of the fkeleton and the track
of the monftrous creature that was obferved to
have come out of the water and paffed by it,
                                                    left

left no room to fufpect a deception.   It will not
feem ftrange therefore, that the officer fhould
advife calling to their affiftance the ferjeant of
marines, the fecond mate and the armourer,
the ftouteft men of the party.   With this rein-
forcement they march'd up the hill in form,
Mr. Hollingfby and Mr. Dixon in front, the
ferjeant and the fentinel in the next line, and
two failors to compofe the rear.   As they approached the fire, the fentinel, peeping from
behind the armourer, beheld the monfter thro'
the fmoke, as tall again as he was before, and
gave the word to the front line to kneel and fire;
but happy it was, that the armourer, fearing
neither devil nor monfter, determined to referve
his fire till he faced his enemy.   He therefore
advanced boldly, and, looking fharply at it
through the flames, took it for a man, and called to it to fpeak.   But what was their aftonifhment, when they beheld the very identical Thomas Trecher, of whom they had been in fearch
fo long, crawling upon all fours, for his feet
were fo bliftered that he could not ftand, and
his throat fo parched that he could not fpeak.
It is hard to fay which was predominant, their
joy, their furprize or their laughter.   No time,
however, was loft in adminiftring relief.   Some
ran to the tents to tell the news and to bring
fome refrefhment, while the reft ftrove to eafe
him, by fupporting him in their arms.   In a
few minutes he was furrounded by the whole

party,

party, eager, fome to learn his ftory, and all
to give him relief; the officers, in particular,
brought him cordials, which they adminiftered
fparingly till he was brought to his fpeech. He
was a moft affecting fpectacle, bliftered from
head to foot by poifonous infects, whofe venomous ftings had caufed fuch an intolerable itch-
ing, that his very blood was inflamed by conftant rubbing. By anointing him with oil,
the acrimony in fome degree abated, and by
frequently giving him fmall quantities of tea,
mixed with a little brandy, they brought him
to his fpeech; but it was fome days before he
recovered the perfect ufe of his fenfes.

As foon as they had recovered him fo far, by
proper refrefhment, as to entertain hopes of fav-
ing his life, they carried him to bed, and ordered one of his mefs-mates to attend him. In
the morning his fever was abated; but there
arofe a difficulty, how he was to be conveyed
more than 12 miles, through a country fuch as
has been defcribed in his weak condition. To
Englifh failors nothing, that is not impoffible,
is impracticable. One of them remembered
that, when a boy, his fchoolfellows and he ufed
to divert themfelves with making fedan chairs
with rufhes, and he thought it an eafy matter
to make fuch a one, with materials from the
thicket, that would anfwer the purpofe. This
was no fooner propofed than executed, and a
machine contrived, in which they took it by
turns

turns to carry him through almost insurmountable obstructions.—The gentlemen had, indeed, discovered a less encumbered passage than that, through which they had made their way the day before; but it reached very little farther than they could see with the naked eye; all the low ground beyond was swampy and reedy, and so abounding with insects of various kinds, that it was even dangerous for the men to open their mouths, without something to defend them. In the evening, inexpressibly fatigued, and their water and provisions wholly expended, they reached the beach, where the Discovery's cutter was grounded, and where likewise the Resolution's boat, that had been waiting all the day before on the opposite side of the peninsula, was arrived. After some slight refreshment, and wishing each other a prosperous voyage, they parted, each party repairing to their own ship, and Trecher being committed to the surgeon's care, recovered gradually, but it was some weeks before he was fit to do duty.

We had now been off this island near seven days, in which time we had taken more than 100 turtle, from 150 to 300 ℔ weight on board; but, not being able to discover any fresh water in it,

On the 1st of January, 1778, about ten in the morning, we unmoored and set sail with the Resolution in company, directing our course N by E. with a gentle breeze from the east.

To

To the island, which we have just left, Capt.
Cook gave the name of Turtle Island. It lies
in lat. 2 deg. 2 min. N. and in long. 208 E.
from Greenwich. It is a low barren island,
and has all the appearance of being burnt up.
The few cocoa-nut trees that were found upon
it produced hardly any fruit, and, except a few
on the borders of the lagoon already mentioned
what they bore were without any kernel.

Early on the 2d of January, Turtle Island
bore E. S. E. as far as the eye could carry, and
as we were now clear of land, and proceeding
with a prosperous gale, and had plenty of provisions on board, the men were allowed turtle
to boil with their pork, which in a few days was
discontinued by the advice of the surgeon, and
turtle substituted in the room of every other kind
of meat. This was found both healthful and
nourishing, and was continued till within a few
days of our arrival at another island, where we
met with fresh provisions, and water equal to
any we brought with us from the Society Isles.

On the 3d the wind shifted W. S. W. and a
storm came on, preceded by a lowring darkness,
that presaged some violent convulsion, and soon
after it broke forth in thunder, lightning, wind
and rain, which in two hours increased to such a
violent degree, as no man on board had ever
known the like. Fortunately it was but of
short continuance; but, in that little time, the
sea broke over our quarter, and cleared the decks

of

of every thing that was loose. Before noon the force of the tempest was abated, but the rain continued, of which we made good use. From the time of our leaving Ulietea to the present day, we had received no fresh supply of water: and, though the still had been constantly at work, our complement began already to run scanty. This afternoon, several indications of land were observed, such as great quantities of sea-weed, and fresh timber floating with the current by the ships. The Resolution made the signal to shorten sail and stand to the southward, which was obeyed; but, no land coming in sight while it was day-light, after eight hours search we left off the pursuit, and resumed our course to the northward, which we continued till

The 13th, when, in lat. 13 deg. 3 min. long. 202 deg. 6 min. we steered to the N. W. in search of land, the signs of which were very striking; but, after continuing that course all night, without succeeding, we again stood to the north. From this time till

The 20th, nothing material happened, some slight storms excepted; we shall therefore resume our relation of what occurred to Trecher, from the time that he parted from his companion, on the 29th of December, till the night he was found on the 3d.

It was, as has already been observed, several days before he could perfectly recollect all that passed in his mind, and all that he suffered

S   in

in his perfon. He confirmed Loreman's rela
tion of what paffed while they remained together, but, in the morning of the 29th, when
they agreed to part, his thoughts ran chiefly on
difcovering fome houfe or place of refort of the
natives, as it ran ftrongly in his mind, that an
ifland, of fuch extent as that appeared to be,
could not be wholly deftitute of inhabitants.
In purfuit of this idea, he determined to make
towards the hill or high land which he had feen
from the top of the tree ; and to obferve the
courfe of the fun for his guide, but he met
with many obftructions that retarded his progrefs. The reeds and the rough grafs were in
many places fo high and thick, that he was almoft fuffocated in attempting to get thro' them,
and was frequently obliged to return, when he
thought he had nearly reached the oppofite fide.
Though there were ferpents, and, he believed,
fcorpions, continually hiffing in almoft all directions, the fear of being ftung by them was
abforbed by the more immediate torture he felt
from the mufketoes and other venomous infects
that faftened upon him, and teized him inceffantly ; add to thefe diftreffes, the bad condition
of his fhoes, which were worn to fhreds, and,
though he had tied them round and round with
cords made of twifted grafs, yet it was hardly
poffible for him to keep them upon his feet for
ten fteps together. In this melancholy fituation,
reft was a ftranger to him, yet fleep would fome-

times

times clofe his eyes, and fill his imagination with horrors ftill more diftreffing than thofe he felt while awake. Towards the evening of the 29th, he thought he heard the howling of dogs; and, a-while after, the growling of fome favage beaft, but of what fpecies he could not tell; however he faw nothing, and thefe might only be the creatures of his own difturbed fancy. Towards night he got together a quantity of broad leaves from the trees to make him a bed, and to cover his face and hands from the black ants. To allay his thirft, he thought of chewing the ftems of a reed, that had a fuecarine tafte, and was probably a wild kind of fugar-cane, which gave him fome refrefhment, and contributed not a little to his prefervation. Soon as day began to dawn, he found himfelf weak and languid, and had very little ftomach to renew his labour. His firft care, however, was to repair his fhoes. This he did by forming wifps of grafs into the fhape of foales, and placing them underneath the remains of the leather foles. He then tied them together round his feet and ancles with cords, made as before; and with thefe he made fhift to fcramble on a-while, but they foon wanted repair. He again had recourfe to his firft expedient, and mounted a tree that over-topped the cover, and got fight of the high land that firft animated his purfuit. He thought it fo near that he could foon reach it, and haftening down made his way with more alacrity than

ever,

ever, being prepoffeffed that, if he could reach
that eminence, his deliverance would be fure.
For fome hours he ftruggled through the moft
formidable obftacles, the cover being now fo
thick and ftrong, and withal fo high, that he
could hardly fee the light over his head through
the leaves and the bufhes.   This happened to
be the outer border that fkirted the lagoon,
which when he had penetrated, and found an
opening, his heart leaped within him, but his
joy was of fhort continuance.   He prefently
difcovered that he had another danger to furmount before he could reach the fummit of his
wifhes.   He attempted the lagoon, and waded
nearly acrofs, without the water rifing higher
than his middle, but all at once plunged over-
head in deep water, and it was next to a miracle, that he faved himfelf from drowning.
He then returned quite exhaufted and dejected,
and breaking through the fedge on the margin
of the lake, he ftumbled upon the fkeleton of
the wonderful monfter, already mentioned, which
he believed was fifty feet long.   He was fo fcar-
ed at the fight of the bones that his hair ftood
on-end, and he thought of nothing now but
being eaten up alive.   Totally difpirited, and
faint for want of food or any thing to drink,
and deprived of all means of proceeding any
farther, he crept along the lake till he came to
a cocoa-nut tree near the edge of the thicket,
which he attempted to climb, but fell down for

want

want of strength to keep his hold, and lay for several hours incapable of motion. He heard, he said, a noise in the cover, in the day, but could neither hollow to be heard, nor follow the sound, though some of the company must have passed very near him; but seenig the fire lighted on the hill in the evening, it encouraged him to make one struggle more for life. Without a shoe to his foot, having lost them in the lake, he made shift to crawl up the hill, as already related.—Few readers will think it possible for a man to suffer so much in so short a time; and yet many have lost their lives by being bewildered in England, and many more on the wild heaths in Scotland, which cannot be supposed to be so dangerous as the thick cover of a desolate island, where no man ever set his foot before. But, be that as it may, such is the account given by Trecher of his suffering during the three days he was absent from the ship. Having been now 17 days at sea, without seeing land,

On the 18th, a very severe storm arose, which blew with irresistible fury for some hours, and obliged us to clue up our main sheets, and scud before it at the rate of 7 or 8 knots an hour; but before noon the wind died away, and a dead calm succeeded. Such is the variableness of the weather near the tropics.

On the 19th, being then in lat. 21 deg. 20 min. N. and long. 198 E. the man at the masthead called out high land, bearing E. N. E. and

in

in a very little time came in fight of more land, apparently of an equal height with the former. As we approached nearer the windward ifland, it prefented no very promifing afpect, being mountainous, and furrounded with reefs, without any figns of inhabitants; we therefore flood off and on till

The 20th, when we bore away for the land we had feen to leeward, but not then in fight·

About 9 in the morning, it was feen the fecond time at the diftance of about 7 or 8 leagues. We were charmed with its appearance as we came near it, obferving it to abound with rivers, and to exhibit a profpect fo full of plenty, that we anticipated the pleafure we expected, by fuppofing ourfelves already in poffeffion of a moft feafonable fupply. We had been for feveral days reduced to the fcanty allowance of a quart a day, and that none of the beft; and now we faw whole rivers before us, our hearts were dilated with joy; yet we had much to· fuffer. We found ourfelves debarred from the thing we moft wifhed-for for feveral days, by fhoals and rocks that to us were impracticable. We coafted along the N. W. fide of the ifland, founding as we went, while the boats from both fhips were employed in fearching for fome bay or harbour, where we might fafely anchor. In the mean time feveral canoes came from the fhore with plantains and dried fifh on board, who parted with what they had for any trifles
that

that were offered them, and at firſt behaved with great civility, but could not be perſuaded to venture on board. At five in the evening we were two leagues from the ſhore ſurrounded by Indians in their canoes, with hogs in abundance, ſome very large, which we purchaſed according to their ſize for a ſpike or a ten-penny nail each.

While we remained at ſea, no people on earth could be more friendly; but our boats had no ſooner landed, than a quarrel aroſe between the natives and our people, which was terminated by the death of one of the former. It was ſaid that the Indians were the aggreſſors, by throwing ſtones at the boats to prevent the people from landing, and that orders being given to fire a gun over the heads of the aſſailants, without doing them any hurt, inſtead of commanding reſpect, it only encouraged them in inſolence, till Mr. W——, our third Lieutenant, preſenting his piece, ſhot one of the ringleaders dead upon the ſpot.

This early act of ſeverity was probably the means of ſaving many lives. The Indians diſperſed immediately, carrying off the dead body along with them. And the boats not having made any diſcovery returned to the ſhips, where they were taken on board, and ſecured till next morning.

On the 21ſt the boats were again ſent out, but to as little purpoſe as before. Little trade was this day carried on, as the natives feemed very fhy. But,

On the 22d, the fhips having found anchorage on the fouth-weft fide, they were no foonet moored, than they were again furrounded with a more numerous multitude of iflanders than before; moft of them in canoes laden with hogs, plantains, bananoes and fweet potatoes, which they readily exchanged as before. Here the failors were fuffered to make what purchafes they pleafed; only women were prohibited by Capt. Cook's order, on the fevereft penalties.--- This created a general murmur among the feamen, whofe pleafure was centered in that kind of commerce, in the new-difcovered iflands wherever they went.

In the afternoon the pinnace was ordered out, and the two Captains landed on the beach, where they were met by the chiefs of the ifland, and more than 2000 of their fubjects, not in a hoftile manner, but in amity, exchanging prefents and eftablifhing trade.

Capt. Cook made figns for water, and was conducted to a moft delightful little rivulet, fo conveniently fituated for fupplying the fhips, that, had not the Refolution been driven from her moorings by the violence of an eafterly wind and ftrong current, nothing could have exceeded our entertainment at this hofpitable port; but unfortunately for her, fhe could never again recover her ftation. When fhe was forced to fea

fhe

she had but half her complement of water; nor
had she fresh provisions sufficient to supply her
people for any length of time.   We in the Discovery were more fortunate.   In the evening of
the 24th we could see the Resolution to leeward
eight or nine leagues, and in the mean time,
while she was beating up, we were employed in
compleating our hold.

On the 25th we were in readiness to sail,
and, having lost sight of the Resolution, we
imagined that, not being able to fetch her former station, she had bore away to another island,
which had been seen to the N. W. distance about
10 or 12 leagues.

On the 26th we weighed, directing our course
to the N. W. but about ten in the morning,
the man at the mast head descried the Resolution at a great distance, bearing S. by W. whereupon we instantly tacked, and stood S. by E.
to join our Commodore.   This being effected,
we remained several days beating up, but in
vain to regain our former birth.

On the 29th we bore away to another lee
island, which abounded with hogs and fruit,
and where the natives were equally hospitable
with those we had just left; but, there being no
water to be procured at a moderate distance,
and the reefs being dangerous, and the surf running high, Capt. Cook, after surveying the
island, and taking possession of it, in the name
of his Royal master, (calling the whole cluster

Sandwich's

Sandwich's Ifles) was preparing to depart, when a ftorm came on from the eaftward, and again obliged the Refolution to put to fea.

The Captain had already exchanged feveral prefents with the chiefs of the ifland, and had, in particular, prefented the king with two fhe-goats and a ram, and had received in return fix large hogs, and an immenfe quantity of yams and fugar-cane, with which thefe iflands feemed to abound; and it was fortunate, that he had fupplied the fhip with fuch provifions as the ifland afforded, before the ftorm came on; for afterwards it would have been equally impoffi-ble for him as before to have recovered his fta-tion here, any more than in the other harbour. Water was now the only neceffary with which he was fcantily provided; however, as he feem-ed to know where he could obtain a fupply, he did not fo much regret the difappointment. Our boats, while the fhore was acceffible, were employed in bringing on board the product of the ifland, and, on the evening of

The 1ft of February, we had more than 250 hogs, befides three months allowance of fweet potatoes, bananoes, plantains, fugar-cane, and vegetables in abundance.

Early in the morning on the 2d we weighed, and foon came in fight of the Refolution; and both took our departure to proceed upon our voyage.

Thefe

These islands, which lie in the latitude of 21 deg. 44 min. N. and in long 199 E. are not, in beauty and fertility, inferior to the Friendly Islands in the southern hemisphere, nor are the inhabitants less ingenious or civilized. Except the first quarrel that happened, of which we have already spoken, we had not the least difference with any of them during our stay. What they had to dispose of they parted with upon the easiest terms; nor did they seem so thievishly inclined as those on the other side the line.

The men in these islands are of the middle size, of a dark complexion, not much tattowed, but of a lively open countenance. They were no otherwise cloathed than decency required, and what they had on appeared to be of their own manufacture, of which there were various fabricks, and of a variety of colours. Some were made with borders exactly resembling coverlids, and others appeared like printed cottons; and, besides cloth, they had many other articles which shewed that they had artificers among them not wanting in ingenuity. One peculiarity we observed among the men, and that was in the cut of their hair, which they trimmed up to a ridge along their heads, in form like what, in horses manes, is called hogging. Others again wore it long, platting it in tails, which hung below the waist; and these we took for marks of distinction among them. Add

to

to this, a kind of fhort cloak worn by their chiefs, in fhape like thofe worn by the ladies in England, and compofed of moft beautiful feathers, ranged in rows, one over another, and narrowing from the lower border till they terminate in a kind of net-work round the neck. The women in general have fhock hair, which they were at great pains to ornament. They had large holes in their ears, that, filled as they were, with moft beautifully coloured fhells made up in clufters, ferved for jewels, and had no bad effect. Their head-drefs confifted of wreathes of flowers, decorated with feathers chiefly red; and having, in general, lively piercing black eyes, white teeth, fmall features, and round faces, were not a little inviting, had not Capt. Cook's fevere prohibition put a check to the predominant paffion of our men.

Their drefs, upon the whole, was more decent than that of the men, and few were without necklaces and bracelets, of which they feemed very fond, and for which our ftrings of beads were well fuited.

Their manufactures the people freely fold for nails, hatchets, fciffars, knives, or iron inftruments of any kind; glafs bowls was a valuable article, fo were beads, buttons, looking-glaffes, china-cups, and in fhort any of our European commodities.

Except the fugar-cane, which appeared indigenous to thefe iflands, and which were rare in

thofe

thofe on the other fide the line, their produce was much the fame, only the cocoa-nuts were by no means fo large, nor in fo great plenty here as at the Friendly Ifles.

Wood was not to be purchafed in plenty, nor did we ftand much in need of that article.

Hogs, dogs, ducks and poultry were here in greater abundance than on the other fide the line, but their plantations were not fo beautifully ranged, nor fo well cultivated. The houfes here are warmer as the air is colder. They are built tent-fafhion, and are covered from top to bottom.

There feems indeed a remarkable conformity between thefe iflands and thofe of the oppofite hemifphere, not only in their fituation, but in their number, and in the manners, cuftoms, arts and manufactures of the inhabitants, tho' it can fcarce be imagined that they could ever have any communication, as the globe is now conftituted, being at more than 2000 miles diftance one from the other, with very little dry land between. From obferving this general conformity among the tropical iflanders, fome have been led to believe, that the whole middle region of the earth was once one entire continent, and that what is now the Great South Pacific Ocean was, in the beginning, the Paradife of the World; but whoever would wifh to hear more on this fubject, will do well to read Burnet's Theory of the Earth, where, if he does not find arguments folid enough to convince his

reafon,

reafon, he will meet with reafoning fufficiently plaufible to amufe his fancy. But to take leave of thefe iflands for the prefent, though we fhall have occafion to mention them again with lefs commendation.

On the 3d of February, the day after we took our departure, we had heavy fqualls, but not fo fevere as to force us to part company.

On the 4th it cleard up, and we purfued our courfe E. N. E. having pleafant weather, and a favouring gale.

On the 5th, our men had pickled pork ferved inftead of their ordinary allowance, one pound *per* man a day, with a pound and a half of yams inftead of bread; and this was continued to them for feven weeks, which they liked much better than their fhip's provifions.

Nothing material occurred till

The 9th, when there appeared the ufual figns of land, but we faw none, and continued our courfe till

The 13th, when we tacked and ftood N.N.W. lat. 30 deg. long. 200 deg. E. But,

On the 14th we ftood again N. by E. with a light breeze. During this interval of fine weather, our fail-makers were employed in getting up and reviewing the fails, when it was found that they were in a miferable condition, being eaten thro' and thro' by the rats in a hundred places; while they were employed in repairing them, our other artificers had work enough to

do;

do; for it was made a point to suffer none to remain idle, when the business of navigating the ship did not require their immediate attendance. The course we were now steering we continued with little or no variation, except what was occasioned by the shifting of the wind till the 21ft. when in lat. 39 long. 209 E. we shortened sail, and steered N. N. W. the whole night, having had strong signs of land to the eastward the whole day; but no land coming in sight, we again renewed our course, and so continued till

The 26th, when a most dreadful storm arose, with such a swell, that though we were not more than half a mile from the Resolution, we frequently lost sight of her amidst the heavy seas. In this gale both ships suffered considerably in their sails and rigging, it being impossible to hand them before we were surprized by the tempest. We were now in lat. 43 deg. 17 min. and in long. 221 deg. 9 min. and were attended by seals, sea-lions, man of war birds, Port Egmont hens, shaggs and sea-guls, which were strong indications of land.

On the morning of the 27th the wind abated, but the swell still continued from the southward, and we proceeded under close reefed top-sails till about ten in the morning, when we shook out the reefs, and made all the sail we could in company with the Resolution.

March

March the 1ſt the wind died away, and being in lat. 45 deg. 95 min. and long. 225 deg. 14 min. we ſounded with 180 fathom, but found no bottom. We now began to feel the effects of an alteration in the climate. From intenſe heat it became piercing cold; and our men, who deſpiſed their Magellan jackets, while within the temperate climates, now firſt began to find the comfort of them in theſe northern regions.

On the 5th, being moderate weather, we ſounded, and at 56 fathom found bottom, loamy ſand and ſhells. At ſix in the evening we ſhortened ſail, and ſtood all night S. ½ W. with the water as white as milk.

On the 6th both ſhips wore and ſtood N. by E. ſhortening ſail in the evening, and ſtanding all night to the ſouthward.

On the 7th we made the land. Cape Blanco, the weſternmoſt known point of Californio, bearing E. N. E. then diſtant about 8 or 9 leagues. It appeared mountainous and covered with ſnow. This day the gentlemen in the gun-room dined on a fricaſſee of rats, which they accounted a veniſon feaſt, and it was a high treat to the ſailors, whenever they could be lucky enough to catch a number ſufficient to make a meal.

On the 8th we wore ſhip, and ſtood N. E. by E. We had heavy ſqualls, with ſnow and rain for a whole week, and after a ſeries of the moſt

tem-

tempeftuous weather that ever blew, and in which the Refolution moft miraculoufly efcaped perifhing upon a funken rock, it was the 28th before we could get fight of a bay, wherein we could anchor ; at length we difcovered an inlet, the mouth of which was not more than two miles over, in which we entered, and found it a found which narrowed as we advanced, tho' it ftill continued of a confiderable depth. About 7 in the evening we anchored 97 fathom water, and was prefently joined by the Refolution. We made figns for fome of the natives to come on board; but this they declined, though fome hundreds foon came about the fhips, to which they appeared to be no ftrangers, as they gave us to underftand, that iron was what they valued moft. We obferved likewife that their weapons were headed with copper, and their arrows with iron, which they could obtain only from the Ruffians, or from trade with the Hudfon's Bay Company. Though they declined coming on board, they were neverthelefs very civil, and when they took their leave faluted us with a war fong. We were now fo far advanced to the northward and eaftward as to be far beyond the limits of European Geography, and to have reached that void fpace in our maps, which is marked as a country unknown.

Early on the morning of the 30th the boats were armed and manned, and both Captains

T   proceeded

proceeded to examine the found, in order to find a convenient place to refit the ships which had suffered materially in the violent gales, which for the laft 20 days they had been combating, at the hazard of being hourly dafhed to pieces upon the rocks, or ftranded upon the fands of this inhofpitable coaft.

In their progrefs they were fortunate enough to difcover a cove the moft convenient that could be wifhed, the entrance of which was about two cables length, bounded by high land on each fide, and furnifhed with wood and water (now much wanted) fo conveniently fituated, that both could be taken on board at lefs than a cable's length from the fhore; but, tho' now within the diftance of four miles, it was four o'clock in the evening before we could get the fhips properly moored, owing to the uncertainty of the weather, and the violent gufts to which this coaft is fubjeft. All this while the Indians behaved peaceably and apparently with much friendfhip. They brought, after a fhort acquaintance, a great variety of valuable fkins, fuch as beaver, foxes, racoons, fquirrels, rein-deer, bears, and feveral others, with which we were but little acquainted, but what they chiefly defired in exchange, were cutlery wares of all forts, edge-tools, copper, pewter, iron, brafs, or any kind of metal, with the ufe of which they were not unacquainted. All our people were now employed in the necefary repairs

pairs of the ships, and in cutting wood and getting water on board, while the gentlemen diverted themselves in shooting and botanizing; when,

On the 1st of April, about four in the evening, there entered the cove a large canoe, in which were 30 armed Indians, who, on their first appearance, began a war-song, and when they had finished, took to their paddles and rowed round the ships, having first stript themselves of their cloathing, except one man, who stood upright in the vessel, delivering an oration, of which not a man on board could understand a word. They paddled round the ships several times, as if led by curiosity, but did not offer to molest any of the workmen, nor did they offer to trade. All hands were instantly ordered under arms; when these new visitors were seen to cloath themselves as before, and to make towards the ships. The orator made not the least hesitation; but mounted the ship's side, and accosted the Captain with much civility, and after receiving some presents, and stopping a little while to observe the artificers, he took a very polite leave, descended to his boat, and was landed on the opposite shore of the Sound.

On the 3d, a large body of Indians were seen paddling along the Sound, mostly armed with spears from 20 to 30 feet long, and with bows and arrows very neatly made. On their nearer approach they too were heard to tune

up

up their war-fong, and to brandifh their weapons, as if in defiance of an enemy. Their
number was alarming, there being not lefs than
between 3 and 400 of them in their war canoes, who we apprehended were come to attack us ; but we afterwards underftood they
were come to attack a body of their enemies
on the oppofite fhore, whom they afterwards engaged, and returned victorious.   We were frequently vifited by fuch parties, who appeared
always in arms ; but never offered the leaft violence. They brought, befides fkins, great
quantities of fifh, with plenty of game, which
we purchafed of them for glafs bowls, looking-
glaffes, nails, hatchets, or whatever utenfils
or toys were either ufeful or ornamental.

The men were of an athletic make, very rough
to appearance, but more civilized than from
their afpect there was reafon to expect. To
iron they gave the name of te-tum-miné, and
to other metals che-à-poté.

On the 5th, the water, which was excellent,
was fo handily fituated, that by erecting a ftage,
and conftructing a fpout, we could convey it
into cafks in the fhip without farther trouble.
This facilitated the labour of the waterers, and
fhortened our ftay, as wood was conveyed on
board with very little more trouble.

On the 6th it blew a ftorm, and the tide came
rolling in at an alarming rate ; it prefently rofe
eight or nine feet higher than ufual, and drifted

feveral

feveral of our materials from the fhore, which we never could recover; and at nine in the morning the Difcovery drifted very near the Refolution, and very narrowly efcaped being bulged.

On the 7th the artificers again refumed their labour. The natives continued their vifits, and befides fifh, furs and venifon, brought bladders of oil, which were greedily purchafed by the men. With this they made fauce for their falt-fifh, and no butter in England was ever thought half fo good.

During our ftay here, which was but very fhort, owing to the time loft in making the land, and the advanced feafon of the year, no people could be more obliging; they were ready to accompany the gentlemen, who delighted in fhooting, in their excurfions, and to fhew them the different devices they made ufe of to catch and to kill their game; they fold them their mafks, their calls, and their gins, and made no fecret of their methods of curing the fkins, with which they carried on a traffic with occafional vifitors; in fhort, a more open and communicative people does not live under the fun. They have, befides fea-fowl in abundance, fwans, eagles, and a variety of other land-fowl, of which we had never feen the fpecies. Nor were their fifhermen more referved than their hunters; they pointed out the haunts of the different forts of fifh, and they were

not

not averfe to helping their new acquaintance to compleat their lading, whenever they had been unfuccefsful in filling their boats.

They had not hitherto difcovered any difpofition to pilfer; but on the 10th day after our arrival, feveral of them being on board, and our people having no fufpicion of their honefty, one of them watched his opportunity to flip into the great cabin, and carry off the Captain's watch; which being foon miffed, all the Indians on board were feized, their boats fecured and fearched; and at length it was found hid in a box on board one of their canoes, which the offender delivered up without the leaft concern. This watch, had he been permitted to carry it off, he probably would have parted with to the firft failor he had met, for a fingle nail. About the fame time another Indian made free with a bolt from the armourer's forge; but was feen in the fact, and an endeavour made to wreft it from him; but he inftantly jumped overboard, and gave it to one of his companions, who was making off with it, till fired at with fmall fhot, which brought him back, and he furrendered it, but with fuch a fiercenefs expreffed in his countenance as fufficiently indicated his intent. In a moment, every Indian in the cove difappeared, and in lefs than three hours, more than 900 of them affembled in the found, and being uncloathed (which is their cuftom when they mean to engage) began their war-fong, and approached the fhips. We

were

were in readiness to give them a warm reception; but seeing our preparations, and perhaps not liking our countenance, they all laid down their arms, and putting on their cloaths, came peaceably round the ship without offering the least incivility.

Being in great want of masts, most of those we brought out with us being sprung, our carpenters were sent into the woods to cut down such trees as they should find fit for their purpose. This they did without the least interruption from any of the inhabitants. They found trees from 100 to 150 feet high, without a knot, and measuring from 40 to 60 feet in circumference. In these trees the eagles build their nests. When they had cut down what best suited their purpose, the great difficulty was to bring them to the shore; and in this labour they were assisted by the natives. It was now their spring, and the weather began to change for the better; when we first arrived the thermometer was as low as $38\frac{1}{2}$, and now

This 20th day of April it is as high as 62 degrees. We have at present the full range of the woods; the snow all melted away, and the rivers open; we found plenty of game, and catch'd fish in abundance.

April 22. This morning we were visited by a large body of distant Indians, who had come from a great distance with furs, and other articles of trade. These were warmly cloathed

T 4   with

with coftly cloaks that reached down to their ancles; and among them was a ftately youth, to whom the reft paid great refpect. Him our Captain invited on board, which he at firft declined; but after fhewing him fome axes, glafs bowls, looking glaffes, and other articles that excited his curiofity, he fuffered himfelf to be handed into the fhip, where he ftayed fome time, admiring every thing he faw. While thefe continued to trade, it was remarked, that no other Indians came in fight; but they had hardly left the fhip, when another body of Indians appeared, more than double the number of the former, who hemmed them all into the cove, and ftript them of every thing they had about them, and then came and traded with us.

On the 26th, having finifhed the repairs of the fhips, we began to prepare for our departure, the tents were ordered to be brought on board, the aftronomers obfervatory, and what live-ftock we had yet left; and, as the laft fervice to be performed, we cut grafs for their fubfiftence, which we were fortunate enough to find in plenty, and to have a pretty good time to make it into hay. We alfo, by the affiftance of Mr. Nelfon, whofe bufinefs, as has already been obferved, was to collect the vegetable and other curious productions of the countries through which we paffed, were enabled to ftock ourfelves with a large proportion of cu-

linary

linary plants, which was of infinite service to us in our more northerly progress. And now having all things in readiness, we began to tow out of the cove into the sound, to which Capt. Cook gave the name of K. George's Sound, and with a light breeze and clear weather to proceed on our voyage : but we had scarce reached the sound, when a violent gust from E. S. E. threw us into the utmost confusion. All our boats were out, our decks full of lumber, and night coming on dark and foggy, our danger was equal to any we had hitherto met with in the course of the voyage, though an especial Providence seemed to attend us, and to interpose in our favour; for by this storm a leak was discovered in the Resolution, which, had it been calm weather, would probably have proved fatal to the crew. Having cleared the sound, we shaped our course to the westward, and so continued till day-light, when, seeing nothing of the Resolution, we shortened sail; and before noon she came in sight, seemingly in distress. The storm continuing, we pursued our course to the north-westward, till

May 1, when the weather became fair, and we proceeded with a pleasant breeze. Being now at leisure to recollect what observations occurred at the harbour we have just left, the curious reader will not be displeased with a short relation. When we first arrived in the sound, the rough countenance of the men seemed to promise no very agreeable entertainment during

our

our ſtay; but when they ſaw our diſtreſs, and that we only meant to repair our ſhips, ſo far from giving us any diſturbance, they gave us every aſſiſtance in their power; they ſupplyed us regularly with fiſh, and, when they found that our men liked their oil, they brought it in bladders, and exchanged it for whatever they pleaſed to give for it. They diſcovered no propenſity to thieve, till they found we were preparing to depart, and then they were ſo covetous of our goods, that they could not reſiſt the temptation, when a fair opportunity offered, to carry off whatever fell in their way.

The cove, in which we anchored, we found to lie in 49 deg. 33 min. N. and in 233 deg. 16 min. E. but whether the Ruſſian diſcoveries had reached ſo far, we could not be able to determine; that the inhabitants were no ſtrangers to the uſe of iron and other metals was, as has already been obſerved, viſible on our firſt approach; but by their manner of uſing what they poſſeſſed, it was not eaſy to diſcover from what quarter it came. In the ſituation we were in, we did not think it ſafe to venture far into the country, having no ſpare hands to attend us. Of their houſes we ſaw but few; and of their manner of living we know but little. That they eat the fleſh of their enemies we had ſome reaſon to ſuppoſe, by obſerving a human head in one of their canoes, and arms and limbs in another; that fiſh, and the fleſh of of the animals they catch in hunting are the principal part of their food, is not to be doubted; their bread is made from the rows of fish, but in what manner they prepared it, we could not learn; their sauces chiefly seal-blubber or oil; we saw none of their houses near the shore, by which it should seem that their winters are severe, and that they chuse the recesses of the woods for shelter as well as safety. Their houses were all built of wood, and hung round with dried fish, and skins of various animals. They have different masks for different purposes; some they put on when they go to war, which are really frightful; some that cover their whole bodies, and give them the appearance of the animals they are in pursuit of, whose cries, while they are young, they are taught to imitate; they have decoys excellently adapted for entrapping both fish and fowl; and they have snares likewise for snaring wild beasts, and contrivances for killing them as soon as they are catched.

We saw no plantations which exhibited the least trace of knowledge in the cultivation of the earth; all seemed to remain in a pure state of nature; shrubs there were in the woods that put forth blossoms; and trees that promised in time to bring forth fruit; but except some currant bushes, wild rasberries and junipers, we saw none bearing fruit that were known to any but Mr. Nelson.

The

The men were not ill made, but they disfigured themselves with greafe and coarfe paint; they were of a dark copper colour, with lank black hair, which they tied in a knot behind, but they fo bepowdered, or rather befeathered it with down, that the colour was hardly difcernable; their cloathing was a cloak made of fkins of beafts, which covered them from the neck to their knees, and gave them a favage appearance; fome of them wore high fur caps; but the chiefs among them had their heads dreffed in a more becoming manner. In that confifted their chief diftinction. Their heads were bound round with fillets, decorated with feathers, which adds fo ftriking a grace to the human figure, that almoft every nation in the known world have agreed, in making plumes of feathers a part of their warriors drefs. Their weapons of war were fpears from 20 to 30 feet long; their bows about three feet and a half; their arrows two feet, pointed with bone or flint, fome few with iron; but they had one horrid weapon peculiar to themfelves, refembling a man's head with hair; it had eyes and nofe, but where the mouth fhould be, a fharp piece of bone or flint about fix inches long was firmly morticed and cemented; in the neck part was a hole, through which they paffed a ftrong cord, and faftened it to the right arm; this we faw none of the warriors without; many of them had befides, a knife about twelve inches long,

of

of which they were very choice. We faw no muſical inſtrument among them ; but ſome had muſical voices, and ſeemed fond of dancing and tumbling in a beariſh way. Their canoes were of an uncommon length, many of them from 30 to 40 yards long, made of the main body of one of their enormous trees, of which we have already ſpoken ; their breadth from four to five feet over in the middle, and gradually narrowing, like all others to both ends, but the ſtem much higher than the ſtern. They were ſtrengthened by bars of wood placed acroſs at certain diſtances, and were rowed by paddles about ſix feet long, ſharp at the lower ends. Some of thoſe canoes were roughly carved and painted with the figures of the ſun, moon, and ſtars, probably the objects of their worſhip ; but what was remarkable, they had no out-riggers to prevent their overſetting, like thoſe in ſouthern iſles.

The women are much more delicate than the men, and dreſs in cloaks curiouſly woven with the hair of wild beaſts, intermixed with the moſt beautiful furs. We faw but few of them during our ſtay, and thoſe who came in ſight were rather in years ; they were, however, much fairer than the men ; and even fairer than many of the men we had on board. Their employ-ment ſeems chiefly confined at home. We faw none of them employed in fiſhing ; nor did we meet any of them in the woods. Beſides the

care

care of their children, and the manufacturing
and making the cloathing, they may probably
affift in curing and preparing the fkins, with
which thefe people certainly carry on a traffic
with ftrangers; though of that trade, for want
of underftanding their language, we could not
fufficiently inform ourfelves.   Be that as it may,
when we left the harbour, we had more than
300 beaver fkins on board, befides other lefs
valuable fkins of foxes, racoons, wolves, bears,
deer and feveral other wild animals; for dogs
excepted, we faw no other domeftic creatures
about them.   But to return.

On May the 1ft, in the morning, the weather
being fine, we fpoke with the Refolution, who
informed us of the danger they were in of foundering in the late gale, by a leak, which increafed
fo faft upon them, that it baffled the utmoft
efforts of all the hands they had on board, gain-
ing upon them confiderably, though every man
in the fhip, even to the Captain, took it in turn
to work at the pumps; but what was aftonifhing, it had now ftopt of itfelf, without the
carpenters being able to difcover either the caufe
or the cure.   However, Capt. Cook gave us to
underftand, that he intended to put in at the
firft harbour he could find.

We were now in high fpirits, not dreaming
of the hardfhips we had yet to fuffer, and we
purfued our courfe at a great rate.   Before
night

night we were in lat. 53 deg. 24 min. N. and in long. 226 deg. 26 min. E. with whole flocks of sea-fowl flying over our heads, among which were strings of geese and swans, all flying to the southward. We had other indications of land, and on

The 2d we came in sight of the main land, being then in lat. 54 deg. 44 min. and in long. 225 deg. 44 min. E. We continued our course to the north-westward as the land trended, till the 10th, when we opened on a very high island, which however appeared rocky and barren, and without inhabitants. We continued our course, sailing between this island and the main, in hopes of discovering some harbour where the Resolution might examine her leaks. We were now in lat. 59 deg. 53 min. and in long. 217 deg. 23 min. the land high and mountainous, and covered with snow.

On the 11th we came in sight of Cape Elias, a vast promontory that seemed to cover its head in the clouds. It bore from us S $\frac{1}{2}$ W.

On the 12th we hauled up to double it, and saw the land trending very much to the northward. About 3, A. M. we tacked, steering N. N. W. and at nine in the morning, opened a large strait, the entrance of which appeared to be about four miles; probably the same called in our maps the Straits of Anian, and placed erroneously in lat. 54 deg. N. and in long. 230 E. About four in the afternoon we entered the

mouth

mouth of the ftrait, and met a ftrong current to oppofe our progrefs; having a ftiff breeze, and the wind much in our favour; before fix in the evening, the Refolution opened a clofe harbour, and was foon followed by the Difco-very. Here both fhips caft anchor, which we had fcarce accomplifhed, before the boats were ordered out, and fome, eager to haul the feine, and others to go a fhooting, were impatient to begin, when unexpectedly they were alarmed by four canoes, in which were between 20 and 30 Indians not more than two miles diftant, and rowing with all their might towards the boats, who not being prepared for fuch an attack, made the beft of their way back to the fhips. As the Indians neared the boats, they began their war-fong, as their cuftom is, and brandifhing their arms, denounced defiance; but by this time other boats armed from the fhips, had joined the fportfmen, who were now fo near the fhips as to be out of danger. The Indians had then time to cool; they re-treated to the oppofite fide of the harbour, and in a very little time returned, with a white cloak difplayed as a fignal of peace, which was an-fwered by a white flag; and then they came on board without the leaft ceremony. Their fea-tures, fize and colour differed little from thofe we had juft left in George's Sound; but they had a flit between their lower lip and chin, through which they could put their tongue,

that

Ounalaschkan Chief

that gave them the appearance of having a double mouth. Add to this, the ornaments they wore in their nofes and ears, of tin and copper, and no figures upon earth could be more grotefque. However, they behaved civilly, and it being near night they took their leave, promifing to vifit us again in the morning, which they accordingly did, bringing with them the very fame forts of fkins which we had purchafed of the Indians at our former harbour, and which they readily parted with for any thing made of iron, though ever fo trifling. Thefe were cloathed with the fkins of wild beafts neatly fewed together, and they had befides a covering made like parchment, which in rainy or fnowy weather was water-proof; fo that no wet could effect them. Their ordinary canoes too had coverings of the fame kind.

They had fome inftruments for fifhing, which we did not obferve among the more foutherly Indians, fuch as harpoons, and giggs, all of which they were very ready to part with, as well as their cloathing, of which, though valuable to us, they made but little account. Thefe were chiefly purchafed by the failors, who found them warmer, and better adapted to the climate than any of their other cloathing. They had fpears headed with iron, very neatly manufactured, and knives, which they kept as bright as filver; but thefe they refufed to exchange for any thing we offered.

U

In the morning of the 13th we weighed and pursued our course to the northward up the strait all day, with the pleasing hope of having found the passage, of which we were in search. In our way we passed several very fine rivers that emptied their waters into that which we were now exploring. About four in the afternoon, we came to an anchor in 18 fathom water, and were surrounded with Indians who came to trade. Here, being safely moored just opposite to a small rivulet of excellent water, the boats were ordered out to fill the empty casks, and the carpenters from both ships were set to work to find out the leak in the Resolution; and after a most painful search, a hole was discovered in the ship's side, eaten quite through by the rats; which, by the working of the ship in the storm, had providentially filled with rubbish, and thereby prevented her foundering.

On the 14th, while we were employed on this necessary service, we were visited by crouds of Indians, persuading us to proceed; but our pinnace being ordered out, with boats to attend her, in order to examine the strait, it was found it be only an inlet through which there was no passage for ships to any other sea. To our great disappointment, therefore, after continuing here eight days, in which time every part of the sound had been searched, we took our leave of it, Capt. Cook giving it the name of Sandwich's Sound.

On the 20th, we returned to sea, and stood along-

along-fhore to the weftward, where we faw land trending as far as S. by E. very high, and the hills covered with fnow. We then ftood S. and S ½ E.

On the 21ft we came up with the fouthernmoft point we had feen the day before, and opened on a fine bay, which trended full to the eaftward, with very high land on both fides. We founded, in 34 fathom water gravelly bottom; then tacked and fteered the whole night N. E. by E.

In the morning of the 22d we tacked again, and ftood to the weftward.

On the 23d, the weather being clear and pleafant, and there being little or no wind the boats were ordered out, and all hands were employed in fifhing, except this gentleman, who preferred the diverfion of fhooting.

On the 24th a ftiff breeze fprung up, attended with very heavy fqualls, with fnow and rain, in which we carried away our main top-gallant-maft in the flings, and received other damage in our fails and rigging. We were now two degrees farther to the fouthward, fteering as the land trended, and examining every bay and inlet as we paffed along.

On the 25th we altered our courfe, to N. by W. the Main trending away to N. E. high and mountainous. At noon we paffed fome large iflands, bearing from W. S. W. to N. W. by W. but foon loft fight of them in a great fog.

On the 26th, at 3 A. M. we perceived the

land very high on both sides of us E. and W.
and saw two burning mountains at a considerable distance.   As the fog cleared up, we found
ourselves in the entrance of a vast river, supposed to be about four miles over, with a strong
current setting to the southward.

On the 27th we found the river to widen as
we advanced, and the land to flatten.   We continued under an easy sail all day and the following night, sounding as we advanced from
30 to 40 fathom, shelly bottom and white sand.
We were once more flattered with having found
the passage, of which we were in pursuit, being now in the latitude of 60 degrees north.

On the 28th, in the morning, we sounded
at 24 fathom, the tide still setting strong to
the southward at the rate of five and six knots
an hour; but the wind dying away, the signal
was made for casting anchor, when both ships
came to in 26 fathom water; but the Resolution expecting to come to with her small stream
anchor, let the whole run out and lost both anchor and hausser, besides the ship's grapnel in
looking for it.   About 8 at night, the signal
was made to weigh and sail; but at ten the
current ran so strong, that both ships were a-
gain obliged to cast anchor in 24 fathom, bottom the same as before.   It was now light all
night, and we could perceive the river to make
W. N. W. very rapid.

On the 29th we made sail with a fresh wind,
and advanced apace, but on trying the water

we

we found a great alteration from falt to frefh. This day we were vifited by feveral Indians, who brought fkins, which they exchanged for trifles. In the night we obferved they made large fires; but the flames from the two burning mountains feemed to darken their light. We were yet at a great diftance from them. We found regular foundings all this day, till opening into a large wide extended bay, the water fhallowed, and we caft anchor in nine fathom water, brown fand and fhells as before. Here the boats were ordered out, and after a fruitlefs fearch to find a paffage, founding from two to four fathom, with the water quite frefh, they returned in the morning, and were taken on board. In the evening they renewed their labour, founding to the north eaftward, as the day before they had founded in the oppofite direction. Here they difcovered a large river, the entrance of which bore from the fhips N. E. by N. but found that it trended away to N. W. with high land on both fides, and with foundings from 8 to $3\frac{1}{2}$ fathom. This they examined for more than 20 miles. It abounded with fifh and fowl; but though the land was high on both fides, moft part of the way, they faw neither houfe nor inhabitant. The water was frefh, and the current rapid; all hopes therefore of a communication with any other fea in this paffage vanifhed; and the fhips returned to fea again by the fame channel. In the mean time, while the boats were founding, a party of us

U 3

with

with the two Captains at our head, attended by a ferjeant's guard of marines, landed on the eafternmoft fhore, in order to take the diverfion of fhooting, and to reconnoitre the country. We had proceeded more than four miles without feeing one inhabitant, and were going to fcour the woods for game, when a body of Indians, to the number of fixty, rufhed out of an adjoining thicket, all armed after their manner with bows and fpears; a few of our marines difcharged their pieces over their heads, which inftantly ftopt their career; and they were retreating as rapidly as they came on, when Capt. Cook advancing fingly, grounded his piece, and made figns for them to halt. One who feemed to have the command of the reft, turning fuddenly about, obferved his motions, and underftood them; and calling to the reft, they all ftopt, and, after a fhort confultation, laid down their arms, and ftripping themfelves quite naked, laid their cloathes down by them. This we underftood they did, to fhow that they had no arms concealed. We then advanced, and entered into a kind of dumb difcourfe, of which we could underftand enough to know that they wanted us to accompany them to their town, which we very readily did; they very deliberately put on their cloaths, and then fhewed us the way.

When we arrived we found a number of wretched huts, with women and children, old men and dogs, who, at firft fight of us, were

more

more frightened than their masters, hanging their tails, and sneaking away. One of these Capt. Cook purchased. These huts consisted of nothing but long poles, rudely constructed into the form of a hovel, and covered over with heathy earth. For a door, they had a hole just large enough to creep in at, which, in cold weather, they close with a kind of faggot. These inner apartments were holes or pits dug in the earth, and divided like stalls in a stable. Their furniture we did not survey. We saw some bladders full of blubber or fat hanging about, and some skins of beasts; also dried fish in plenty; we likewise saw several wooden utensils, besides their arms; and we saw quantities of salt in wooden troughs. They had dried flesh too, probably the remains of their winter provisions, which we understood they eat raw, and some of which they offered us for dinner. In these huts or holes they burn no fire; but in the winter they shut themselves up close, and have lamps, which they continually keep burning: for here, during the winter months, they scarce ever see the sun. We were not a little surprised at the sight of some of their children, who were as fair, and their skins as white as those of many children in England; their dark coppery complexion is therefore owing to their anointing and greasing their children when they are young, and exposing them to all weathers while they have light, and shutting them in their smoaky

U 4

caverns

caverns when it is dark. We found no difference between the people in this found, and thofe
we have defcribed in the other. Having gratified our curiofity we returned to our fhips;
and having nothing farther to detain us,

On the 1ft of June, in the afternoon, we
fet fail. We were now in lat. 61 deg. 15 min. N.
and in long. 209 deg. 55 min. E. many leagues
within land, and it was not till the 6th that we
cleared the channel.

On the 4th, being his majefty's birth-day,
we kept as a day of rejoicing.

On the 5th we paffed the burning mountains.

The 6th we cleared the ftrait to the unfpeakable joy of the failors, who, during the whole
time from our entrance till our return, worked
with incredible labour, anchoring and weighing
as the winds and the tide afforded opportunity.
During our paffage we had frequent interviews
with the natives, who, the nearer we approached
the fhore, were better cloathed, and fhewed
fome manufactures of their own, and other nations; and were in poffeffion of a greater variety of fkins than thofe within land, which
were ftrong indications of a foreign trade, but
by what conveyance carried on, all our endeavours at this time could not difcover. On this
day our courfe was S. E.

On the 7th we ftood S. by E. ½ E. and about
2 P. M. we paffed two very large iflands, having paffed feveral fmall ones before. We continued

tinued this courfe with very little variation till the 10th, when the Refolution, in coafting along the main, ran foul of a dangerous reef, that appeared juft above water clofe under her lee bow. Her good fortune ftill accompanied her, for fhe flid off without damage.

On the 11th we were alarmed by the clafhing of the waves, as if fome great building was tumbling in, and, looking round the fhip, we faw ourfelves involved among fhoals of feals and fea-lions, who prefently fet up the moft frightful howlings that poffibly can be conceived; at the fame time we obferved a large whale to pafs along, at which we fired a fwivel, but without effect. We this day ftood to the north-eaft as the land trended.

On the 12th we purfued the fame courfe, and faw the land bear N. E. to a great diftance. The extreme of the eaftward point bore E.S.E.

On the 13th, at 2 P. M. we altered our courfe, and ftood to the fouth.

On the 14th in the morning we faw the eaftward point diftant 7 or 8 leagues, lat. 56 deg. 23 min. long. 205 deg. 16 min. We directed our courfe along-fhore.

On the 15th, the weather hazy, we loft fight of land, founded and found no ground at 100 fathom. A ftorm came on, and both fhips ftood to fea.

On the 16th it abated, the weather clear, ftood W. S. W. with a ftiff breeze.

On

On the 17th ſtood in, and ſaw land trend
S. ½ E. as far as the eye could carry. We
were now about 2 leagues diſtant from the
ſhore, which was covered with geeſe, ducks,
ſhags and ſea-fowls innumerable.

On the 18th we coaſted along-ſhore, and
paſſed many dangerous rocks and ſhoals, which
we ſaw project from the main into the ſea to a
great diſtance. We were now in lat. 55 deg.
26 min. long. 200 deg. 58 min. E. and about
3 P. M. had paſſed all the land to the Southward, when, being within half a mile of the
main, we obſerved three canoes making towards us, in which were ſix Indians. When
they came along ſide, they made ſigns for us to
drop our anchors, intimating, that the people
on ſhore would be glad to ſee us ; at the ſame
time we thought we heard the report of a gun.
Little notice, however, was taken of what
paſſed. The people from the gang-way talked
with the men, one of whom made ſigns for letting down a rope, to which he tied a neat box,
curiouſly made up with a ſmall twine ; for which
he would take nothing in return. The man
who took it in looked upon it as a great curioſity, and, after the Indians were gone, began to examine the contents, when a note was
found in the inſide, which was immediately
carried to the Captain, and a conſultation was
held on the quarter-deck to endeavour to decy-
pher the contents ; but none on board the Diſcovery

covery could make out a letter. The ship was then hove-to, three guns fired, and a jack hoisted at the mast-head for stopping the Resolution. This being observed, all on board were struck with fear for the safety of the Discovery, thinking that some fatal disaster had happened, and that she was going to the bottom. Their boat was instantly hoisted out, and Mr. Williamson, 3d Lieutenant, came in all haste to learn the cause. With him our Captain returned, and related what had happened, and shewed Capt. Cook the note, who likewise held a consultation upon it, and it was handed from the quarter-deck to the gang-way, where every man in the ship might see it, but not a man could make out more than something like the date 1778, of which they were not clear. We therefore continued our course along the coast as the land trended; but saw no opening nor any inhabitants. About midnight, we saw a vast flame ascend from a burning mountain, and observed several fires within land. Lat. by observation, 54 deg. 47 min. N. long. 197 deg. 52 min. E.

On the 20th early in the morning, looking out a-head, we saw something like a reef before us, and fired a gun for the Resolution to tack; happy that day-light had enabled us to escape the danger.

On the 21st we steered S. W; but at 8 A. M. finding the land to trend more to the southward,

we

we altered our courſe to S. S. W. The extreme
of the land in ſight bearing W. by S. ſeven or
eight leagues, very high land and much ſnow.
About two in the afternoon we came again in
ſight of the two burning mountains which we
had before ſeen, but at a great diſtance, bearing N. W. by N. Our courſe during the night
was S. S. W. During the courſe of this day,
the weather being fair, and but little wind, the
men were employed in fiſhing, and in leſs than
four hours caught more than three ton weight
of cod and holybut, ſome of the latter more
than a 100 pounds weight.

On the 22d our men were employed in ſalt-
ing and barrelling up, for future uſe, what the
ſhip's company could not conſume while freſh,
which proved a moſt acceptable ſupply. All
this day we kept our courſe S. W. by S.

On the 23d in the evening we ſhaped our
courſe more to the weſtward, the weather thick
and hazey.

On the 24th, little wind and hazey. Saw
no land ; but, looking over the ſhip's ſide, obſerved the water to change colour to a milky
white. Sounded, and found ground at 47 fathom. About 4 P. M. we ſaw two very high
iſlands bearing N. W. diſtance about 5 leagues,
and could diſcern the main land contiguous.
We bore away under the lee of the weſternmoſt,
and continued ſteering all night S. by E.

On

On the 25th, in the morning we changed our courfe, fteering S. W. as the land trended. At ten the fame morning we had a full view of the land, for many miles but faw no figns of houfes or inhabitants; but doubtlefs, tho' the country appeared rugged and barrren, and in many places white with fnow, there were many people in the inland parts. About 7 in the evening we could fee land at a great diftance, bearing due fouth, which had the appearance of a large ifland. Hitherto we had been exploring the coafts of an unknown continent, unknown at leaft to our European geographers; though we fhall fee by the fequel, that it was not wholly unexplored by the Afiatic Ruffians. Towards night, tho' it had been perfectly clear all day, the air began to thicken, and by 10 at night, the fog was fo thick that we could not fee the fhip's length. We kept firing guns, burning falfe fires, and ftanding off land all night, as did the Refolution, and in the morning of the

26th, when the fog difperfed, we found ourfelves in a deep bay, furrounded by high lands, and almoft afhore under a high mountain, which we had not before difcovered. Both fhips inftantly dropt anchor in 24 fathom water, blew muddy bottom within two cables length of the fhore, and among fhoals and breakers, from which we moft miraculoufly efcaped. For fome time we ftood in amazement how we could poffibly

poffibly get into fuch a frightful fituation. But being in it, for our own fafety we moored both fhips ; and happy it was we ufed that precaution ; for a gale came on, when our whole exiftence depended upon the goodnefs of our cables.

On the 27th, at 3 A. M. it ceafed blowing, and the weather began to clear. At 6 we unmoored, and failed under clofe reefed topfails, directing our courfe N. W. for an opening we faw at about a league diftance, but at nine the wind dying away, we anchored again in 25 fathom water, loamey fand. It being a dead calm our boats were ordered out, and fome gentlemen went on fhore to examine the land. In their fearch they found fomething like an Indian manfion, being a deep pit funk in the earth, with fome poles placed acrofs it after their manner, and covered with fods and a hole to creep into it about two feet fquare. In it they found the bones of dried fifh, and of birds, and near it a place where there had been a fire, but all had the appearance of being long deferted. They alfo found the rib of a whale about eight feet long, which it was not eafy to account how it could come there. About noon the gentlemen returned on board, and a breeze fpringing up from the eaftward, we weighed and took leave of this dangerous bay, to which Capt. Cook gave the name of Providence Bay, as it was owing to providence that we were here

mira-

miraculously preferved from perifhing. We had pleafant weather all day, and the land high all round us. We founded all the afternoon from 18 to 36 fathom, moftly fandy bottom. In the evening we faw a large body of Indians towing a whale which they had ftruck, who were too bufy to mind us till late, when two canoes came along fide and traded. We were furprized when they afked us for tobacco, and more fo when they fhewed us fome, together with fnuff in their boxes. As tobacco was a precious commodity on board, we could fpare them little, but for that little they were thankful, and departed. We paffed feveral iflands to the eaftward, very high and mountainous.

On the 28th in the morning Mr. Nelfon, accompanied by feveral other gentlemen, went on fhore botanizing; they found great variety of plants and flowers peculiar to the country, befides others with which we were all well acquainted, fuch as primrofes, violets, currants, rafberries, juniper and many other northern fruits, which were now all in bloffom. They found alfo a bird's neft, with five fmall eggs, not unlike a fparrow's. After fome ftay they came again on board, and the wind dying away, and the Refolution having got far a-head, our boats were employed in towing us, when a ftrong current meeting us right a-head baffled their endeavours. This current ran with fuch force that the Refolution, unable to ftem it,

caft

caſt anchor, and ſoon after was joined by the Diſcovery. Here ſeveral canoes came from the land to trade, and made ſigns for more tobacco, of which our own men were in great want. About noon we opened on a fine harbour to the weſtward of us; but we were the whole afternoon in working up the Race, as it was called, from the rapidity of its motion, and the ſtrength with which it ſet againſt us. Our firſt attempt to ſtem it proved fruitleſs. We were driven as far back as the place from whence we ſet out. On the tide's turning in our favour, we made a ſecond attempt and ſucceeded. About ſix in the evening, we caſt anchor in 12 fathom water, and ſoon after came to moorings. We were, in leſs than an hour, ſurrounded with more than 30 canoes, with rock fiſh and dried ſalmon, which they exchanged for beads, ſmall nails, or any thing we offered them.

On the 29th, the boats were employed in watering the ſhips, and the ſail-makers, &c. began to over-haul the rigging, and all hands were employed in different repairs. In the mean time ſeveral Indians hovered round the ſhips with fiſh ready dreſſed, which they preſented to any indiſcriminately who would accept them; but would take nothing in return, except tobacco or ſnuff were offered them; neither did they offer to ſteal or take any the moſt trifling thing away; and what was remarkable not a woman was to be ſeen, nor did any come

near

near the ship during our stay. Our Captain taking notice of two that seemed superior to the rest, he invited them on board, and with much intreaty prevailed on them to enter. He made them presents of a few beads, and two or three hands of tobacco each, for which they in the most submissive manner expressed their gratitude. All this while our botanist and his attendants were busily employed, and sent plenty of celery and other wholesome herbs on board, as well for the use of the great cabin, as for those of the subordinate tables down even to the lowest of the ship's company.

On the 1st of July the signal was given to unmoor; but, the wind shifting to N. N. E. it was

July the 2d, before we could clear the harbour, to which Capt. Cook gave the name of Providence Harbour, in lat. 54 deg. 18 min. but more of this hereafter. About noon, we saw the land trend to E. S. E. we hauled up to E. N. E. and continued all night in that course.

On the 3d, at 2 A. M. we wore ship, and stood to the southward till day-light, and then tacked, and steered E. N. E. At noon we saw the extreme of the land, bearing E. ¼ S.

On the 4th, at 2 A. M. we steered N.N.E. At ten sounded at 70 fathom, blue mud, shelly bottom. At noon we had an observation, lat. 55 deg. 48 min. N. long. 195. 34. Course all night N. E.

X

On

On the 5th, we faw the land very low and even, trending away to the fouthward of the eaft. We. were diftant from the northernmoft fhore 3 or 4 leagues, and from this day we began founding till our arrival in watering harbour. This day all hands employed in fifhing; and as our people were now put on 2-thirds allowance, what each catched he might eat or fell. Fortunate for them, they caught fome tons of fine fifh which proved a moft feafonable fupply; for the fhip provifions, what with falt and maggots eating into the beef and pork, and the rats, and weavils devouring the heart of the bread, the one was little better than putrid flefh, and the other, upon breaking, would crumble into duft. At noon, this day, we directed our courfe N. N. E. being now in lat. 57. deg. 4 min. long. 199 deg. 40 min.

On the 6th we continued the fame courfe, and, founding, found ground at 12 fathom. We tacked, and ftood to the S. E. and, founding again, found ground at 3½ fathom. We were now in Bhering's Straits. We tacked again, and ftood to the north, having had another providential efcape from running upon the rocks. We were now in a moft perilous and laborious navigation, which would afford little entertainment to the generality of readers. Till

The 15th we continued founding and tacking night and day, in moft tempeftuous weather, and through a Race of fhallow water, with a ftrong cur-

current againſt us, when, about ten in the morning, the weather clear and fine, we came to an anchor in 17 fathom water, lat. 58 deg. 20 min. long. 197 deg. 51 min. Here the cutters from both ſhips were manned, and all the gentlemen went on ſhore. We ſaw no other inhabitants but bears and foxes, and ſome wild deer; we heard in the adjoining woods the howlings and yellings of wolves and other wild beaſts; but thought it neither ſafe nor ſeaſonable to purſue them. After ſpending the greateſt part of the day in botanizing with Mr. Nelſon, we returned on board; leaving on the bluff part of a rock a bottle behind us, in which were encloſed ſome blue and white beads with a note of the ſhips names, the date when left, by whom, and on what expedition. We were no ſooner returned than a breeze ſprang up, when we weighed, and again made ſail, with the ſhips heads W.N.W. We continued ſounding, and on

The 16th, the water ſhallowed ſo faſt, that it was thought prudent to drop anchors again, and to ſend the boats out with a compaſs to examine the ſtrait to a conſiderable diſtance a-head. In half an hour a gun was fired from the boats, as a ſignal not to proceed, and the man at the maſt-head ſaw land appear juſt above water This proved a barren ſpot, not above an acre wide, with nothing but ſhells and the bones of fiſhes on it. The boats having ſounded from W. to N.W. by N. from two to one fathom and a half, returned with their report, that no paffage could be found in that direction. From this day to the 20th the boats were continually founding in all directions amidft the moft dreadful tempeft of thunder, lightning and hail, that ever blew; but fuch was our danger, that Capt. Cook himfelf fhared in all the labour; and what added to our misfortune the Refolution parted her beft bower within ten fathom of the anchor, and it was wonderful that fhe was not wrecked.

On the 17th all hands that could be fpared were employed in fweeping for the anchor, but in vain; being quite worn down with fatigue, they were forced to give over, and men from the Difcovery were ordered to fupply their places.

On the 18th the anchor was recovered, when every officer on board both fhips was obliged to do the duty of common men. No pen can defcribe our danger from the horrible fituation we were in.

The 19th was wholly employed in founding, without fuccefs.

On the 20th Capt. Cook himfelf, in founding to the S. E. found a narrow channel, regular foundings, from 8 to 10 fathom. Hope took place of defpair, and all hands returned to their labour with frefh fpirits. We prefently weighed, and purfued our courfe with a fine breeze. The day continuing clear, at noon we had

had an obſervation in lat. 59 deg. 37 min. long.
197 deg. 16 min E. This day we were viſited
by ſome Indians, who had little to part with,
except ſome dried fiſh and their cloaks.

On the 21ſt, about noon, both ſhips brought
to, the wind and current both uniting to oppoſe
our progreſs.

On the 22d we were overjoyed, on ſounding,
to find the ſea deepen to 40 fathom ; but, before night that joy was much damped by a prodigious fall of ſnow, of which it was with difficulty that the deck could be kept clear, tho'
the watch was conſtantly employed in ſhovel-
ling it off during the night. This weather continued till

The 26th, when it began to clear up.

On the 27th, we had clear weather, and regular ſoundings, from 25 to 35 fathom water,
white ſandy bottom.

On the 29th, the man at the maſt-head called out land very high, diſtance about 2 leagues
right a-head. We tacked and ſtood off.

On the 30th we continued along-ſhore, courſe
N. N. E. to N. E. ſounding in very unequal
depths from 10 to 30 fathom.

Auguſt the 1ſt, the ſea began again to deepen,
but the land trending to the ſouthward obliged
us to change our courſe. We were now in lat.
61 deg. 14 min. N. long. 191 deg. 33 min. E.

On the 2d we again bore away N. W. all the morning, and at noon tacked to N. E. by N. which courfe we purfued till

The 3d, when we ftood N. N. E. This courfe we purfued, with a little variation to the eaftward, till the evening, when we faw land, bearing . S. W.

The 4th at noon, founding from 15 to 20 fathom, we came again in fight of land, which bore from us W. to N. $\frac{1}{2}$ E. At noon we founded, and found only 8 $\frac{1}{2}$ fathom. In the evening we came to an anchor in 15 fathom.

On the 5th, word was brought us from the Refolution, of the death of Mr. Anderfon, the furgeon. His funeral was performed with the ufual fea ceremonies, and our furgeon, Mr. Law, was appointed in his place ; and Mr. Samuel, furgeon's mate of the Refolution, fucceeded Mr. Law. This day we came to in 12 fathom water, under the lee of a fmall but high ifland, to which Capt. Cook gave the name of Sledge Ifland, as a fledge and the remains of an Indian town were found upon it ; but no inhabitants. There were likewife found fome Indian fnow-fhoes. Mr. Nelfon, and his affociates found great quantities of wild celery, and a kind of wild fetch or chichilling, of which the fhip's company made the proper ufe. We were now in lat. 64 deg. 44 min. long. 192 deg. 42 min.

Early on the 6th we weighed, and ftood W. by N. As we coafted along fhore, feveral Indians

dians were feen on the oppofite fide of the ifland, who were, to all appearance, preparing to pay us a vifit. We hove-to; but, after waiting an hour, and none coming, we continued our courfe. We foon came again into fhallow water, founding from 4 to fix fathom water, fix leagues from the main land.

On the 8th we had a violent ftorm of hail, rain and fnow, which continued all the morning; but the wind dying away about noon, we were drifted to leeward clofe in fhore, under a very high track of main land, and among rocks and breakers. Both fhips inftantly came too in 9 fathom water, the Refolution with her beft bower, and the Difcovery with her coafting anchor. Fortunately a breeze fprung up in our favour, and relieved us from this perilous fituation. Seeing the land trend away to the N.W. we directed our courfe accordingly, till, having doubled the wefternmoft point, we fteered again to the eaftward.

On the 9th about 2 A.M. we came again to an anchor, a ftrong current from 5 to 6 knots an hour fetting againft us; but the fhips pitching bows under, and the water from the upper deck running, as through a fieve, to the lower deck, in lefs than half an hour, every thing between decks was afloat; fo that the poor men had not a dry rag to put on. This obliged us to weigh as faft as poffible; but, in our fituation, that was a work of no fmall labour and

X 4 diffi-

difficulty, as at this time many of our hands, through fatigue, and being conftantly expofed to the rain and fnow, and in a damp fhip, were ill of colds, attended with flow fevers, which rendered them incapable of duty. Out of 70 hands, officers included, we could only mufter 20 to the capftern. We had with difficulty weighed our fmall bower, and had made two unfuccefsful attempts at the fheet anchor, when the Refolution left us, making all the fail fhe could carry, to furmount the current. We were now in the utmoft diftrefs; but by contriving feveral additional purchafes we at laft fucceeded, but we had the misfortune to have two of our ableft hands wounded, and it was next to a miracle, that none were killed. The Refolution was now out of fight, but, judging our diftrefs, fhe lay to amidft a clufter of iflands, of which we told no lefs than feven very fmall but very high. As foon as we came in fight, fhe made fail, and we followed with all the fail we could crowd till about midnight, when we were furprifed by a fudden fquall, which fplit our main top-fail, and fhivered our jeb to ribbons; it was, however, of fhort continuance.

On the 10th, we had fine weather and a calm fea, and were proceeding at a great rate, when, unexpectedly, we opened into a deep bay, where we faw at the diftance of a few leagues, a large Indian town, of which, probably, our Commodore was in fearch, as the Ruffians, in their

late

ate difcoveries, had found a town upon the extremity of the Afiatic coaft, to which they had given the name of Helenefki; but called by the natives   This bay, by obfervation, lies in lat. 66 deg. 27 min. N. and in long. 188 deg 3 min E. near which the Ruf-fians have fixed the north-eafternmoft point of the Afiatic continent, and which we have now proved to join the main continent of America, having traced that continent from Cape Blanco, the wefternmoft known Cape of Californio, to the prefent bay, without being able to find any communication with Hudfon's bay, or any o-ther fea whatever.   But of this more hereafter.

Here we caft anchor, and both Captains, at-tended by a proper guard of marines, went on fhore, and were met by an old Indian, at the head of a numerous body of his countrymen, all dreffed in the fkins of beafts.   He had in his right hand a fpear 12 feet long, and over his left fhoulder hung his bow and fhaft of ar-rows.   He addreffed the ftrangers in a fpeech of half an hour, at the conclufion of which he difplayed a cloak of white feathers, as a fig-nal of peace, which Capt. Cook anfwered by waving his white handkerchief.   Thefe preli-minaries over, the Indian made figns to his followers to ground their arms, and fet them the example by laying down his own, and making his fubmiffion.   The parties then approached each other, and Capt. Cook prefented the Indian

with

with a few European trifles, such as knives,
sciffars, needles, pins, beads, and small looking-glaffes, which were found more acceptable
here than iron, or more coftly merchandize,
with which the Indian was fo pleafed, that he
ftripped himfelf of the garment which he wore,
and prefented it with his weapons of war, to
the Captain in return, making figns at the fame
time to the company to accompany him to the
town, where we fhould meet with things more
worthy our acceptance. This invitation both
Captains, with their train, accepted, and, after
walking little more than two miles, we came to
the town, of which the old Indian appeared to be
chief. Here we trafficked for furs of various
forts, fables, martins, foxes, beaver, and fome
deer fkins, dreffed in a particular manner, on
both fides, two of which we purchafed for drum
heads. They had dogs in abundance of a
large breed, but we faw no other domeftic animal. Their houfes, or rather holes, were built
much like thofe we had feen all along the coaft.
After ftaying about two hours, the company
returned to the fhips, the Indians accompanying
us to the fhore, where they took their leave,
kneeling when we parted. We were no fooner
embarked, than the fignal was made to weigh,
and get under way, fhaping our courfe N.N.E.

On the 11th we paffed feveral large iflands to
the eaftward of us, and at the fame time left
the extreme point of the northern cape of the

Afiatic

Afiatic fhore to the eaftward of us very high and very barren. We then bore away to the north-eaft, founding from 5 to 6 fathom; and about 3 P. M. finding the fea to change of a milky colour, and at the fame time to fhallow very faft, we came too in 7 fathom water, and fent the boats out to found, who foon returned finding the fea to deepen as they proceeded.

On the 12th we altered our courfe, and ftood to the N. W. till noon, when we again ftood to the E. leaving feveral iflands on our ftarboard bow. In the evening we croffed the arctic circle, and ftood all night W. by S. as the land trended. But

In the morning of the 13th we ftood once more to the eaftward. We were now in lat. 66 deg. 35 min. long. 189, the weather warm and fine.

On the 15th, finding ourfelves near land, on a fhallow and rocky coaft, we ftood off W.S.W. when prefently we were attacked by a heavy ftorm of wind, attended with rain, which lafted the whole day. At night we ftood again N.N.E. and fo continued till morning.

On the 16th at noon we found ourfelves in lat. 69 deg. 46 min. long. 192 E. We then ftood from N. N. E. to N. E. founding from 22 to 23 fathom water.

On the 17th the weather began to grow piercing cold. The froft fet in and froze fo hard, that the running rigging was foon loaded with ice,

ice, and rendered almoſt impoſſible to make the ſheafs or blocks traverſe without the aſſiſtance of ſix men to do the work of one. But what is moſt remarkable, the ſudden tranſition from heat to ſuch ſevere cold. The day before was warm and pleaſant, but in the evening of this day the ice was ſeen hanging at our hair, our noſes, and even at the men's finger's ends, if they did but expoſe them to the air for five or ſix minutes: And ſtill the farther they ran to the eaſtward, the colder it grew, and the ice the more connected.

On the 18th, hot victuals froze while we were at table; and this weather continued for ſome days. We were now advanced as far as lat. 69 deg. 46 min. N. and in long. 192. E. and involved among iſlands of ice, ſome of which hung over our heads as we paſſed them, and excited very frightful apprehenſions. On ſome of theſe iſlands, many ſea morſe, and other ſea animals were ſeen. Being now well in with the ice, and having loſt ſight of land, we ſtood on to the northward till

The 19th, when looking round in the morning, as ſoon as the fog cleared away, we ſaw nothing but fields of ice covered over with whole herds of ſea lions, ſea horſes, and other amphibious animals, to the number, as it was thought, of ſome thouſands. Thus ſurrounded, a ſignal was made from the Reſolution to bring too, and to load the great guns, while
the

the boats were getting ready to attack thefe hideous looking creatures with mufkets. This by the failors from both fhips was accounted fport; and they went to the attack with as much alacrity as if to a match at foot-ball. Orders were given, as foon as the great guns were difcharged, to quicken the attack with the mufketry as faft as poffible. In a few minutes not a creature was to be feen upon the ice, but fuch as were killed, or fo feverely wounded, as not to be able to crawl to the open fea. Some lay growling on the ice not quite dead, with two or three balls through their heads, aud others tumbling about with horrible vindictive looks, threatening deftruction to whoever fhould approach them. All hands were employed to collect the carcaffes, and to carry them on board; but what was thought an ill reward for their labour, orders were next day given by Capt. Cook to fubftitute the flefh of thefe fea-monfters in the room of all other provifions, flower only excepted. This was ftrongly oppofed by the crew of the Refolution, and Capt. Clarke remonftrated againft it. He was told by Capt. Cook, that he might do what he pleafed on board his own fhip ; but the ftate of the provifions on board the Refolution made it neceffary; and that he himfelf fhould fet the example. Capt. Clarke endeavoured, but in vain, to enforce the order. and the matter paffed on without any ferious confequences.

On

On the 20th we tacked ſhip and ſtood to the weſtward, the wind much againſt us. We tacked every two hours, ſtill working over to the Aſiatic ſhore, with a view to examine the coaſts on both ſides, before we returned to the ſouthward. We were now in lat. 70 deg. 9 min. long. 194 deg. 55 min.

We continued labouring among the ice till the 25th, when a ſtorm came on, which made it dangerous for us to proceed; a conſultation was therefore held on board the Reſolution as ſoon as the violence of the gale abated, when it was unanimouſly reſolved, that as this paſſage was impracticable for any uſeful purpoſe of navigation, which was the great object of the voyage, to purſue it no farther, eſpecially in the condition the ſhips were in, the winter approaching, and the diſtance from any known place of refreſhment great. On obſervation being had at noon, we found we were in lat. 71, and long. 197, when the ſhips put about.

About 2 in the morning of the 26th we obſerved a great body of ice nearing us very faſt, and in a few hours after, we ſaw the ice all cloſed as far as the eye could carry, bearing from N.E. to S.W. we continued to ſail W.S.W

On the 28th ſeveral pieces of looſe ice paſſed us, one of which came foul of the Diſcovery, and ſhook her whole frame; it was feared ſhe had received conſiderable damage, but upon the carpenter's examining her fore and
aft,

aft, nothing was found amifs. We now took leave of the ice for this feafon, directing our courfe S. S. W.

On the 29th we faw land in the morning, which bore from N. N. W. to S. W. very high and covered with fnow. In the evening we were in with the land; not a fhrub to be feen, but birds innumerable.

On the 31ft we came in fight of the eaftern cape, bearing S. S. E. very high and covered with fnow; at three in the afternoon we faw two fmall but very high iflands, bearing from N. N. E. to N. W. we were then in lat. 68 deg. 10 min. and long. 182 deg. 2 min.

Sept. 1, we continued coafting to the fouthward.

On the 3d we opened into the great bay, where we anchored the 10th of laft month, lat. 66 deg. 31 min. long. 188 deg. 17 min. E.

On the 5th we loft fight of the main continent of Afia, which we left the day before.

On the 6th we faw land from W. N. W. to E. N. E. very woody, and covered with fnow in the valleys. Here we found the continent of America and the Afiatic fhore not above 6 leagues diftant, lat. 63 deg. 58 min. long. 192 deg. 10 min.

On the 7th, there came two canoes from the fhore, with four Indians in them, though we were full four leagues diftant. We hove too for their coming up; but when along fide, they

had

had little or nothing to part with, except fome dried fifh. They were invited on board, but could not be perfuaded to enter. The Captain made them prefents of fome trifles, with which they departed well pleafed. They were cloathed in fkins after the manner of all the inhabitants of the weftern coafts of America, among whom we found no remarkable diftinction of drefs or colour.

On the 8th we fteered E. ½ N. paffing feveral bays and fine harbours all day, found the country pleafant, and the coaft delightful. Here we found a ftrong current to fet to the S. E. at the rate of 5 knots an hour.

On the 9th the land opened all round, from one fhore to the other, and we found ourfelves in the middle of a deep bay, but very fhallow, fometimes 3, but never above 5½ fathom water. We faw the bay to run as far as the eye could carry, but impoffible to proceed, as in many places the water fhallowed under three fathom. We fent the boats out to found, at the fame time land appeared from S. E. to E. like two iflands, which we afterwards found to join to the land.

On the 10th, having a ftiff breeze, we ran right acrofs the mouth of the bay, for the N. W. fhore, and juft before night the Refolution narrowly efcaped running upon a rock. We were now again in Bhering's Straits.

On

On the 11th we came to an anchor in 6 fathom water, the easternmost point of the bay bearing N. E. by E. distance 8 miles very high land. In the night we saw several fires, but no Indians came off to us.

On the 12th, in the morning, the boats from both ships were sent on shore, where they saw some houses of a wretched construction; a small sledge, and several other articles belonging to the Indians; but none of the natives. About ten they returned with a load of wood, which they found drifted on the beach, but no water; the wood had drifted from the southward, for we saw no trees but black spruce. We then stretched over to the other shore, and the boats were again sent out, and about nine in the evening returned, loaded with wood, which the men were obliged to carry through the water on their shoulders, as the boats could not come within half a mile of land for breakers. This was a grievous task, as many of them had but just recovered their late illness. This day several natives came from S. S. E. in large canoes, having great quantities of salmon dried and fresh, which they exchanged for blue and red beads, needles, pins, knives or scissors, or any European trinkets that were offered them; but what they valued most was *tobacco*. For this they would exchange their bows and arrows, their warlike instruments, and whatever else they valued most; but of this commodity,

Y   as

as has already been noticed, we had but little to spare. We were again obliged to change our station, and stretch to the other shore, where a safe anchorage was discovered, near which we could wood and water with the greatest ease. Here our great cutter was sent out, properly provided with a compass, and six days provision to survey the bay, in order to determine whether that land, which the Ruffians have laid down as Heleneski, joins to the American continent, or whether there might not be a passage to some other sea intervene.

On the 13th, while the cutters were on this service, the boats were busy in wooding and watering, and before the return of the former, the latter had got more than 20 tons of water on board the Discovery, and near double that quantity on board the Resolution, with a proportionable quantity of wood. The men had then leave to go ashore, by turns, to gather berries, which they now found ripe, and in great abundance, such as rasberries, blue berries, black and red currants, huckle berries, with various other sorts, all in full perfection. A party was likewise sent out to cut spruce, to brew into beer for both ships. Of this liquor, however, the men were not very fond in this cold climate, especially when they were given to understand that their grog was to be stopped, and this beer substituted in the room of it. This occasioned great murmuring, and it was

found

found neceffary to give it alternately, fpruce one day and grog another.

On thefe excurfions, the parties were always well armed and had marines to attend them, and their orders were never to go out of hearing of the fhips guns, but to repair inftantly on board on the proper fignals. Thefe precautions, however, feemed unneceffary, as they never met with any moleftation from the natives, who were not numerous upon the coaft.

On the 17th, the party that were fent out to furvey the bay returned, after a diligent examination of two days and two nights. Their report was, that it extended within land above 40 leagues, that they coafted it round, founding as they went, that they found the foundings regular from 5 to 3½ fathom; that it had no communication with any other fea, nor any current that indicated a paffage to any other continent whatever. This report being confirmed by the officers who commanded the cutters from both fhips, the boats were all taken on board and fecured, and

On the 18th we weighed and failed, retracing the coafts we had before explored, without making any material difcovery.

On the 25th we met with a dreadful tempeft of wind, rain and hail, or rather ice, between two and three inches fquare, by which feveral of our men, who were obliged to keep the deck, were feverely wounded. In this long run, we paffed feveral re-

markable

markable promontories and iflands, particularly
in lat. 63 deg. 30 min. N. we paffed two headlands, diftance from each other about half a
mile. We hove-to, and our boats founded
acrofs, in fome places not above 1 ½ fathom.
In lat. 62 deg. 56 min. we came in fight of a
clufter of iflands as we imagined, but on our
nearer approach, found them all in one, barren, and without a fhrub or tree. In lat. 60
deg. 22 min. we came up with a ftupendous
rock or high ifland, almoft covered with fnow,
and without any other inhabitant, except birds
and feals; to this laft Capt. Cook gave the
name of Winter Ifland, from its dreary appearance.

On the 26th, the Refolution made the fignal
of diftrefs. On haleing her, we were informed,
that fhe had again fprung a leak, in the late
violent gale; and that all hands were employed
at the pumps and in baleing; and that it was
with difficulty they could keep her above water.
Lat. 58 deg. 39 min.

On the 29th we were again vifited with a fevere ftorm, and involved in heavy feas, our
hull being fometimes entirely under water,
and the waves rifing to the yard-arms. A-
bout midnight it came on to fnow, and the
Refolution kept making fignals and firing guns
all night. At day light we faw her diftant 5
or 6 miles. We fhortened fail, and waited for
her coming up. And,

On

On the 30th, being both in company, the ftorm abated and the fea quite calm, both fhips hove-to, and, while the carpenters were employed in ftopping the leak in the Refolution, the people were bufied in fifhing. Thofe on board the Difcovery caught 40 large cod, befides turbot, which were the more acceptable to officers and men, as our falt provifions were now very bad. Lat. 55 deg. 27 min. N.

On Sept. 1. we continued our courfe to the fouthward. And

On the 2d, about 5 in the morning, we made land; and hauled our wind in fearch of Providence Harbour, of which we had miftaken the entrance. About fix in the evening we came in fight of a large Indian town in a deep bay, where we found ourfelves furrounded with whales of a prodigious fize. We founded, and found no bottom at 100 fathom. Here fome of our former friends came off to us, and being informed, that our defign was to anchor in our late harbour, they undertook to be our pilots, and one of them flept all night on board the Difcovery.

On the 3d, in the morning, we found ourfelves right a-breaft the Race, and faw the Refolution juft within the entrance. About 2 in the afternoon, the wind and tide both uniting in our favour, we fafely anchored in our late birth.

Y 3   All

All hands were now fet to work, the carpenters in ftripping the fheathing from the Refolution to examine her leaks, and the fail makers, caulkers and riggers in their refpective employments, for which there was great need, both fhips having fuffered much in their fails, feams, and rigging, in the late tempeftuous weather, and in the icey northern feas; but what gave the greateft pleafure to the feamen, was the fuccefs they met with in fifhing, whenever the weather was fuch as to fuffer them to haul the feine. At the mouth of the harbour, they could at any time, in three or four hours, fill their boats with holybut of an enormous fize; one of them, fent on board the Refolution during our ftay, weighed 220 lb. Each mefs had now a fmall cafk with a quantity of falt given them, in order to make fome provifion to help out their fhort allowance, which it was found neceffary to continue till their arrival in the tropical iflands, where the fhips might again be furnifhed with a frefh fupply.

On the 4th our Capt. went on board the Commodore, where he was acquainted by Capt. Cook with the diftrefs of the Refolution, which ever fince the hard gale on the 26th had been ready to founder; on that day, on founding the pumps three feet water were found in the well; and judging it to proceed from the fame place as before, the carpenters were employed in fearch of it, when, to their great furprize, they found

the

the full casks afloat, and great quantities of
provisions utterly spoilt. Their first care was
to skuttle the balk-heads, and to let the water
down into the hold, and then the pumps were
kept constantly at work to pump it out; but
this was beyond their power; they could gain
but little with incessant labour, and when they
came into harbour had 28 inches still in the hold.
The carpenters had already stript the sides of the
Resolution 16 feet from the counter forwards,
where they found the inside timbers so much de-
cayed, that their report was, that if their continuance at sea had been necessarily protracted
but a fortnight longer, she must have gone to
the bottom.

We had still much to do, our articles for the
tropical trade were nearly all exchanged, and
we could expect no supplies of provisions without an equivalent. We therefore sent a small
spare bower anchor on shore, and set our armourers
to break it up, and make it into spikes, axes,
hatchets, nails, and other tropical merchandize.

While every thing was getting ready, the officers diverted themselves as usual with shooting,
and surveying the country; and here they found
amusement enough, having discovered a Russian
settlement in an adjoining island, divided only
by a neck of land, about 15 miles over, and a
bay of about 12 miles, which they had to cross.
To this settlement several of our gentlemen, led
by curiosity, repaired. They were conducted

by

by two Kamſhatſkadale indians, who had been ſent by the Ruſſians to learn what they could concerning us, having before ſeen us paſs in our courſe to the northward. When they firſt diſcovered us at a diſtance from the ſhore, they were apprehenſive that we were Japoneſe, with whom their nation was at war ; but on our nearer approach, they were convinced from the trim of our ſhips that we were ſtrangers ; they were therefore encouraged, by the report of the natives, to make themſelves known, and to offer their aſſiſtance as far as lay in their power.

The road acroſs the neck of land was rather rugged, but when that was ſurmounted, our gentlemen were met by a Ruſſian barge of 12 oars, commanded by an officer, who received them politely, and when they landed, directed them to the factory, where, beſides the fort, they found a Ruſſian bark of about 50 or 60 tons, eight ſmall ſwivels and one 3 pounder laid up for the winter, and intended for Kamſchatſka the enſuing ſummer. Our gentlemen were here ſhewn the ſtores belonging to the factory, conſiſting of ſkins and oil ; their coppers for boiling the oil, with the ſmall ware with which they trafficked with the natives by way of exchange. Iron inſtruments of war are prohibited, nor do they ſuffer any offenſive weapons of any kind to be introduced among them. It is probable therefore, that the long knives we ſaw in the poſſeſſion of the more ſoutherly Indians,

dians, were some that were taken from those unfortunate Ruffians, who on the first difcovery of this continent, fell a facrifice to the favage barbarity of the natives. It was a little unfortunate, that we had not one perfon on board either fhip that had the moft diftant knowledge of the Rufs language; every thing was to be gathered by figns. Our officers could juft make out, that a Ruffian Captain had been murdered by the natives, and that the Ruffians had taken a fevere revenge, and had laid the country under contribution, and obliged the inhabitants to pay a certain annual tribute in fkins, but to what extent they had fubdued the country, or in what year, they could not at all underftand. They learnt, that the name of the ifland was Elafkah, that they had another fettlement to the fouthward, and other veffels that were conftantly employed in trading with the natives, and collecting their fkins and oil; that the factory was fuppofed to clear about 100,000 rubles annually by this trade; and that it was increafing; that their only guard confifted of about 40 Kamfhatfkadale Ruffians, and 300 natives, over whom they were obliged to keep a watchful eye. Our gentlemens entertainment there was rather friendly than fumptuous; they had dried venifon and great variety of fifh, but dreffed after the Ruffian manner; their bifcuit was black, and their bread rye; their butter not extraordinary; their wine and brandy the Indians

who

who conducted the gentlemen carried from the
ships, with which the Ruffian officers made very
free. The evening being fpent in mutual enquiries, by which neither fide could receive much
fatisfaction, they were fhewn to the apartments
prepared for them, where they flept undifturbed.
In the morning they renewed their enquiries,
and the Ruffians, by exhibiting the chart of their
difcoveries and conquefts, gave our gentlemen
more fatisfactory information than they could
otherwife have obtained. They obferved a remarkable conformity between thofe charts exhibited by the Ruffians as far as they went, and of
their own. The Ruffian difcoveries extended
from the 49th to the 68th degree of northern
latitude, by which the impracticability which
we had difcovered of a north-weft paffage by
any ftrait or found communicating with any
other fea was fully confirmed.

They were now equally communicative to
each other, the Ruffian gentlemen were defirous
of knowing the names of the navigators and
ships, with the expedition they were engaged
in; and they were invited on board to receive
further information. To this they readily a-
greed; and as foon as our gentlemen had fatis-
fired their curiofity; had vifited the Ruffian
houfes, which were built with timber, and thofe
of the natives built with poles and earth; had
remarked the fimplicity of the latter, which
feemed but one degree above the level of the

beavers

beavers they hunted; and of the former, that was little more than a degree above those of the natives; they set out upon their return to the ships, accompanied by the Ruffian gentlemen, by whom they had been entertained.

About five in the evening, they all came on board the Refolution: the Ruffian gentlemen were received by Capt. Cook with that familiarity and politenefs that was natural to him; they were taken into the great cabin, where both Captains with their principal officers and gentlemen were affembled to entertain then, and where the bottle was pretty brifkly pufh'd about, as that was the principal fubject in which the ftrangers could bear a part. Here they were interrogated as to the time generally taken up in making the voyage to Kamfhatfka, which they anfwered by dividing the year into twelve parts, and pointing to the two middlemoft. As the mafter of the veffel which lay at Elafkah was of the company, he was afked at what time he expected to arrive at Kamfhatfka. He anfwered about the 9th month, meaning in July. He was then requefted to take letters with him to be forwarded to England through Ruffia, fhould it fo happen, that he fhould arrive at that port before us. This charge he readily undertook; and, being pretty well plied with liquor, they flept on board the Refolution, and next day came on board the Difcovery, where they dined, and,

and, being amply supplied with grog, went jovially away in the afternoon.

Before our departure, we were visited by the Principal of the Russian factory, who came from the southward, accompanied by a number of Indian canoes, laden with skins, who on coming ashore in the harbour, instantly began erecting a tent, which in half an hour they finished, covering it with skins. He was received on board the Resolution with the respect due to his rank, and by his deportment it was easy to perceive that he was of family. He was a young gentleman of a fair complexion, and graceful stature, and, though differing but little in point of dress from those by whom we had been visited before, he was, notwithstanding, very different in his manners and behaviour. He had travelled much, but chiefly in these savage countries and in the northern parts of Asia, and understood, and could talk the language of the natives, but could speak no European language, except his own. He was handsomely entertained on board both ships, and had every attention paid him that, in our situation, he had reason to expect; nor was he insensible of our civilities. He wrote a letter, directed to the Governor of Kamshatska, which he requested Capt. Cook to deliver. It contain'd, as we afterwards understood, a detail of his own mercantile affairs, and a representation of us, as trading with the Indians. He told us, that his residence fidence was on the coaft off which we had received a note in a little box, and that he was the perfon who wrote that note and fent it. Some prefents reciprocally paffed : thofe on his part were cloaks and fkins ; on ours, tobacco and fpirituous liquors, of both which we obferved the Ruffians to be immoderately fond.

After fleeping on board the fhips two nights, and obferving, with an attentive eye, the different employments of the artificers, and examining the various conveniences and accommodations which we had on board, he took his leave on the 26th, intending to make fome ftay at the fettlement of Elafkah, which the gentlemen of the Refolution had juft vifited.

The repairs of both fhips being nearly finifhed, we were preparing to fail with the firft fair wind, when a ftorm arofe, which retarded our departure till it abated. Happy that we were got in a fafe harbour, unaffected by its violence, though the waters of the race came tumbling in with unexampled fury.

On the 29th, the wind fair to carry us to fea, we weighed, and, having cleared the harbour, made fail, directing our courfe for Sandwich's Ifles, near the northern tropic, where we intended to winter, and to fupply the fhips with provifions to enable us to purfue the remaining part of our voyage.

On the 30th we were overtaken by a violent gale, which carried away our fore and main-
tacks,

tacks, and, endeavouring to save them, John Mackintosh, seaman, was struck dead, and the boatswain and four men much wounded. We at the same time sprung a leak.

On the 1st of November we were again within the race, but the wind offering fair, and our leak not being dangerous, we once more stood to sea. After which no other accident, or any thing worth relating happened, from the time of clearing the harbour of Samganuida, so called by the Russians, and by Capt. Cook Providence Harbour, till our arrival on the coast of O-why-e on the 26th of the same month. We were then so much in want of provisions, that Capt. Clarke, much against his inclination, was under the necessity of substituting stock-fish in the room of beef, but we were no sooner well in with the land, than we were visited by many of the inhabitants, who came off in their canoes with all sorts of provisions which their island afforded, and every man on board had leave to purchase what he could for his own indulgence. This diffused a joy among the mariners that is not easy to be expressed. From a sulleness and discontent visible in every countenance the day before, all was chearfulness, mirth and jollity. Fresh provisions and kind females are the sailors sole delight ; and when in possession of these, past hardships are instantly forgotten ; even those whom the scurvy had attacked, and had rendered pale and lifeless as

ghosts,

ghofts, brightened upon this occafion, and for
the moment appeared alert. This flattering
beginning, however, yielded no fubftantial relief. The boats that were fent to found the
fhore and to look for a harbour, went out day
after day, without being able to difcover fo
much as a fafe anchorage, and we were longer
in finding a harbour than in making the coaft.
Nothing could be more toilfome or diftreffing
than our prefent fituation; within fight of land,
yet unable to reach it; driven out to fea, by one
ftorm, and in danger of being wrecked on the
breakers by another. At length, after having
examined the leeward fide of the ifland, Capt.
Cook made the fignal to ftand out to fea. This
was on the 7th of December, when it was determined to take a long ftretch, in order, if poffible, to get round the S E. extremity and to examine the weathermoft fide where we were told
there was a fafe harbour. In this attempt we
fplit our main-top-maft ftay-fail, and loft
fight of the Refolution. The weather continuing tempeftuous for many days, heavy complaints again prevailed among the fhip's company. Their fufferings, from inceffant labour
and fcanty provifions, were grown confeffedly
grievous. Their grog, that had been ftopped
as foon as we arrived upon the coaft, was again
dealt out to them as ufual, and it was with
the kindeft treatment from their officers that the
men could be kept to their duty; yet on Chriftmas

mas day, when each man was allowed a pint of brandy, and free leave to enjoy himself as he liked, not a murmur was heard; they the very next day returned to bufinefs, and continued it without repining, till

The 16th of January, when, after a feries of the moft tempeftuous weather that ever happened in that climate, the boats from both fhips were fent out to examine a fine bay, where we were informed there was a harbour, in which we might fafely moor, and where we fhould be fupplied with materials to refit the fhips, and provifions to victual them. In the evening the boats returned with the joyful news, that they had fucceeded in their fearch, and that the harbour promifed fair to anfwer all that had been faid of it.

On the 17th our boats were employed in towing the fhips into harbour in fight of the greateft multitude of Indian fpectators in canoes and on fhore, that we had ever feen affembled together in any part of our voyage. It was concluded, that their number could not be lefs than 2 or 3000. While we were hovering upon the coaft, we had often been vifited by 200 canoes at a time, who came to trade, and who brought us provifions when the weather would permit; and befides provifions they brought us great quantities of cordage, falt and other manufactures of the ifland, which the Captains purchafed for the ufe of the fhips, and with-

out

out which we could not have proceeded; for during the tempestuous weather our cordage snapped rope after rope, so that our spare hands were incessantly employed, night and day, in knotting and splicing, of which there was no end.

This day, before two o'clock, P. M. we were safely moored in 17 fathom water, in company with the Resolution, which a few days before we had given over for lost. From the time of attempting to get round the island, till the 8th of January, we had never been able to get sight of her, though both ships were constantly looking out to find each other. They had suffered much in their masts and rigging, and were happy at last, as well as ourselves, to find a convenient harbour to refit. We were scarce moored, when the prince, son to the O-ro-no, the great king of the island, came along-side, and after an oration, and the usual ceremonies of peace had passed on both sides, he came on board, bringing with him a small barbicued hog, some ready-dressed bread-fruit, and a curious mantle of red feathers as presents to the Captain; and in return was complimented with several axes, looking glasses, bracelets and other shewy articles which took his fancy. While he was busy in admiring every thing he saw on board the Discovery, the pinnace was ordered out, and he with his attendants were taken to Capt. Cook, who re-

Z   ceived

ceived them with all poffible refpect. And after entertaining them with mufic, and inviting
them to partake of fuch refrefhments as the
fhip afforded, and making them fome handfome prefents he acquainted them with his
wants, by fhewing them the condition of his
fhip, and requefting a fmall portion of ground
to land his materials, and to erect his tents.
This requeft the young prince readily granted,
at the fame time giving the Captain to underftand that his father was abfent, that he had
lately been at war with the king of the neighbouring ifland of Maw-whee, that he was employed in fettling the terms of peace, and that in
lefs than ten days, he was expected home. That
the ftrangers might, notwithftanding, land whatever they thought fit, and that the ground they
had occafion for fhould be marked out and
taboo'd, that is appropriated to their ufe without any of the natives to encroach upon it.
Both Captains very readily embraced the offer,
and prepared to accompany the young prince to
the town near which they wifhed to pitch their
tents. Upon their landing, feveral vacant plats
of ground were fhewn them, and, when they
had made their choice, ftakes were ordered to
be driven at certain diftances, and a line to be
carried round, within which the common people were forbidden to enter, under the fevereft
penalties. Matters being thus amicably fettled, no time was loft on our part to get every

thing

thing on fhore. The tents, the armourer's
forge, the mafts, the fails, the rigging, the
water-cafks, the bread, the flour, the powder,
in fhort every article that wanted either to be
reviewed or repaired were all fent on fhore ; and
not the leaft interruption was given to the boats
employed in the carriage, or infult offered to the
perfons who conducted them. On the contrary,
the chiefs offered fome empty houfes, that were
conveniently fituated near the new dock (if
that may be fo termed where our artificers were
fet to work) for the fick to lodge till their recovery.
No ftrangers were ever more hofpitably received.
On the morning after our people landed, fix large double canoes were feen
entering the harbour at a great rate, having not
lefs than 30 paddles to each canoe, with upwards
of 60 Indians, moft of them naked.
Seeing them on their nearer approach making
towards the fhips, the Captains ordered the
guns to be fhotted, the marines to be drawn
up, and every man to be ready at his poft ;
the Indians affembled fo faft, that before noon,
the fhips were furrounded with more than 100
canoes, in which there were not lefs than 1000
Indians. They at firft traded friendly, having
hogs in abundance, and plenty of breadfruit,
plantains, bananoes, and whatever elfe
the ifland produced, but they had not been
there long, before a large ftone was thrown at
the cabin-window, by an invifible hand. A

watch

watch was inftantly fet, and in lefs than half an hour another ftone was thrown at the caulkers, as they were at work on a ftage on the fhip's fide. The offender was feen, and in fight of the prince, the chiefs, and the whole multitude, he was feized, brought on board, tied to the fhrouds, and punifhed with 50 lafhes. In a few minutes, fuch was their fright, there was not an Indian to be feen near the fhips:—Like unlucky boys, when one is apprehended for fome naughty trick, the reft commonly fly the place. —And in fact, thofe people are in many things like children, and in none more than in this inftance. Before the day clofed, they all again returned to trade, and, when night approached, not a male was to be feen ; but fwarms of females, who came to fleep on board, though much againft the will of Capt. Cook, who, upon the firft arrival of the fhips upon the coaft, wifhed to have prohibited all commerce with the women of the ifland, but he foon found that, if that commerce was forbidden, all other trade muft ceafe of courfe, and not a pig could be purchafed, without a girl was permitted to bring it to market.

There are, who have blamed Capt. Cook for his feverity to the Indians ; but it was not to the Indians alone that he was fevere in his difcipline. He never fuffered any fault in his own people, tho' ever fo trivial, to efcape unpunifhed: If they were charged with infulting an Indian, or injuring him in his property, if the fact was proved, the offender was surely punished in fight of the Indians. By this impartial diftribution of equal juftice, the Indians themfelves conceived fo high an idea of his wifdom, and his power too, that they paid him the honours as they did their Et-hu a, or good fpirit.

The caulkers, who have already been mentioned, when they came round in courfe to the after-part of the Refolution, they found that, befides the feams that wanted clofing, there were other more material defects. The rudder eyes were almoft eaten through with ruft, and the bolts ready to tumble out. This was an alarming defect, and all other bufinefs was fufpended till that was repaired.

Every thing went on now as fmoothly as could be wifhed. The chiefs, if they faw any of their own people mifbehave, would themfelves give information, and bring them to punifhment; they were fo very obliging, that, feeing us in want of wood to burn, they made an offer of a high fence, that furrounded the Morai, adjoining to the town, for a prefent fupply.

On the 19th, being the fourth day after our arrival, feveral very large canoes were feen to come from the S. E. We at firft thought they were the friends, with whom we had traded on the other fide of the ifland, but on their

nearer

nearer approach, we found they were all armed
and cloathed in the military ftyle, after their
country manner. This gave us caufe to fufpect fome traiterous defign, but our fears were
in fome meafure diffipated by the affurances we
received from the young prince, that they were
fome of the warriors that had accompanied his
father in his expedition againft the king of
Maw-wee, and that they were now returning
home in triumph; but, nothwithftanding this
affurance, it was thought prudent to be upon
our guard, and the rather as the women who
were on board, told us, that their people defigned to attack us, and to mattee, that is, to
kill us every one.

Next day, before nine o'clock, more than
four thoufand Indians furrounded the fhips.
The Captain ordered two great guns to be fired
over their heads, in order to try what effect that
would have in difperfing them. In lefs than
three minutes, there were a thoufand heads to
be feen above water, fo many having jumped
from their canoes into the fea, frighted on the
fudden report of the guns; neither did a fingle
canoe remain about the fhips, nor came near
us for fome days after. Several of the women
however remained on board, who never could
be prevailed on to fhew themfelves upon deck
in the day-time, but whether from fear of their
countrymen or of the guns is uncertain, as all
trade was now ftopt, and nothing brought on
board

board for our fubfiftence. Capt. Cook went on fhore to expoftulate with the chiefs, and by fome trifling prefents to engage them to trade as before; threatening at the fame time to lay their country wafte, if they refufed to fupply the fhips with the provifions they ftood in need of. His remonftrances had the defired effect, and next day we purchafed not lefs than 60 large hogs with great quantities of fruits and vegetables for the fhip's ufe.

In a few days after this, the old king was feen to enter the harbour, on his return from Maw-wee. He was attended with more than 150 large war-canoes, himfelf at the head of them in a moft fuperb veffel, in which were four idols, two at each end, reprefenting men of a monftrous fize, covered with mantles of feathers, interwoven with various colours, red, black, green, and yellow. Thefe they call E-ah-tu-a, fignifying their warrior gods, without which they never engage in battle. They paffed the fhips, and feemed to take very little notice of them; when they landed, they hauled up all their canoes on the beach, drew up in martial order, and led by the king, marched in ranks to their place of worfhip, diftant from our tents about fifty yards; but, feeing the ground taboo'd by fmall green boughs, that marked the boundaries, they all made a circle round with their images in proceffion, till they

Z 4   arrived

arrived at their Morai, where they placed their deities, and depofited their arms.

This ceremony over, the king, attended with ten of his chiefs, came on board the Refolution. When he entered the fhip, he fell on his face, as a mark of fubmiffion to Capt. Cook, as did all his attendants, and after having made an oration, which none of us underftood, he prefented the Captain with three barbicued hogs, who, in return, put a necklace, compofed of feveral ftrings of various-coloured beads, round his neck, and gave him two looking glaffes, a large glafs bowl, with fome nails, and other trifles, which he received with much feeming fatisfaction, and immediately difpatched a meffenger on fhore, who foon returned with feveral large hogs, and cocoa-nuts, bread-fruit, plantains and fugar-canes, as much as our fmall cutter could carry. Having remained upon deck the fpace of an hour, admiring the conftruction of the fhip, he was conducted into the great cabin, where wine was offered him, which he refufed : neither was there any thing he would tafte, except a head of bread-fruit ; but he appeared delighted with every thing he faw, and did not return on fhore till the evening, He was of a graceful ftature, about fix feet high, rather corpulent, and tattowed in feveral parts of his body, in manner like that of other warriors. His fkin was remarkably fcaley ; his hair grey, and cut

quite

quite fhort. He had very little cloathing, except a thick mat thrown over his fhoulders,
and on his head he wore a cap of feathers.
Before he departed he gave us to underftand,
that he had 6000 fighting men, always in readinefs to war againft his enemies.

Next day both Captains, accompanied with
feveral of their officers, went to pay the king a
vifit on fhore. They were very refpectfully received, and having dined after the Indian manner, the king rofe, and clothing Capt. Cook
with a mantle, fuch as is worn by the great
E-a-thu-ah-nu-eh, conducted him to the place
of worfhip, where a garland of green plantain
leaves was put upon his head, and he was feated on a kind of throne, and addreffed in a long
oration by a prieft cloathed in a veftment of
party-coloured cloth, who concluded the ceremony with a folemn fong, in which he was joined by all the natives prefent; this part of the
ceremony over, they fell at his feet, the king
acquainting him, that this was now his building, and that he was from henceforth their E-
a-thu ah-nu²eh. From this time an Indian
Chief was by the king's order placed at the
head of his pinnace, at whofe command the Indians
in their canoes as he paffed them were all filence,
and would proftrate themfelves till he was out
of fight; and this they would do when the Captain was alone, but the Indian had orders from
the king whenever the Captain came afhore in his
pinnace,

pinnace, to attend him, and conduct him to his houfe, which the failors now called Cook's Altar.

When we firſt approached the coaſt of this iſland we were aſtoniſhed at the ſight of a mountain of a ſtupendous height, whoſe head was covered with ſnow. This was ſo rare a ſight in an iſland between the tropics, that ſeveral of the officers and gentlemen from both ſhips were deſirous of taking a nearer view of it, and for that purpoſe they requeſted the king's permiſſion, and a guide to attend them, which was readily granted, and no leſs than twenty Indian chiefs contended which ſhould accompany them.

On the 26th Mr. Nelſon and four other gentlemen ſet out in the morning on this expedition, which they afterwards found attended with no ſmall fatigue, and not a little danger ; for after travelling two days and two nights thro' a ſavage country, they were obliged at laſt to return, without being able to ſatisfy their curioſity. On the way they were inſulted by the rabble, who without offering any violence to their perſons, would make faces, twiſt their mouths, and uſe the ſame contemptuous geſtures, with which it is their cuſtom in war to provoke their enemies.

On the 29th they returned to the ſhips, and the only advantage that accrued from their journey, was, a curious aſſortment of indigenous plants and ſome natural curioſities, collected

by

by Mr. Nelson. During their abfence every thing remained quiet at the tents, and the Indians fupplied the fhips with fuch quantities of provifions of all kinds, that orders were given to purchafe no more hogs in one day than could be killed, falted, and ftowed away the next day. This order was in confequence of a former order, to purchafe all that could be procured for fea ftock, by which fo many were brought on board that feveral of them died before they could be properly difpofed of.

On the 1ft of Feb. 1779, William Watman, gunner's mate, died. His body in the afternoon was carried on fhore in the pinnace, and buried according to his own defire in the Morai belonging to the king. The Indians who dug his grave about four feet deep, covered the bottom of it with green leaves. and when the corpfe was depofited in the earth, the chiefs who attended the funeral, put a barbicued hog at the head, and another at the feet, with a quantity of bread fruit, plantains and bananas. More was going to be added, when Capt. Cook ordered the grave to be covered up, and a poft erected to the memory of the deceafed, infcribed with his name, the date of the year, day of his death, and the nation to which he belonged. From this circumftance, Capt. Cook gave this port the name of Watman's harbour. The next day the Indians rolled large ftones over his grave, and brought two barbicued hogs, plan-

tains

tains and bananas, cocoa-nuts and bread-fruit, which they placed over his grave, upon a ſtage erected for that purpoſe.

We were now preparing to depart, when our Captain was preſented by the king, with 12 large hogs, three boats-load of bread-fruit, potatoes, ſugar cane, and cocoa-nuts; and the ſame preſent was made to Capt Cook.

This day, Feb. 2, the king came on board, attended with twenty of his chiefs, and gave the Captains of both ſhips, with their officers, an invitation to an heiva, to be performed in the evening, by moſt of the royal family. Capt. Clarke excuſed himſelf from ill health; but Capt. Cook and all the other gentlemen promiſed to attend.

The ſame day the king and his chiefs dined on board the Reſolution, and were entertained with muſic, the whole band having orders to play all the while they ſat at dinner. They were highly delighted with the muſic, and would not ſuffer the performers to reſt a moment.

About four in the afternoon the pinnaces from both ſhips were ordered to be in readineſs to take the company a-ſhore, with their pendants and colours diſplayed, to do honour to a king and people, by whom we had been ſo hoſpitably entertained. More than 200 canoes attended us to ſhore, where a number of chiefs were ready to receive us, who all obſerved a

pro-

profound filence at our landing, and conducted us to the place appointed for the entertainment. But we were much difappointed by the performers, who were far inferior to thofe of the fouthern iflands.

The only part of the performance that was tolerable was their finging, with which the heiva or play concluded, the young princeffes, the chiefs, and even the king himfelf joining in the chorus.

The play being ended, Capt. Cook acquainted the king that, with his permiffion, he would exhibit fome fireworks, that, if they did not affright, would very much aftonifh him. The king readily gave his confent; and the engineer was ordered to begin his exhibition as foon as it was dark. On the rifing of the firft fky-rocket, the indians fled precipitately, and hid themfelves in houfes, or wherever they could find a fhelter, at firft there were fome thoufand fpectators, but in lefs than ten minutes there were not fifty to be feen, the king and his attendants excepted, whom the Captain and the gentlemen with the greateft difficulty perfuaded to ftay. When the fecond rofe up in the air, lamentations were heard from every quarter, and when the water rockets were played off, the king and his chiefs were hardly to be reftrained. Other fireworks it was found dangerous to exhibit, as thefe had already ftruck the fpectators, the king as well as his people, with

with a general panic. We therefore took leave
of the king and royal family, and returned on
board our respective ships. The king having
been made to understand that we should sail
the first fair wind, came next morning to visit
the captains of both ships, who were now preparing to sail. This being publicly known,
the Indians in general expressed their concern,
but particularly the young women, whose lamentations were heard from every quarter.

In the evening of the 4th of Feb. all hands
were mustered, and none were missing.

In the morning of the 5th we cleared the
harbour, shaping our course for Maw-wee, as
we had been informed by the king, that in that
island there was a fine harbour, and excellent
water. We had not been long under sail, when
the king, who had omitted to take his leave of
our Captain in the morning, as not suspecting
our departure so sudden, came after the ships,
accompanied by the young prince in a sailing
canoe, bringing with them ten large hogs, a
great number of fowls, and a small turtle, (a
great rarety) with bread fruit in abundance.
They also brought with them great quantities
of cocoa nuts, plantains, and sugar canes.

Besides other persons of condition who accompanied the king, there was an old priest,
who had always shewn a particular attachment
to Capt. Clarke, and who had not been unre-
warded for his civility. It being rather late
                                              when

when they reached the ſhips, they ſtaid on board but a few hours, and then all departed except the old prieſt and ſome girls, who by the king's permiſſion were ſuffered to remain on board till they ſhould arrive at ſome of the neighbouring iſles. We were now ſteering with a fine breeze, but juſt at the cloſe of the evening, to our great mortification, the wind died away, and a great ſwell ſucceeding, with a ſtrong current ſetting right in for ſhore, we were in the utmoſt danger of being driven upon the rocks. In the height of our diſtreſs and trouble, the old prieſt, who had been ſent to ſleep in the great cabbin, leapt over-board unſeen, with a large piece of Ruſſian ſilk, the Captains property, and ſwam to ſhore.

The next day, ſeeing a large canoe between us and the ſhore, we hove to for her coming up, and to our great ſurprize perceived the old king, accompanied by ſeveral of his chiefs, having in their veſſel the prieſt who had ſtolen the ſilk, bound hand and foot, whom the king delivered to the Captain, at the ſame time requeſting that his fault might be forgiven. The king being told that his requeſt was granted, unbound him, and ſet him at liberty; telling the Captain that, ſeeing him with the ſilk, he judged it was none of his own, and therefore ordered him to be apprehended; and had taken this method of expoſing him for injuring his friend. This ſingular inſtance of Indian Generoſity and Juſtice ought not to be forgotten. As

soon

foon as they had delivered the filk, which the
Captain would have had the king to accept,
they departed, and had fcarce reached the fhore
when a heavy gale came on, with thunder,
lightning, and hard rain. We wore fhip, and
continued working off the land all night, and
foon loft fight of the Refolution, who, as well
as ourfelves, continued beating about the ifland
for feven days fucceffively, in dread every moment of being wrecked upon the coaft. On
the fourth day after we had loft fight of the Refolution, the ftorm being a little abated, we
obferved her under a high part of the ifland,
lying with her fore-top-gallant-maft down, her
fore-top-fail yard upon the cap, and the fail
furled; which gave us reafon to fuppofe that
fome accident had befallen her, and as we expected fo we found it. We ftood down for
her with a heavy gale, but it was not till the
next day that we could come to fpeak with her.
Capt. Cook himfelf being upon deck when we
came up, informed us that he had fprung his fore-
maft in two different places, that the fhip was
leaky, and that it was with the greateft difficulty they kept her above water. He further
faid, that on the 7th in the morning, they difcovered the leak, that at that time, they made
thirty inches of water in three hours; and that
ever fince all hands had been conftantly employed night and day in baleing and pumping;
we likewife underftood, that they had fplit their

main-

main top-fail, and that they were now bound
to our late harbour, to repair their damage.
We pursued the same course; but it was not
till the 11th, when we opened on the bay in
which lay our port. We were very soon surrounded with old friends, who brought us hogs,
bread-fruit, plantains, bananoes and cocoa-nuts,
which they threw on board, without waiting
for any recompence. We were likewise visited
by the old king, the prince, and many of the
chiefs, who came to welcome us, and who
were seemingly glad of our return. About
ten in the morning both ships moored near
their old birth, and presently all hands were
set to work to strip the mast, and to carry it on
shore to be repaired.

The next day the king came again on board,
and mutual presents and mutual civilities were
continued as usual: but about five in the afternoon there came along-side a large canoe, with
about 60 of their fighting men all armed, with
little or no provisions on board, and who seemed to have no good design. The Captain observing their motions, ordered the guns to be
shotted, and every man to his post. About six
they departed, without offering the least insult;
but soon after we saw, upon a high hill, a large
body assembled, who were observed to be gathering stones, and laying them in heaps. At
dark they were seen to disperse; but great
lights and fires were kept burning all night.

A a   In

In the morning of the 13th they again affembled, and began rolling the ftones from the brink
of the hill, in order, as we fuppofed to annoy
the fhips, which, however, were at too great
a diftance to receive any damage.   Our Captains looking upon this as an infult, ordered
the guns to be levelled and fired among them,
and, in ten minutes, there was not an Indian to
be feen near the place.

In the afternoon the king came on board the
Refolution, and complained to Capt. Cook of
our killing two of his people, intimating, at
the fame time, that they had not the leaft intention of hurting us.   He continued on board
fome hours, amufing himfelf with feeing the
armourers at work, and, when he departed,
requefted that they might be permitted to make
him a Pa-ha-we, (an inftrument they ufe in battle, when they come to clofe quarters) which
was readily granted.

From this time forward the natives became
very unruly, and ftolen every thing they could
lay their hands on.   They were fired upon,
but that only enraged them; one who had
juft ftole the armourer's tongs and an iron chif-
fel, with both which he was making to fhore,
was intercepted by Capt. Cook himfelf, who,
with a few marines, endeavoured to feize him as
he was landing, but the Indians feeing his defign
came rufhing in a body to the water-fide, a-
mong whom the fellow found means to fecrete
himfelf

himself; and the multitude, instead of delivering him up, attacked the boats that were in pursuit of him, seized their oars, broke them, and forced our whole party to retreat.

Capt. Cook, having only a few marines with him, part of those who were placed as a guard to the carpenters employed upon the mast, did not think proper to renew the attack; but returned to the tents, ordering a strict watch to be kept during the night, and his whole force to be kept under arms till matters should be accommodated. For this purpose, Mr. Edgar, our master, was sent with a message to the young prince, who from the beginning had behaved friendly, to acquaint him with the cause of the fray, and to demand the delinquent to be delivered up. The prince, instead of listening to his remonstrances, assumed another countenance, and Mr. Edgar was very roughly handled, and glad to make his escape with a good beating.

The temper of the Indians was now totally changed, and they every day became more and more troublesome.

On the 14th a vast multitude of them were seen together making great lamentation, and moving slowly along to the beating of a drum, that scarce gave a stroke in a minute. From this circumstance it was supposed, they were burying the dead, who had been killed the day before. No violence, however, was either done or attempted this day, though the girls that

were

were on board made us to underftand, that they only waited for a favourable opportunity to attack the fhips.

On the morning of the 15th, our great cutter, which was moored to the buoy, was miffing from her moorings, and, upon examination, the boat's painter was found cut two fathoms from the buoy, and the remainder of the rope gone with the boat.

This gave caufe to fupect that fome villainy was hatching, and, in order to prevent the ill-confequences that might follow, both Captains met on board the Refolution, to confult what was beft to be done on this critical occafion. The officers from both fhips were prefent at this council, where it was refolved to feize the king and to confine him on board till the boat fhould be returned.

With this view, early on the morning of the 14th, Capt. Cook, with 20 marines went on fhore under cover of the guns of both fhips. The Indians obferving our motions, and feeing the fhips warping towards the towns, of which there were two, one on each fide the harbour's mouth, they concluded that our defign was to feize their canoes. In confequence of which moft of their large war canoes took the alarm, and were making off, when our guns, loaded with grape and canifter fhot, drove them back ; and the Captain and his guard landed without oppofition. We obferved, however, that their

warriors

warriors were cloathed in their military dress, tho' without arms, and that they were gathering together in a body from every direction, their chiefs assuming a very different countenance to what they usually wore upon all former occasions. However, Capt. Cook, attended by Mr. Philips, Lieut. of Marines, a serjeant, and ten privates, regardless of appearances, proceeded directly to the king's residence, where they found him seated on the ground, with about twelve of his chiefs round him, who all rose in the utmost consternation on seeing the Captain and his guard enter. The Captain addressed the king in the mildest terms, assuring him that no violence was intended against his person or any of his people, except against those who had been guilty of a most unprecedented act of robbery, by cutting from her moorings one of the ship's boats, without which they could neither conveniently water the ships, nor carry on the necessary communication with the shore; calling upon the king, at the same time, to give orders for the boat to be immediately restored; and insisting upon his accompanying him to the ships, till his orders should be carried into execution. The king protested his total ignorance of the theft; said he was very ready to assist in discovering the thief, and should be glad to see him punished; but shewed great unwillingness to trust his person with strangers, who had lately exercised very unusual severities against his peo-

ple

ple. He was told that the tumultuous appearance of the people and their repeated robberies
made some uncommon severities necessary ; but
that not the least hurt should be done to the
meanest inhabitant of his island by any person
belonging to the ships, without exemplary punishment; and all that was necessary for the
continuance of peace was, to pledge himself
for the honesty of his people. With that view,
and that view only he came to request the king
to place confidence in him, and to make his
ship his home, as the most effectual means of
putting a stop to the robberies that were now
daily and hourly committed by his people,
both at the tents and on board the ships, and
were now so daring as to become insufferable.
The king, upon this remonstrance, was preparing to comply ; but the chiefs, taking the
alarm, began to steal away one after another,
till they were stopped by the guard. In about
half an hour the king was ready to accompany
Capt. Cook on board ; but by that time so great
a body of Indians were got together and lined
the shore, that it was with difficulty they could
break through the multitude, who now began
to behave outrageously, and to insult the guard.
Capt. Cook, observing their behaviour, gave
orders to the officer of marines to make way,
and if any one opposed, to fire upon and instantly dispatch him. This order Lieut. Philips endeavoured to carry into execution, and

a lane

a lane was made for the king and his chiefs to get to the boats, but they had scarce reached the water-side, when the word was given, that Tu-tee was about to carry off their king to kill him. In an instant a number of their fighting men broke from the crowd, and with clubs rushed in upon the guard, four of whom were presently dispatched A ruffian making a stroke at Capt Cook, was shot dead by the Captain himself, who, having a double barrelled gun, was aiming at another, when a savage came behind him and striking him on the head with his club felled him to the ground; and then thrust his Pa-ha-he (a kind of poignard made by our armourers at the request of the king, the day before) through his body with such force that, entering between his shoulders, the point of it came out at his breast. The quarrel now became general. The guns from the ships began to pour in their fire upon the crowd, as did likewise the marine guard, and the marine from the boats; and tho' the slaughter among the savages was dreadful, yet, enraged as they were, they stood our incessant fire with astonishing intrepidity, insomuch that, in spite of all our efforts, they carried off the bodies of the dead, as a mark of triumph.

Besides Capt Cook, whose death was universally deplored, corporal Thomas, and three privates, Hinkes, Allen, and Fadget fell victims to their fury. But it seemed as if it was against our Commodore that their vengeance

A a 4   was

was chiefly directed, by whofe order they fuppofed their king was to be dragged on board,
and punifhed at his difcretion. For, having once
fecured his body, they fled without much regard-
ing the others, one of which they threw into the fea.
Thus ended the life of the greateft navigator that
this or any other nation ever could boaft, after having fuccefsfully led his crews of gallant Britifh
feamen thrice round the World ; had reduced to
a certainty the non-exiftence of a Southern
Continent, about which the learned of all nations were in doubt : had fettled the boundaries
of the earth and fea; and fhewn the impracticability of a N. W. paffage from the Atlantic
to the Great Southern Ocean, for which our
ableft navigators had contended, and in purfuit
of which vaft fums had been fpent in vain,
and many valuable mariners had miferably perifhed.—Reader, if thou haft any feeling for
thy country in the lofs of fo great, fo illuftrious
a navigator, or any tendernefs for thofe whom
he has left to lament his fate, thou wilt drop
with me a tear at this melancholy relation;
efpecially when thou reflecteft, that he, who
had braved dangers, and had looked death in
the face in a thoufand forms, fhould at laft be
cut off by the hands of a cowardly favage,
who, dreading the impetuofity of his rage,
came behind him, and, ruffian-like, ftabbed him
in the back.—But of this enough.——

The

The dead being paſt recovery, the diſtreſſed ſituation of the living was now to be regarded. The Reſolution was without her maſt, and lay in a manner at the mercy of the ſavages, who, it was every moment expected, would have cut away her moorings and drifted her on ſhore. It was therefore the firſt care of Capt. Clarke, who ſucceeded to the command, to float away the maſt, and to get the tents and all our other baggage on board. For this purpoſe no time was to be loſt. While many of the Indians lay dead upon the beach, it was judged the propereſt time to take advantage of that interval of inactivity, which always ſucceeds any conſiderable exertion of Indian ferocity. Our whole force was therefore collected, and, being well provided with arms and ammunition, we made one bold effort to accompliſh our purpoſe. Having landed under cover of our guns, we marched with bayonets fixed, and took poſſeſſion of the Morai, which ſtood on elevated ground, and gave us an advantage over the ſavages, who could not approach us from the ſhore, neither could they attack us from the towns, without being expoſed to our fire from the ſhips. They made ſeveral unſucceſsful attempts to diſlodge us, but were repulſed with loſs. After ſuſtaining an unequal conflict for three hours, in which more than thirty of them were killed, without being able to make any impreſſion on our ſmall body; and without

our

our lofing a man, though feveral were much hurt by the ftones from their flings; they at length difperfed, and left us mafters of our tents and of all our other property.

Our bufinefs now was to decamp; all hands were therefore employed in that fervice, and happy we thought ourfelves when we had got every thing fafe on board.

Our next care was to recover our dead. A ftrong party were fent out in the pinnaces and boats, with a white flag in token of peace, to endeavour to procure their bodies They were met by Ow-a te, a man of chief note among the favages, at the head of a vaft multitude without anfwering our fignal, who informed us, that the warriors were then on the back of the hill, cutting up and dividing the bodies, but that if Ta-tee, the name they gave Capt. Clarke, would land, what remained of Tu-tee fhould be delivered to him; but our party being inconfiderable in proportion to the numbers of the enemy that were then affembled, we were apprehenfive of fome treacherous defign, and therefore our Commander very wifely declined the invitation. While we remained in our boats, feveral other chiefs came to the water-fide; and one in particular, with Captain Cook's hanger, which he drew in a vaunting manner, and brandifhed it over his head; others fhewed themfelves with the fpoils taken from the dead, one having a jacket, another a fhirt, a third a third a pair of trowfers, and fo on; infulting us, as it were, with the trophies of their victory.

At this time it was thought prudent to ftifle our refentment, and to referve our vengeance till a more favourable opportunity. We were now in want of water, our fails and rigging in a fhattered condition, our cordage bad, and our repairs not near finifhed; all therefore we had to do, was to remain upon the defenfive till we were better provided.

Towards the clofe of the evening, we faw from the fhips, at a confiderable diftance, a canoe with eight or nine Indians making towards us from the N. W. and, on their nearer approach, obferved one of them ftanding up with our late Commanders hat on, and apparently daring us, by firft clapping his hands, and then applying them, with a quick motion, to different parts of his body; by which we afterwards difcovered, that nothing more was meant than a kind of joy that he had fomething to give, which he thought we would be glad to receive. Under the firft mifapprehenfion of his meaning, a gun was fired at him from the Refolution, which wounded him in the leg; but, notwithftanding this, the canoe came clofe under the fhip's ftern, haling us, and at the fame time the whole crew calling out Tu-tee, Tu-tee, as loud as they could bawl. This excited every one's curiofity, and orders were given

ven to admit them on board. When the wounded man produced a piece of flesh, carefully wrapped up in a cloth, which he solemnly assured us was part of the thigh of our late Commander; that he saw it cut from the bone, but believed that all the rest was eaten. He was instantly carried into the surgery, had his wound dressed, and during the operation was questioned closely concerning any other part of the Captain's remains, all which he declared had been divided among so many of the warriors, as he called them, that he supposed by that time every other part must be devoured. He was then asked if he knew what became of the other dead bodies; which he answered in the negative. As soon as his wound was dressed, he desired to be set at liberty, which was granted; and when the canoe departed, the Indians were desired to bring us hogs and provisions, and to trade as before. Their answer was, they were taboo'd.

On the 15th, the different promotions took place, and according to their succession, the officers changed ships, Capt. Clarke went on board the Resolution; and Mr. Gore, 1st Lieut. of the Resolution, took the command of the Discovery.

In the evening of the 16th, the flesh belonging to the deceased commander was deposited in a box, and with much solemnity committed to the deep.

On

On the 13th both ships were again warped near the shore, and a spring put upon their cables, in order to cover the boats, who were sent to compleat our stock of water, lest the people of the neighbouring isles, hearing what had happened to us here, should refuse to supply our necessities. On this movement crowds of inhabitants were seen to flock together with a large black flag displayed, which we interpreted as a signal for war; but we afterwards found, that it was part of their ceremony in burying their dead. Under this mistake a few guns were fired from the ships to disperse them, by which the king's second son, Mea-Mea was killed, and a poor woman lost her arm. This made a strong impression on the whole body of Indians, and we were left in quiet both this and the next day, to pursue our repairs and compleat our hold.

On the 19th they began again to be troublesome. In the morning while the boats were loading at the well, the stones came about the crews like hail, some of them of more than a pound weight; one in particular was seen to come from an invisible hand, which being attended to, an Indian was observed to creep out of a hole, who as soon as he had discharged his stone, retired back to his place of shelter. Him we marked, and returned to our ships; and it being now apparent, that nothing was to be gained by fair means, orders were given to strike terror among them, by pursuing them with fire and sword.

fword. About two in the afternoon all who were able to bear arms, as well failors and artificers as marines, were muftered, and preparations made to fuftain them, while with lighted matches they rowed on fhore, and fet fire to the S.E. town, purfuing the frighted inhabitants while their houfes were in flames, with unrelenting fury. Many were put to death without mercy, and all driven to feek fhelter in the other town; fcarce a houfe in this having efcaped the fury of the flames. In this general defolation, the hut or hole of the crafty Indian whofe cowardice had been one principal caufe of the deftruction that followed, was not forgotten. His hole had been marked, as has already been obferved, and on feeing our failors approach it, fuch was his malice, that he heaved a huge ftone at the affailants, one of whom he dangeroufly wounded, but was inftantly difpatched by the difcharge of three mufkets, and a bayonet run through his body. Our orders being fully executed, we returned to the fhips before night, loaded with Indian fpoils, confifting of bows and arrows, clubs and arms of all kinds which they ufe in battle, and having the heads of two of their fighting men, of which the obnoxious Indian was one, ftuck at the bows of the pinnaces, as a terror to the enemy from ever daring again to moleft us.

It is however not a little remarkable, that the father and mother of two girls who were on board our fhip, came in the dead of night, in their

their canoe, loaded with cocoa-nuts and bread-fruit, which they had been gathering in the day for their own subfiftence, and acquainting us with a treacherous defign of their countrymen. to cut our cables and drift the ships ashore, at the fame time imploring our protection, as not knowing where to shelter themfelves with fafety. They were taken on board, and remained prifoners till morning, when not an Indian was to be feen near the harbour, but fuch as were old and feeble, and knew not how to make their efcape. The informers were tenderly treated, had prefents made them, and afterwards difmiffed at their own defire, upon a neighbouring ifland, with every token of kindnefs. The waterers now filled their cafks in quiet; and it was not long before the chiefs of the ifland came to fue for peace.

About four in the afternoon of the 20th, ten girls came down to the well, where the waterers were bufy, with quantities of fruit, as much as they could carry, for which they would take nothing in return, only praying to be taken on board. This was denied them, as peremptory orders had been given by Captain Clarke, forbidding their admiffion.

On the 21ft, a chief, never before feen on board either ship, attended by about 300 of his people, with a white flag difplayed, and carrying boughs and green branches in their hands, came finging and dancing to the water fide. On feeing his enfign anfwered by a white flag at each mizzen-top-maft-head, he, accompanied

with

with three other chiefs, came on board, having some cocoa-nuts, plaintains, and bread-fruit, as presents to the commander, for which they would accept of nothing in return. This chief, whose name was A-nu-a, came to make submission, and, as a token of his sincerity, promised to collect the bones of our deceased warrior, as he called him, and to bring them, and lay them at his feet. This was the token of the most perfect submission that an Indian warrior could make to his conqueror; and this was accepted on the part of our commander. In this manner, and on these conditions, peace was to be restored.

At nine in the morning of the next day, the same old chief returned, attended by a more numerous suite than before, having several large hogs added to his peace-offerings, and with him, likewise, he brought the bones of Capt. Cook, those of his back bone and feet only excepted, which he promised to produce the next visit he made. On examination, the head appeared to have been scalped; the face was entirely gone; the hands had the flesh on, but scored and salted; and, as he assured the Captain, most of the flesh besides was eaten. Our Commander made signs to return the cutter; but was told, it was broke up and burnt for the iron. Some presents were made to this friendly chief, who departed well satisfied. We were now preparing to depart, when provisions

of

of all forts came pouring in upon us faster than we could consume them. The Indian kept his promise, and

On the 23d brought the bones of the Captain that were missing: these were all placed in due form in a case made for the purpose, and under a triple discharge from the ships buried in the bay. The terror of the Indians on this occasion was increased by a four pound ball being loaded by mistake, which fortunately did no other mischief, than that of exciting the jealousy of the Indians that our professions of peace were not sincere, which possibly might be the case with him who loaded the gun, as the sailors in general could hardly be restrained from violence, whenever an Indian came within their power. Nothing more remained now to be done. The repairs being compleated, so far, at least, as our circumstances would allow, we bent our sails in the morning, and were visited by many of our former friends, among whom was the king's youngest son, a boy of about fourteen years of age, of whom Captain Cook was remarkably fond, and the boy, in return, was no less attached to the Captain. He came to express his sorrow for the accident that had happened, which he did by a plentiful flow of tears. He gave us to understand, that his two brothers were killed, and that his father was fled to the adjoining island. Captain Clarke made him some presents that were plea-

sing

fing to him, and he departed very much comforted.

About 7 in the evening, a breeze fpringing up in our favour, we unmoored, and foon left the harbour, fhaping our courfe to the N. W. Nothing remarkable till

The 28th, when we opened upon a fine bay, in one of the Leeward Iflands, called by the inhabitants O-aa-ah, where the fhips came to an anchor, and where both Captains landed but made a very fhort ftay. Several of the inhabitants came on board, who were fo immoderately fond of iron, that they endeavoured to wrench the ring-bolts from the hatches. Here we put afhore the family that accompanied us from O-why-e, and here we purchafed a few fmall fwine, bread-fruit and plantains, and a quantity of a root, called Ta-ee, not unlike fern-root, but of an enormous fize, fome weighing from 60 to 70 pounds. It is an excellent anti-fcorbutic of the faccharine kind. Pounded, we made an excellent liquor from it, very pleafant and exceedingly wholefome: we had quantities of it when we reached Kamfhatfka, and as good as when firft purchafed. Having found nothing elfe to engage our attention in this ifland, we fet fail in the evening, and

This day, March 1, about noon, we arrived at the Ifland of Ne-hu, and moored in our old birth, where we victualled and repaired the winter before. Here we were received with

seeming

feeming kindnefs. Hogs and the produce of the ifland were brought us in abundance; but when our cafks were landed, in order to exchange our water, (that of O-why-he being both bitter and brackifh, and the water here excellent)the coopers were no fooner fet to work, than one Indian fnatched up his adze, another his bucket, a third his bag of nails, and fo on; and this among a croud of natives of more than 4 or 500 in number. To put a ftop to thefe depredations, orders were given to fire over their heads; but this not having the defired effect, a gun from the fhips threw them all into confufion. Two were feen to drop, and by the fhrieks and cries of the women, more were fuppofed to have been killed or wounded. For a while the multitude retreated; but being rallied by fome of their chiefs, who doubtlefs had heard that we were not invulnerable, they returned in greater numbers than before, when it was thought prudent to lay afide watering, and to provide for our own fafety. All hands were now ordered to their pofts, and an engagement commenced in earneft, when the Indians inftantly gave way, after a few being killed and wounded by our fire, and they never again offered the leaft violence during our ftay. A perfect agreement took place, and prefents were mutually exchanged on both fides. Here all the bad water was ftarted from both fhips, and a plentiful ftock of good water taken on board, to

ferve

ferve us during our long run to Kamfhatfka, for
which we were preparing. Here one of the
chiefs, named Noo-oh-a exprelfed a defire to
accompany us in our voyage, when, being
told that we were never more to return to that
ifland, he lamented the opportunity he had loft
when we were here before ; and pointing to the
fun, feemed to fuppofe that we fhould vifit that
luminary in our courfe, and that the thunder
and lightning of our guns, and that which
came from the heavens were both derived from
the fame fource.

From this harbour we failed on the 9th, and
vifited the oppofite fide of the ifland, where
we had likewife paffed a part of the former
winter. Here we were received with much
kindnefs and hofpitality ; and here we purchafed yams and potatoes for our fummer's confumption, which the companies of both fhips
were glad to exchange for their allowance of
bread, that part of their food being both fcanty
and bad. Befides the natural productions of the
country, we purchafed in thefe iflands many
tons of falt ; much of their cordage and cloth ;
and a great variety of artificial curiofities, fuch
as their weapons of war, their inftruments for
fifhing ; their cloaks and coverlids ; their caps,
mafks, nets, inftruments of mufic ; their needles, thread, working-tools, bracelets, ear-jew-
els, and, in fhort, almoft every thing that was
new to us, or which was peculiar to them ; a-
mong

mong which were some houshold utensils, and prints for impressing their cloth. The island we are now preparing to leave lies in lat. 21 deg. 49 min. N. and in long. E. from London 193 nearly.

On the 15th we came to sail, and soon after we were informed that Capt. Clarke was taken ill. We at first stood to the westward, veering a little to the south, in search of a small island, which we were told abounded in turtle. We continued this course till

The 30th, when we were in lat. 20 deg. 19 min. N. long. 180 deg. 40 min. per watch. We now altered our course, and steered N. W.

April 1, we continued steering N. W. ½ W. lat. 21 deg. 46 min. N. long. 180 deg. 2 min.

On the 3d we crossed the Northern Tropic, long. 176 deg. 39 min. E. steering N. W. by N. in a direct course for Kamshatska. On the third day after leaving the Island of Ne-hun, it began to blow a hard gale, which continued with very little intermission till the present day, when our ship became very leaky, and we were informed, that the Resolution was much worse than the Discovery.

On the 9th, for the first time, since our leaving Ne-hun, we had an observation, and found ourselves in lat. 32 deg. 16 min. long. 167 E.

On the 10th we observed a tropic bird hovering about the ship, and by her motions we expected her to light, being far to the north-

ward

ward of her proper climate; however she left us, and made for the Resolution. In the evening it began to blow with heavy rain, and continued an unremitting gale till

The 13th, when we were in lat. 39deg. 50min. very cold and foggy. As we now began to approach the higher northern latitudes, the flannel jackets, that had been stored up while we were among the Tropical islands, were again brought into use, and were of infinite service to the poor men. We now altered our course to the eastward, having great signs of land on our larboard beam.

On the 15th, being in lat. 41 deg. 59 min. the signs of land increased. The weather being fine and clear, we seized this opportunity to search for the leak, and, knowing it to be forwards, we moved the sails from the fore-sail room, and found them wringing wet; but the leak was out of our reach; however, when the weather was fine, it gave us very little trouble.

On the 16th the Resolution's boat came on board, and Capt. Gore and our 1st Lieutenant went to visit Capt. Clarke, who still continued very ill. On their return, they brought a dismal account of the condition of the Resolution; she became leaky on the 7th, when it blew a tempest. On the carpenters going down to the cockpit for lights, they were alarmed by finding themselves over their shoes in water, and, upon further examination, the casks in the

the fish-room and spirit-room were driving one against another, by which two casks of French brandy were staved. They then searched forwards, where they found the coal-hole six feet deep in water, and the ship's whole complement of paint destroyed; several casks of shells and curiosities staved, the light-room deck blown up, and the bulk-head between the gunner's store-room and the coal-hole burst open. In this alarming situation they continued during the whole time that the stormy weather lasted, pumping night and day, and every officer in the ship (the Captain, who was ill, only excepted) took his turn with the common men, who were sickening apace with fatigue; nor were they then relieved from hard duty, when our gentlemen left the ship; which was the reason we could make no stay, to examine the extent of De Gama's or Company's Land, which, however, we discovered, by our run, not to extend farther to the eastward than it is marked in our ordinary maps. Their misfortune did not end with the damages above recited; much of their bread was spoiled, and they were forced to take from us a ton of yams to supply its place.

On the 18th we lost sight of the Resolution; but by every appearance, were at no great distance from land. Large pieces of timber drifted by us, and land-birds innumerable were seen to the westward. We were now in lat. 46

deg. 10 min. running at the rate of 7 or 8 knots an hour.

On the 19th we came in fight of the Refolution: and, though it blew hard, they threw out the fignal for us to make fail, from whence we concluded that their leak ftill diftreffed them. At noon we were in lat. 48 deg. 38 min. and long. 159 deg. 10 min.

On the 20th we had a deep fnow, attended with froft, by which our men were expofed to incredible hardfhips. It fell fo heavy upon the decks and rigging that it was next to impoffible to keep them clear, or, not being clear, to make the ropes traverfe. Fortunately it ceafed freezing in the night.

On the 20th we were in lat. 49 deg. 48 min. when we began to get every thing in readinefs for coming to anchor.

On the 22d we were in the latitude of London; the water of a milky colour, but no foundings at 85 fathom. In the evening the Refolution made the fignal to tack fhip, and we never afterwards faw her till our arrival at our deftined harbour.

On the 23d we came in fight of land, very barren, very rugged, and covered with fnow; from whence we were diftant not above a league with our ftarboard tacks on board, the water near the fhore black with wild-fowl, and a fheet of ice fkirting the land, covered with fea-lions, feals and other amphibious animals. At half

paft

paft 10, P. M. we put about, finding by our log-book and watch that we were 50 miles to leeward of our port.

On the 25th we were out of fight of land, with a heavy gale, a fall of fnow, piercing cold, and 20 of our hands froft-nipped.

The 26th it blew hard from the N. E. We kept working to windward, which doubled our labour, and our concern for our Commodore increafed fo much the more, as we judged by our own fufferings, what muft be the fate of the Refolution, that was much lefs able to ftruggle with the ftorm than the Difcovery. The ftorm continuing with fleet and fnow, three men could fcarce do the work of one.

Amidft thefe complicated diftrefles, our leak increafed to an alarming degree.

On the 28th we made 17 inches in 3 hours. The wind dying away, we tried the current, and found we drifted half a mile an hour to the fouthward. A man was fent up to the maft-head to look round for the Refolution, but without fucceeding. We now gave her over for loft.

On the 29th we ftood in for the land, and at 2 in the afternoon, we came in fight of the en-trance of the bay of Kamfhatfka, then diftant between feven and eight miles to the fouthward. We made fail and ftood right in ; but finding it frozen over, we judged that the Refolution could not poffibly be there, and therefore con-cluded that fhe muft have gone to the bottom.

Early

Early next morning we once more attempted
the entrance of the bay, and finding the ice
drifted, we conceived hopes, that we might be
able to force a paffage through the loofe ice,
which, now the weather was fine, did not appear fo formidable as before. About noon a
pleafant breeze fprung up, and we directed our
courfe to a flag we faw difplayed juft within the
bay, and happily fucceeded, dropping our anchor in 20 fathom water, within lefs than three
leagues of our intended harbour. In about
half an hour, while our boats were ftill looking out for a paffage, we obferved at a diftance
two boats making towards us, one of which we
knew to belong to the Refolution. The other
belonged to the Ruffians. No joy could exceed that, which the news of the fafety of the Refolution fpread through the whole fhip's company
of the Difcovery. She had been in port ever
fince the 27th and had given us over for loft,
never expecting to fee us more. She had met
with fome damage in her fails and rigging ; but
by her fortunately hitting the harbour, fhe had
efcaped much of the diftrefs that we fuffered
from the feverity of the weather.

Early on the firft of May, we weighed, having the Refolution's boat to direct us. Soon
after day-light, we were within the light-houfe
near the entrance of the harbour, but were oppofed by a ftrong tide from the fhore, which
drifting huge pieces of floating ice againft us,
made our further progrefs both dangerous and

fatiguing ;

fatiguing; but, having the wind fair, about five in the evening we came to in fight of the town, and foon after dropt anchor near the Refolution.

On the 2d the Refolution unmoored, and both fhips came to, and moored within a mile of the town, and within a cable's length of the ice, which entirely fhut up the head of the bay. Here we found only one fmall floop, about 50 tons, which, as foon as the ice was clear, was bound on a trading voyage to the northward. We had no fooner dropt anchor than our boat was ordered out, and our Captain, with feveral other gentlemen, went to vifit Capt. Clarke, and to take his orders for our future proceedings. We found him ftill growing weaker and weaker; we therefore fhortened our ftay.

On the 3d both Captains, attended by the principal officers and gentlemen, went on fhore, and were received by a fubaltern who now had the command of the fort, fituated clofe by a little miferable town, called A-watch-a, which, by its appearance, could not be fuppofed to furnifh provifions for the fhips crews a fingle week. We foon learnt that the governor lived at a town called Bolchaia-reka, diftant about 70 miles, and that an exprefs had been fent to him to notify our arrival. The fubaltern, in the mean time fhewed us every civility. We found on our landing, a fledge drawn by dogs in readinefs to receive our Commodore, who was in fo

weak

weak a ftate as not to be able to walk, and to
conduct him to the refidence of the governor
when at Kamfhatfka, where moft of the officers
and gentlemen had apartments allotted them
during our ftay. It was not however a little
ftrange, that though we were expected, and
that the emprefs of Ruffia had given orders to
her governor, to furnifh us with every accommodation in his power, that not a creature was
to be found that underftood any other language
than that of the natives of the place, and of
Ruffia; neither of which languages was intelligible to any of us, fo that having no interpreter, every thing was to be learnt by figns.

Capt. Clarke, with fome gentlemen who attended him, flept on fhore for the benefit of
the air. They were entertained with ftewed
fifh, venfon-foups, and other difhes, dreffed
after the manner of the country; and the officer who now acted as deputy governor, behaved
with an uncommon degree of civility, or more
properly, fervility, by paying every attention
that his circumftances would admit, to make
the Captain's accommodations comfortable. He
made him underftand, that at the diftance of a-
bout 16 wrefts, at a town called Parantanka there
lived a prieft who might poffibly be able to converfe with him; and with that view he the very
next day fent an exprefs to invite him to the
fort, at the fame time intimating, that the governor was a German, who could talk all languages,

guages, which accounts for the omiffion before complained of; and indeed, as it afterwards appeared, we were expected here the preceding fummer, and that our arrival now was unlooked for. On board, the carpenters were bufy in ftripping the fhip's bows, and the failors in getting the fick on fhore, with every part of the fhips ftores that ftood in need of revifal; and though the weather continued piercing cold, no time was loft in forwarding the repairs.

On the 4th one of our boats, in putting the aftronomer's affiftant on fhore at the influx of the tide, was fuddenly encircled by the floating ice in fuch a manner, as not to be able to move one way or the other, another boat fent to her relief was foon enclofed in the fame manner, and till the return of the tide both were forced to remain in that deplorable fituation, not a perfon on board daring to truft himfelf among the floating ice to endeavour to make his efcape. About 12 at night they were releafed, and the icey prifoners returned on board almoft perifhed with cold.

On the 5th fix gentlemen arrived from Bolchaia-reka, among whom was a merchant who came to trade for fkins, fome of which he purchafed from us, as we thought, at great prices; but as we afterwards found for little more than half their value. Thefe are all monopolized by the Ruffian Company already mentioned in our account of the laft fummer's voyage, and not a fkin to be had from the Kamfhatfkadales.

The

The gentleman was accompanied by the governor's secretary, who could speak both German and Dutch, and who brought a letter from the governor, written in German, complementing the Commodore on his arrival, tendering his best services, and excusing his absence; adding at the same time, that when he was made acquainted with the necessaries of which we stood in need, he would give immediate orders for their supply as far as was in his power, and that he would then embrace the first opportunity of waiting upon the Commodore. It happened, that Mr. Webber, our draughtsman, was master of the German; and on reading the letter it was thought more respectful, as well as more suitable to the occasion, for Capt. Gore, in the illness of our commander, to be the messenger himself, as he could give a more particular account of our many wants, than could possibly be transmitted in a letter. On the 6th the Russian gentlemen were entertained on board the ships, Mr. Webber acting as interpreter to the merchant, and the governor's secretary being master of the French, was well enough understood to make the conversation and the bottle pass jovially round. About ten at night the company parted; and

In the morning of the 7th Capt. Gore, attended by lieut. King, of the Resolution, and Mr. Webber, and accompanied by the merchant and Russian secretary, set out for Bolchaia-reka, where, after a most fatiguing journey, they

they arrived on the 13th, and were received by the Governor with a politeness that did honour to the post he filled.

After the usual salutations, they entered into general conversation, when our gentlemen soon discovered that the governor was not only a man of breeding, but of general knowledge; that he had been made acquainted, by his court, with our intention of touching at Kamshatska; but that the character of our first commander, Capt. Cook was known to him, by the account given of his former expeditions; and the whole route, that he was supposed to pursue in the present expedition, he had deduced from his own conjecture. Capt. Gore, when he came to speak of our north-west course, put the letter into his hands, which our Commodore received from the Russian factor at Samganuida (of which notice has already been taken,) and which chiefly related to the business of the factory, having only slightly touched upon the civilities he had received from us, and had represented us as merchant ships, engaged in a new line of commerce, which he apprehended might be injurious to that in which the factory was engaged. Such is the jealousy the Russians entertain of the trade to the north, which they now look upon as we did formerly upon the trade to America, as of right belonging to them;—founding their claim on their priority of discovery, Bhering having first traced the way to the north-west continent of Ameri-

ca,

ca, though he loft his life in the pursuit. This obfervation however being foreign to the fubject of his commiffion, Capt. Gore paffed unnoticed; and having dined and fpent the day of his arrival agreeably, he next morning took occafion to deliver to the governor, a lift of thofe articles of which the fhips ftood moft in need; reprefenting at the fame time the fhattered condition of the fhips, and how much they were in want of fails and cordage, as well as provifions, having met with no fupply of beef or bread from the time they left England in 1776, to the prefent day; nor of tobacco, a chief article with our failors, tho' for three months they had been under the neceffity of fubfifting without. The governor heard him with attention, and affured him, that he had her imperial majefty's pofitive orders to furnifh the Britifh fhips upon Difcovery with every affiftance in his power; and that his inclination as well as his duty, led him to do his uttermoft to comply with his requeft; that he would ranfact the country round as far as his jurifdiction reached, to fupply him with rye meal, but that wheat meal could not poffibly be procured, becaufe the country produced none; nor would it be eafy to fupply the fhips with beef, except for prefent confumption, as the time of the year was unfuitable, none being killed there in the winter, nor any fit to kill till the grafs in the fummer had recruited their flefh. He added, that tobacco was not among the articles allowed

by

by Her Imperial Majesty, but that he would for
their use spare 400 weight from his own
stores; and what canvas and cordage the magazines could produce should be at the Commodore's service, whose ill state of health he most
sincerely regretted. These civilities were accompanied with the most lively expressions of
esteem; and, when Capt. Gore took leave, he
complimented him with his own carriage, ordered a horse round for the Commodore to ride
out for the benefit of the air, and a cow to supply him with fresh cream and milk. And recol-
lecting afterwards that the gentlemen might,
probably, be in want of tea and sugar, he
sent 100 weight of the latter, and 20 lb. of
the former for a present supply.

We should be wanting in justice to this worthy Governor, were we to pass over his behaviour to us unnoticed, which was such as did
honour to his feelings as a Man, and to Her
Imperial Majesty as an Officer.

Our gentlemen had not been returned many
days, when they were followed by the Governor himself, who, after enforcing his orders for
our immediate supply from the country, came
to examine what could be spared from the
fortress. He was received by Capt. Clarke,
on board the Resolution; and every mark of
attention paid him, which his services so well
deserved. 9000 weight of rye meal was soon
after collected from different districts at a great

C c   distance,

diftance, and conveyed to us at no inconfiderable expence, accompanied with 20 head of horn-
ed cattle. Thefe our failors rejoiced to fee, and,
tho' fkeletons compared with thofe of England,
were received by us with an eagernefs not eafily to be exceeded; for not having had the
relifh of frefh beef for more than three years,
the very fcrapings of the bones would have
been to our failors, at this time a treat infinitely
more grateful than at home they would have
thought the moft profufe feaft.

It was the 23d before the Governor arrived
at Parrantanka, in the vicinage of which the
prieft refided, of whom we have already fpoken. With him the Governor fpent the afternoon, but when night came he flept at the
fort.

On the 25th the pinnace from the Refolution was manned and properly equipped to
bring him on board. He was faluted with 11
guns from the Refolution, and the fame number from the Difcovery; and when he entered
the fhip he was received with mufic, and with
all the honours that circumftances would admit;
and he was fo well pleafed with his reception,
that he ftaid two days and two nights on board:
during which time he had but very little fleep.
Capt. Clarke, being ill, flept on fhore, and
left the care of his entertainment to his officers,
who did not fail to make it agreeable. Some
very noble prefents were made him at his departure,

parture; confifting of curiofities collected from every part of the world, with a gold watch, two fowling-pieces, a brace of filver-mounted piftols, and other valuable articles of Englifh manufacture; to all which were added, near 100 gallons of brandy from the fhip's ftores, as a prefent from the failors out of their allowance, in lieu of the tobacco that he had generoufly ordered to be divided amongft them gratis, which at that time was in fuch eftimation, that he, who had been provident enough to make a referve, fold it nearly at the price of filver.

Orders were now given to get every thing on board, and prepare to fail as faft as poffible; both fhips had been ftripped of their fheathing to the water's edge; but the leak of the Difcovery was found much lower, being a hole worn in her bow, which, had not the hull been cleared, could never have been come at.

Having now got the meal on board, the crews were ferved with an allowance of half rye and half flower; which, however, not being accuftomed to it, they did not very well relifh, though it was found to be very wholefome. The Governor had made Capt. Clarke a prefent of a cow, for which it was neceffary to provide provender; and large quantities of ducks, geefe and poultry were taken on board to fupply the want of other live-ftock; for here they had no fheep, nor any other domeftic animal, except dogs, which ferve the natives both for horfes

and

and hunting; nor was there a cow in the country, that we faw, except that the Governor fent
by Capt. Clarke, and one in poffeffion of
the prieft.

We had now been here a month, when

On the 4th of June, being his Majefty's birth-
day, the fame was celebrated with great magnificence on board and on fhore. The fhip's were
dreffed with ftreamers and with the colours of
all nations; and a flag was difplayed at the
tents. The Ruffian gentlemen were fumptu-
oufly entertained on board; and the common
men were ferved with double allowance of meat
and liquor, and, being permitted to divert
themfelves on fhore, many of them made parties and traverfed the woods in purfuit of game,
with which they were told the country abounded.
But, as they were ignorant of their haunts, they
met with no fuccefs.

Before our departure, pacquets were entrufted to the care of the governor, to be forwarded
to England by the way of Peterfburgh, both
for government and to private friends; thefe
we have fince found were carefully tranfmitted.
And now, having all things in readinefs, our
full complement of wood and water on board,
and of every neceffary the country afforded, and
waiting only for a wind,

Early on the 12th of June we weighed and
failed, directing our courfe to the northward;
but were detained in the bay till

The

The 15th, when we were alarmed with a noise louder than the loudest thunder, and presently were almost blinded with a fall of ashes, which, in lefs than an hour, covered the decks all over from stern to stern, among which were mixed pumice stones as large as walnuts. We were all driven down between decks; but about ten in the morning were releafed by the shower ceafing. On looking round, we found they iffued from a volcano at the diftance, as we fuppofed, of about 20 miles, then bearing from us W. S. W. During this eruption, we were not only obliged to retire ourfelves, but to bettan down the hatches fore and aft; fo that what with the clofenefs of our confinement, and the fulphureous fmell from the flames, we were almoft fuffocated. But we were no fooner releafed, than we weighed anchor and fteered to the eaftward.

On the 17th and 18th we continued our courfe E. and E. by N.

On the 19th fteered E. by N. Lat. 54 deg. 56 min. N.

On the 20th came in fight of land, high, and covered with fnow; called by Bhering, Kamtfchatfka-nofs, but found that Cape a degree more to the fouthward than he had laid it down. Lat. 55 deg. 52 min.

On the 21ft we continued to fteer E. N. E. faw a whale, two feals and a number of fealions.

C c 3

On

On the 22d we ftood to the N. E. and, feeing a change in the colour of the water, we founded, but found no ground in 100 fathom. We continued the fame courfe till the 25th, when we were in lat. 59 deg. 9 min. and long. 168 deg. 30 min. E.

On the 26th we changed our courfe E.N.E. and finding the fea covered with gulls and fhags, we founded, but found no ground at 120 fathom.

On the 27th we ftood E. $\frac{1}{2}$ N. and found ourfelves by obfervation in lat. 59 deg. 57 min. long. 172 E. We changed our courfe, and ftood N. N. W.

On the 28th, early in the morning, we came in fight of land, very high and covered with fnow, the extreme point of which bore N. E. diftance about 6 leagues. We continued our courfe along fhore, with regular foundings at about 54 fathom, free from reefs, and a very bold fhore. We fteered this courfe till

The 30th, at noon, when we were in lat. 62 deg. 1 min.

On the 1ft of July, the weather began to grow hazy, with thick fogs. We ftill kept coafting on till

The 3d in the morning, when the fogs left us and it began to rain. At ten in the morning, faw a very high point of land, bearing from us N. N. E. diftance about 7 leagues. We

We hauled upon a wind, and ftood E. N. E.
till two in the afternoon, when we paffed a
fmall ifland, called by the Ruffians, St. Ni-
cholas; in fome parts very high and covered
with fnow. Lat. 63 deg. 45 min. long. 187.

On the 4th at one in the morning, we bore
away N. ½ E. and about noon, the next day,
faw land from W. to N. E. appearing like two
iflands. At four o'clock we hauled up to
W. N. W. being near land, and founding from
26 to 29 fathom.

On the 6th we continued coafting from
N. ½ W. to N. ¼ E. with the land to the weftward high and fnowy. Lat. 67. deg. 10 min.
long. 187 E.

On the 7th, faw ice in a large body to the
eaftward, diftance about 2 or 3 leagues, and
about noon paffed feveral large fields of ice.
We tacked and ftood N. W. by W. with a
ftiff gale and heavy fnow.

On the 8th fell in with the ice again in a folid body; at the fame time bore away S. S. W.

On the 9th, at three in the morning, we
hauled up along fide the folid ice, freezing cold
all day. Lat. 69 deg. 12 min.

On the 10th continued our courfe all the
morning, and at nine paffed a large field of
loofe ice, diftance about 3 miles, and at noon
went through it.

On the 11th we found ourfelves furrounded
with ice. We kept working to the S. E. paf-

fing

fing many large fields of ice, covered with fea
cows. We kept luffing up and bearing away,
till with fome difficulty we got through. Lat.
obferved 67 deg. 40 min. long. 186 deg. 10
min. We continued working through the
ice till

The 14th, when by obfervation we were in
lat. 69 deg. 37 min. We continued bearing
away to the northward, till

The 18th, when by obfervation we were in
lat. 70 deg. 28 min. and, being very near the
ice, a large white bear paffed us in the water;
but made for the ice at a great rate. In half an
hour, we faw multitudes of them upon the ice,
making to the eaftward, when we obferved the
fea-cows, as the bears approached them, flying
like fheep purfued by dogs.

On the 20th we came in fight of land at the
diftance of about 5 or 6 leagues, bearing from
S. to S. E. founded from 24 to 21 fathom.

On the 21ft we ftood from W. $\frac{1}{2}$ N. to
W. N. W. and at fix o'clock we paffed a large
ifland of ice, on which were whole herds of
fea-cows of an enormous fize. We fired feveral
mufkets among them, which fent them to the
water with dreadful yellings. At nine in the
evening we came in fight of the American
fhore, diftant about 6 leagues. We fteered
all night W. by N. and next morning found
ourfelves almoft furrounded with fields of ice
drifting to the fouthward. At twelve o'clock
we

we hauled our wind to the southward, and, by the alertness of our seamen, we passed it with very little damage.

On the morning of the 23d it came on to blow very hard, and, before noon, we found ourselves closely blocked up in the ice, and could see it all round us in a solid body, to a great distance. At the same time we saw the Resolution bearing N. E. $\frac{1}{2}$ E. some miles off, which was the last sight we had of her, during the whole day. In this horrid situation, we handed all our sails, unbent our fore-topsail, and moored ship with both our ice anchors, one to each bow.

We now began to reflect on our condition; The winter drawing on apace; our provisions short, and what we had but very indifferent; and no relief to be expected; our people's spirits began to sink, and it was with difficulty that they were persuaded to exert themselves for their own deliverance. Fortunately for us, we had, in the evening, a shift of wind from W. N. W. with a steady breeze, when our Captain, looking over our starboard quarter, discerned the ice to the southward, seemingly to leave the ship, and soon heard a crash, as if a thousand rocks had been rent from their foundations; which we afterwards perceived to be the parting of the ice in different directions; and soon after found ourselves released. We instantly got up our ice-anchors, and shaped our course from

S. E.

S. E. to E. S. E. but were frequently stopped by large pieces, which carried away great part of our sheathing forward, and damaged our stern, so that the ship made water at the rate of three inches an hour.

On the 24th we continued our course E. S. E. and came in sight of the Resolution, which had likewise received much damage about her bows. We were now clear of the ice, and, till three in the afternoon, sailed in company, till we came up with a solid body, on which we saw a number of amphibious animals, some of them very large. We instantly got out and manned our boats, and in three hours returned with eleven of the largest, about which all hands were employed the next day in skinning and cutting them up for blubber.

On the 25th we passed several fields of ice. And at noon was at the extreme of the easternmost land in sight. Being then in lat. 69 deg. 12 min. and, by lunar observation, in long. 187 deg. 16 min E. of London.

On the 27th we found ourselves involved again among the loose ice, some of which it was out of our power to escape, and the leak still continuing rather to increase than abate, our Captain, with Mr. Bailey the astronomer, and Mr. Burney, our 1st lieutenant, went on board the Resolution, to report our situation to the Commodore, whom they found so ill as to be past all hopes of recovery. Upon calling
ling

ling a council of officers, it was unanimously agreed, that we should proceed as fast as possible to some port, where we might repair our damages, and Kamshatska was appointed our place of rendezvous. We were now in lat. 68 deg. 10 min. and in long. 183.

On the 28th, at two in the morning we came in sight of the Asia shore, very high and covered with snow, distance about 7 or 8 leagues, we made sail and stood to the southward. About noon we found ourselves in lat. 67 deg. 11 min. and in long. by double altitudes 188 deg. 10 min. E. The extreme of the easternmost land distant about 6 leagues. At ten at night we saw a great number of ducks, geese, and sea parrots very near us, by which we judged land could not be far off.

On the 29th at noon we were in lat. 65 deg. 50 min. and long. 188 deg. 27 min. but no land in sight.

On the 30th we steered till noon to the S. E. with a steady breeze, and came in sight of two islands right a-head, distant about five or six leagues. The weather then became thick and hazy, and though we were certain that the main land of Asia and America were at no great distance, we could see neither till about four o'clock in the afternoon, the weather clearing up, we saw a passage or streight, to which we bore away, and found the two continents at seven o'clock on each side of us. This streight was called

Bhering's

Bhering's ftreight, the entrance of which we found the fame as has been already defcribed; and the current at this time fetting to the N. W. very ftrong, made our paffage not only difficult but dangerous.

On the 31 we paffed Ifchutiolfkoi-nofs, called by the failors Tufkan-nofs, and foon came in fight of Cook's town, which we vifited the laft feafon, as has already been mentioned.

Nothing remarkable till Auguft the 5th, when we had an obfervation, and found ourfelves in lat. 62 deg. 37 min.

On the 7th at noon we were by obfervation in lat. 61 deg. 12 min. and in long. 183 deg. 45 min. and at no great diftance from the land. At four o'clock having a dead calm, the companies of both fhips employed themfelves in fifh-ing, and very fortunately caught a number of large cod, which were equally diftributed a-mong the crews. To this place we gave the name of the Bank of Good Providence; and as foon as the breeze fprung up, we made fail and ftood to S. W.

On the 9th at noon we were by obfervation in the long. of 183 deg. 36 min. 14 fec.

On the 10th we continued our courfe, and on the 12th at noon we were in lat. 56 deg. 37 min. with the fhip's head to the S. W.

In the evening of the 13th we had the Refo-lution's boat on board, to compare time, who

brought

brought the difagreeable news of the Captain's being given over by the furgeon.

On the 13th being in foundings, and the weather calm, we hove to, in order to get fome fifh for the fick, and a few cod were caught and diftributed accordingly.

On the 17th the wind that had been againft us for fome days paft fhifted in our favour, and at nine in the morning the man at the maft head called out land to the N. W. which was foon known to be Bhering Ifland, lat. at noon 53 deg. 50 min.

Nothing remarkable till the 21ft, when early in the morning the man at the maft head again came in fight of land. It was then at a very great diftance, and upon our ftarboard bow, but before night we were only diftant from the mouth of Kamfhatfka bay, 12 or 13 leagues.

On the 22d at nine in the morning we had the Refolution's boat on board, to acquaint Capt. Gore with the death of our Commodore. We were then within fight of the flag, at the mouth of Kamfhatfka bay, of which mention has already been made, and the wind being favourable, we continued our courfe for the entrance of the harbour, which then bore from us W. S. W. lat. at noon 52 deg. 54 min.

On the 23d a little before midnight we came to anchor within the light-houfe.

On the 24th our Capt. being now Commodore, made the fignal to get under way by towing

ing, all the boats were accordingly got out, and the Commodore went on board the Refolutoin, where it was refolved, for the greater convenience of repairing the fhips, and for erecting the tents and forge to go within the upper harbour. And about four in the afternoon both fhips came too, and were moored in three fathom and a half water, muddy bottom.

Early next morning the tents were erected, and the fick were got on fhore.

From the time we fet fail out of this bay in June, till the prefent day, we had been in no harbour to refit; and had been driven from ifland to ifland among the ice, till our fhips had in a manner loft their fheathing, and were otherwife in a miferable condition; we were therefore happy in arriving fafe.

Auguft 25, an exprefs was fent to Balchaia-reka, to acquaint the governor of our arrival, and of the death of our late Commander; at the fame time another exprefs was fent to Parrantanka, to defire the attendance of the prieft, in order to confult with him concerning the interment of Capt. Clarke, whofe defire was, to be buried in his church; while we were waiting the iffue of thefe meffages, the feveral promotions took place that followed in confequence of the Commander's death. Mr. Gore went on board the Refolution, and Mr. King, firft Lieut. of the Refolution, took the command of the Difcovery. Other promotions took place, which the reader will remark by the fequel. The firft
care

care of the commanders of both ships was to provide for the recovery of the sick, and the repairs of the ships; and for that purpose a house was procured for the reception of the former, and a contrivance made for heaving the latter dry.

The weather being now temperate and the country delightful, the officers and gentlemen rather chose to sleep in their Marquees on shore, than in the apartments in the fort, or in the houses in the town. It was however thought expedient to shew every mark of respect to the Russian officers, who, though not of the first rank, were notwithstanding the only people with whom we had any concern, or with whom we could have any communication; they were therefore frequently invited to dinner, and they as often attended.

On the 26th the priest arrived, when Capt. Gore acquainted him with the death of our commander, and of his desire to be buried in his church. The good old gentleman seemed much concerned; but started several difficulties; and appeared very unwilling to comply with the dying request of the deceased. He urged several reasons to shew the impropriety of it; those of most weight were, that the church was soon to be pulled down; that it was every winter three feet deep in water; and that in a few years no vestage of it would remain, as the new church was to be erected near the town of A-watch-a,

upon

upon a drier and more convenient spot. He therefore advised the remains of the Commander to be deposited at the foot of a tree, the scite of which was to be included in the body of the new church, where the Captain's bones might probably rest for ages undisturbed. These reasons, whether real or fictitious, the officers who had charge of the funeral could not disprove, and therefore people were sent to dig the grave, where the priest should direct.

The 30th was appointed for the interment; and to make the funeral the more solemn, every officer was desired to appear in his uniform; the Marines to be drawn up under arms, and common men to be dressed as nearly alike as possible, in order to attend the corpse from the water-side to the grave. All this was readily acceded to, and the procession began about ten in the morning, when minute guns from the ships were fired, and the drums, muffled as usual, beat the dead march. When the corpse arrived at the grave, it was deposited under the triple discharge of the Marines; and, the grave being covered, it was fenced in by piles driven deep in the ground, and the inside afterwards filled up with stones and earth, to preserve the body from being devoured in the winter by bears or other wild beasts, who are remarkable for their sagacity in scenting out the bodies of dead passengers, when any happen to perish and are buried near the roads.

This

This ceremony over, an escutcheon was prepared and neatly painted by Mr. Webber, with the Captain's coat of arms properly emblazon'd, and placed in the church of Parrantanka, and underneath the following inscription.

There lies interred at the Foot of a Tree, near the Ostrog of St. PETER and PAUL, The BODY of CHARLES CLARKE, ESQUIRE, COMMANDER of His Britannic Majesty's Ships, the Resolution and Discovery; To which he succeeded on the Death of JAMES COOK, Esquire, Who was killed by the Natives of an Island we discovered in the South Sea, after having explored the Coast of America, from 42 deg. 27 min. to 70 deg. 40 min. 57 sec. N. in search of a North-west Passage from EUROPE to the EAST-INDIES.

The Second Attempt being made by CAPTAIN CLARKE, who sailed within some few Leagues of Captain COOK; but was brought up by a solid Body of Ice, which he found from the America to the Asia Shore, and almost tended due East and West.——He Died at Sea, on his Return to the Southward, on the 22d Day of APRIL, 1779. AGED, 38 Years.

D d   Another

Another infcription was fixed upon the tree under which he was interred. This tree was at fome diftance from the town and near the hofpital, round which feveral people had already been buried; but none fo high upon the hill as the fpot pointed out for the grave of Capt. Clarke. The infcription placed on this tree was nearly the fame as that in the church of Parrantanka, and was as follows :

Beneath this Tree lies the BODY of
CAPTAIN   CHARLES   CLARKE,
COMMANDER of His Britannic Majefty's
Ships, the Refolution and Difcovery.
Which Command he fucceeded to, on the 14th
of February, 1779, on the Death of
Captain JAMES COOK,
Who was Killed by the Natives of fome
Iflands he Difcovered in the SOUTH
SEA, on the Date above.

CAPTAIN CLARKE Died at Sea,
of a lingering Illnefs, on the 22d Day of
AUGUST, 1779,
In the 38th Year of his AGE.
And was INTERRED on the 30th, following.

Cn

On this occasion the inhabitants of both towns, and those of the whole country for many miles round, attended; and the crews of both ships were suffered to continue ashore, and to divert themselves, each as he liked best. It was the Captain's desire that they should have double allowance for three days successively, and all that while to be excused from other duty, than what the ordinary attendance in the ship required, but the season being far advanced, and a long tract of unknown sea to traverse before they could reach China, the officers representing the hardships and inconveniences that so much lost time might bring upon themselves, they very readily gave up that part of the Captain's bequest, and returned to their respective employments early the next day.

On the 2d of September the Governor arrived at Parrantanka, and with him an officer called by the Russians Proposick, the same as in England is called Collector or Surveyor.

They informed Capt. Gore, that a sloop was daily expected from Janeska, laden with provisions and stores of all sorts for our use; but expressed some apprehensions for her safety, as the boats had been looking out for her several days. This news was of too much importance to be slighted. Accordingly

On the 3d the pinnaces and boats from both ships were sent to the entrance of the bay, to

assist

affist her, in case she should be in sight, in towing her in; but it was

The 11th before she arrived. She was a bark
of about 100 tons, and had two guns mounted,
which she fired as a salute, when she dropt anchor, and was answered by a volley from the
garrison, which consisted of a subaltern and 25
soldiers. She was no sooner moored, than the
Captain waited on the Governor for instructions,
and then came on board the Resolution. He
was introduced to the Commodore, to whom
he delivered the invoice of his lading; among
which was wearing apparel and tobacco, two
articles that were above all others acceptable to
the ships companies. As soon as the Governor
had executed his commission, and delivered up
the stores to the Commodore, he took his leave,
and returned to Bolchaia-reka, and the ships
being lightened before, and their bows heaved
up dry, so that the carpenters could get at the
leaks, the Captains and principal officers finding
little else to amuse them, made a party to scour
the woods for game; but this proved the worst
season in the year for hunting. They had been
told, that rein-deer, wolves, foxes, beavers,
and stone-rams every where abounded in the forests of this country; and they had promised
themselves great sport in pursuing them; but
after staying out full two days and nights, during which time they had been exposed to several severe storms, they returned much fatigued,

without

without having been able to kill a single creature. The parties who had been sent out to wood and water had succeeded much better. As soon as the ships were ready to launch, they were ready to compleat the hold. In short, the utmost dispatch was made to hasten our departure, so that by the latter end of September we were in readiness to put to sea. The cattle with which we were now supplied, one would have thought, had dropt from another region. It is among the wonders of nature, with what celerity every vegetable and every animal changes its appearance in this climate. On the 12th of June, when we left the harbour of Kamshatska, the spring had but just begun to announce the approach of summer by the budding of the trees, and the sprouting of the grass; but now, on our return, it was matter of surprize to find the fruits ripe, and the harvest in full perfection. The cattle were mere skin and bone, which we were glad to accept at our first coming; but those that were now sent us were fine and fat, and would have made no bad figure in Smithfield market. The grass was in many places as high as our knees, and the corn, where any grew, bore the promising appearance of a fine crop. In short, from the most dreary, barren, and desolate aspect, that any habitable country could present, this was become one of the most delightful; Mr. Nelson reaped a rich harvest of rare plants, and had the additional

D d 3 pleasure

pleafure of gathering them in their moſt exalted ſtate.

In this interval of idle time, between compleating our repairs, and clearing the harbour, we had leiſure to take a view of the town near the ſhore, where we firſt moored, and that of Parrantanka, where the prieſt lived, and where the church was ſituated. Theſe towns have received ſome improvement, ſince they became ſubject to the Ruſſians; but are ſtill moſt wretched dwellings. The houſes are built (if we may call that building, which is half dug out of the earth, and half ſet upon poles) in two different forms; one for their ſummer, and the other for their winter reſidence.

Their winter habitation is made by digging a ſquare hole in the earth, about five or ſix feet deep, the length and breadth being proportioned to the number of people that are to live in it. At each corner of this ſquare hole they ſet up a thick poſt, and in the intermediate ſpace between theſe corner poſts, they place other poſts at certain diſtances, and over theſe they lay balks, faſtening them together with ſtrong cords, which they make of nettles prepared in the manner of hemp. Acroſs theſe they place other balks, in the manner of a bridge, then cover the whole with thatch, leaving a ſquare opening in the middle, which ſerves at once for door, window, and chimney. On one ſide of this ſquare is their fire-place, and on the oppoſite ſide is

ranged

ranged their kitchen-furniture. On the two other sides are a kind of broad benches made with earth, on which each family lie, and in one of these huts or houses there live several families. To enter these huts by the only opening at top, they use a ladder, not made with rounds between two sides, like ours, but consisting only of narrow slips of wood fastened to a plank. This ladder the women mount with great agility, with children at their backs, and though the smoke would blind and suffocate those who are not used to it, yet the Kamschatskadales find no inconvenience from it.

Their summer huts, called Balagans, are made by fixing up pillars about 14 feet above ground, and laying balks over them as before. On these they make a floor, and then raise a roof, which they thatch with grass. To these balagans they have two doors, which they ascend by the same kind of ladder.

In the winter they use the balagans for magazines, the thatch secures what they lay up in them from rain, and, by taking away the ladder, it becomes inaccessible to wild beasts and vermin.

It being summer, we had no access to their winter dwellings, which were all shut up, and they were not over-fond of exposing their poverty; for, though they have little to boast of, they are not without pride. The whole furniture of the commonalty consists of dishes, bowls, troughs and cans; their cans are made of birch bark, their other utensils of wood,

D d 4 which

which, till the Ruffians introduced iron among them, they hallowed with inftruments made of ftone or bone; but with thefe tools their work was tedious and difficult. In thefe bowls they drefs their food, though, being wood, they will not bear the fire.

In the winter the men are employed in hunting, making fledges, and fetching wood; and the women in weaving nets, and fpinning thread.

In the fpring, the rivers begin to thaw, and the fifh that wintered in them go towards the fea; the men therefore in this feafon are bufied in fifhing, and the women in curing what they catch.

In the fummer, the men build both their winter and fummer huts, train their dogs, and make their houfhold utenfils and warlike inftruments; but the women make all the cloathing, even to the fhoes. Their clothes, for the moft part, are made of the fkins of land and fea-animals, particularly deer, dogs and feals; but fometimes they ufe the fkins of birds, and frequently thofe of different animals in the fame garments. They commonly wear two coats, the under one with the hair inwards, and the upper one with the hair outwards. The women have befides an under garment, not unlike Dutch trowfers, divided and drawn round the knees with a ftring.

They are filthy beyond imagination; they never wafh their hands or faces, nor pare their nails.

hails. They eat out of the fame difh with their dogs, which they never wafh. Both men and women plait their hair in two locks, which they never comb; and thofe who have fhort hair, fupply the locks with falfe. This is faid of the Kamfhatfkadales who live more to the north; thofe in the towns which we faw, had learnt of the Ruffians to be more cleanly.

They are very fuperftitious; and the women in particular, pretend to avert misfortunes, cure difeafes, and foretel future events, by muttering incantations over the fins of fifhes, mingled with a certain herb, which they gather from the woods in the fpring with much labour. They pretend alfo to judge of good and bad fortune, by the lines of the hands, and by their dreams, which they relate to each other as foon as they wake. They dread going near the burning mountains, left the invifible beings that inhabit them fhould hurt them, and think it a fin to drink, or to bathe in the hot fprings with which their country abounds, becaufe they fuppofe thofe fprings to be heated by the evil fpirits that produce them. They are faid never to bury their dead; but, binding a ftrap round the neck of the corps, drag it to the next foreft, where they leave it to be eaten by the bears, wolves, or other wild inhabitants. They have a notion, that they, who are eaten by dogs, will drive with fine dogs in another world. They throw away all the cloaths of the deceafed, becaufe they

believe

believe that they who wear them will die before their time.

The country is said to abound with wild beasts, which constitute the principal riches of the inhabitants; particularly foxes, sables, stone foxes, and hares, marmots, ermins, weasles, bears, wolves, rein-deer, and stone rams; but our gentlemen were much disappointed, who went in pursuit of them. They have a species of weasle, called the glutton, whose fur is so much more esteemed than all others, that they say, the good spirits are cloathed with it. The paws of this animal are white as snow; but the hair of the body is yellow. Sixty rubles (about 12 guineas nearly) have been given for a skin; and a sea-beaver for a single paw.

Of the bears, the inhabitants make good use; of their skins they make their beds, coverings, caps, collars and gloves; and of their flesh and fat their most delicate food.

The Kamshatskadales, all along the northern coasts, have a particular manner of dressing their food; which is the very reverse of that of the Indians in the south. There they roast or stew with stones made hot and buried, as it were, in the earth with their meat, by which its relish is said to be much improved. But here they boil it with hot stones immersed in water, by which its flavour is rendered more insipid. The same necessity, however, seems to have pointed out the same means to the people of the torrid

and

and of the frigid zones; for both being equally unacquainted with iron, and wood being incapable of refifting fire, when brought in contact with it, though the principle was obvious, the application was difficult; thofe therefore of the torrid zone would naturally be led to call the warmth of the earth to their aid: while thofe in the frozen climates would think water a more ready affiftant; add to this, that the colder regions abound with hot fprings; fome in Kamfhatfka, in particular, are fo hot, as to approach nearly to the degree of boiling water; but thefe they think it finful to ufe, as we have already obferved.

The dogs of this country are like our village curs, and are of different colours. They feed chiefly on fifh, and their mafters ufe them to draw fledges, inftead of horfes or rein-deer.

The feas and lakes abound with a variety of amphibious animals, of which feals and fea-horfes and fea-cows are the moft numerous, and the moft profitable. Of the fkins of the feal they make their canoes, and on their flefh and fat they feed delicioufly. Whales are fometimes caft upon the fhores, but very feldom, unlefs wounded.

With the teeth and bones of the fea-horfe and fea cow they point their arrows, and weapons of war; and of their fat and blubber they make their oil. They have otters in their lakes, but their fkins bear a great price.

They

They have birds of various kinds in great abundance. Among the sea-fowl, they have the puffin, the sea crow, the Greenland pigeon and the cormorant. They have swans, geese and eleven species of ducks; and they have plovers, snipes, and small birds without number. They have likewise four kinds of eagles; the black eagle, with a white head; the white eagle; the spotted eagle, and the brown eagle. They have vultures also, and hawks innumerable.

This country swarms with insects in the summer, which are very troublesome; but they have neither frog, toad nor serpent. Lizards are not rare; but they believe these creatures to be spies sent from the infernal powers to inspect their lives, and foretel their death; and therefore whenever they see one, they kill it, and cut it in small pieces, that it may not carry back any intelligence to their hurt.

But what is most remarkable, and deserves the attention of the curious, is, the remarkable conformity between the Kamschatskadales towards the east, and of the Americans, that live on the opposite coast just over against them, in their persons, habits, customs, and food; both dress exactly in the same manner, both cut holes in their faces in the manner already described, in which they put bones like false teeth; and both make their canoes exactly in the same manner. They are about 12 feet long and two broad, sharp at the head and stern, and flat at the bottom; they consist of flat pieces

of

of wood, joined at both ends, and kept apart in the middle by a tranfverfe piece, thro' which there is a round hole, juft big enough for the man to fet in his legs, and to feat himfelf on a bench made on purpofe; this fkeleton is covered with feal-fkin, dyed of a kind of a purple colour, and the hole is fkirted with loofe fkin, which, when the man is feated, he draws clofe round him, like the mouth of a purfe, and with a coat and cap of the fame fkin, which covers his whole body, makes the man and his boat appear like one piece; and thus clad, and thus feated and furrounded, he fears neither the rougheft fea, nor the fevereft weather.

And now we have had occafion to mention this fimilarity between the inhabitants on the oppofite fhores of Afia and America; we fhall embrace this opportunity, to correct a very material error in our account of our laft year's voyage, where, fpeaking of the Ruffian Difcoveries, we took notice, after examining Bhering's Straits, though the Ruffians fuppofed that the lands were parted, here we found the continent to join, by which the Reader will, no doubt, imagine, that we have afferted, that the two continents of Afia and America join, which they do not; but are feparated by a ftrait between two promontories, which, in clear weather, are fo near as to be feen, in failing thro', with the naked eye. But what is meant is this. When Bhering made his Difcovery, in coafting along the American fhore, he difcovered a found or

ftrait

ftrait, which having furmounted, he found himfelf in a great bay, which he imagined was another fea, and that the land which he had paffed was not the American Continent, but a great ifland feparated from the continent by the found or ftrait juft mentioned. This found therefore, and this bay we examined, and found that what the Ruffians had miftaken for an ifland, is actually a part of the American Continent. Hence it appears that, notwithftanding all that was written againft it, Bhering is juftly entitled to the honour of having difcovered all that part of the N. W. continent of America, that has been hitherto marked in our maps as parts unknown.

It remains now only to give a fhort defcription of the bay and harbour where we repaired ; which at the entrance is between two very high bluff rocks ; on the ftarboard as we enter is the light-houfe, of which mention has already been made, and at the diftance of about 20 miles the volcano, from whence flames and afhes are fometimes emitted to a great diftance, and to the great terror of the inhabitants. The bay is about 8 leagues deep, and lies from S. E. to N. W. And from N. E. to S. W. It is about 4 leagues. It is inacceffible during the winter, by reafon of the ice ; but very fafe and convenient during the fummer.

The harbour where we lay to careen and repair, would contain about 20 fhips of the line in perfect fafety, being clofely furrounded with high ills, except at the entrance. The people are

civil,

civil, and in their way very obliging; but their manner of living affords nothing very inchanting for failors.

Our ships being now in as good repair as we had reason to expect from the length of the voyage they had passed, the rigorous weather to which they had been exposed, the boisterous seas they had shipped; and, above all, from the violent concussions of the ice that had shaken their very frame, and had stript them of their sheathing: and being likewise plentifully provided with provisions and stores, by the generosity of her Imperial Majesty of Russia, and by the care and benevolence of her governor and officers,

On the 9th of October, 1779, we weighed, and soon were without the light-house, shaping our course to the southward, and

On the the 10th were in lat. 52 deg. 36 min. when we had a dead calm, and went to fishing for cod, with good success. Thermometer 52.

On the 11th we pursued our course, and by noon were in lat. 51 deg. 1 min.

On the 12th we stood S. W. and at night founded at 62 fathom, having in the afternoon passed three small islands to the westward of us. Lat. 50 deg. 19 min. Thermometer 48 deg. 52 $\frac{1}{2}$ min.

On the 13th we were in lat. 50. Course as before.

On the 14th we still continued the same course. Lat. 48 deg. 30 min.

The 15th we altered our course in search of
some

fome Iflands, which the Ruffians faid were inhabited by people of a gigantic fize, who were
covered with hair; but who notwithftanding
were very civil, and would fupply us with cattle and hogs, with which their iflands abounded.
Thefe iflands, however, we never found, though
we continued fearching for them till

The 19th, when a ftorm came on, and we
loft fight of the Difcovery; but next day were
in company, and refumed our courfe, the gale
continuing till

The 22d, when we found ourfelves in lat.
41 deg. and long. E. from London 149 deg.
20 min. The wind which had abated in the
day, frefhened again about 9 at night, and foon
increafed to a gale, when we were obliged to lie-
to, as we imagined, from the ufual figns, and
founding at 80 fathom, that we muft be near
land.

In the morning of the 23d we ftood N.N.W.
in fearch of land, but found none. At noon
by double alt. lat. 41 deg. 48 min. long. 146
deg. 17 min. E. About 10 at night we altered
our courfe W. S. W. and fo continued till

The 25th, when, by the time-piece, we were
in long. 145 deg. 29 min. E. and continued
our courfe with an eafy fail. At 3 in the afternoon a large piece of timber paffed us to
the northward. And

On the 26th, early in the morning, the man
at the maft-head called out Land, diftant about

7 or

7 or 8 leagues, bearing E. by N. to N.W.
We then found ourfelves within fight of Japan.
Lat. 40 deg. 56 min. long. 140 deg. 17 min. E.
Thermometer 52 deg. 55 min.

Early in the morning of the 27th we faw a
fail, feemingly very large, making towards us
from the fhore. We cleared fhip, and made
the fignal to the Difcovery to do the fame.
She was a fquare rigged veffel with two mafts,
very fhort, and built much in the manner of
the Chinefe junks. We hoifted Englifh colours.
She looked at us, but made fail to the weftward, and we continued our courfe.

On the 28th we faw land bearing W. N. W.
to S. half W. diftant about 6 leagues. We
then founded 64 fathom, and ftood from S.
to S. E. by E. Lat. 39 at noon, long 140
deg. 10 min. Thermometer 59 and a half.

On the 29th we again ftood S. half W. and
in the morning obferved another veffel making
to the eaftward at a great diftance. We again
hoifted Englifh colours, but fhe paid no attention to them, and we purfued our courfe.

On the 30th we were in lat. 36 deg. 41 min.
fteering S. W. Thermometer 64 and a half.

On the 31ft faw land very high, from W.
half N. to N. W. at a great diftance. Lat.
34 deg. 35 min.

November 1, fteered all day from S. to
S. W. faw a high mountain, which feemed to
be a volcano; but at a great diftance. Tacked
and ftood to the northward.

E e

On

On the 2d we again tacked, and stood E. half S. and, finding the water of a milky colour, sounded, but had no ground at 150 fathom. Lat. 36 deg. 30 min. Thermometer 70 and a half.

The 3d, the wind from the S. S. E. we still continued working to the southward; but made little way.

The 4th, the wind being against us, we advanced but slowly; being at noon in 35 deg. 49 min. only; with a great swell from the S. W. Thermometer 72 and a half.

The 5th we had only advanced 2 min.

On the 6th, the wind shifted to the N. E. made sail and stood all day S. by W. to S.S.W. Lat. 35 deg. 15 min.

The 7th, the sea all round was covered with pumice stones floating to the northward. We now approached the climate where bonettoes, albatrosses, sharks, dolphins, and flying-fish are seen to play their frolicks.

On the 8th we saw sea-weed, pieces of timber, great quantities of pumice, and other signs of land; but none came in sight. At night we shortened sail.

On the 9th we stood the whole day S. W. Lat. 32 deg. 48 min. Thermom. 71 and a half.

The 10th, blew a heavy gale from N.N.W. Hauled our wind to N. E.

On the 11th bore away again S. by W. but, the gale increasing towards night, hauled our wind to the northward.

The

The 12th the gale continued, lay-to, with the ships heads to the westward. Shipped many heavy seas, and the rain fell in torrents.

. The 13th the storm abated. Stood S. S. W. all day. Lat. at noon 25 deg. 56 min. long. 140 deg. 18 min. E.

On the 14th made sail, W. S. W. At 11 A. M. the Discovery made the signal for land, which we answered. It then bore S. W. distant 7 or 8 leagues, and appeared like a burning mountain, from whence proceeded, as we supposed, all the pumice we had seen. In the night saw volumes of flame proceeding from it, very awful.

On the 15th lost sight of the volcano; but in the evening another made a still more awful appearance. We were now in lat. 23 deg. 56 min. long. 139 deg. 20 min. E. Thermometer 72 and a half.

On the 16th we bore away W. half S. Wind fresh from E. N. E. at noon found ourselves in lat. 24 deg. 25 min. having, by the variation and setting of the current gone 20 miles to the northward. Long. by watch, 138 deg. 16 min. 20 sec. E. Thermometer 75 and a half.

Early on the 17th, being near the tropic, and expecting the weather to continue fine, we shifted our canvas and running-rigging, and bent our old ones, knowing what we had still to expect before we reached our native shores; and we made the signal for the Discovery to go

on

on our hull beam in search of land, but found none.   Lat. at noon, 23 deg. 46 min.

On the 18th we stood the whole day W.S.W. with a stiff breeze.   And

On the 19th were in lat. 22 deg. 30 min.

The 20th continued our course without any thing material.

The 21st we were in lat. 21 deg. 42 min. a hard gale and heavy rain.

The 22d we kept our course the whole day. Lat. at noon, 20 deg. 46 min.

The 23d altered our course, and stood W. by N.   Lat 21.

The 24th hauled our wind, and stood N. N. W.   Hard gale from N. E.

The 25th, the gale increasing, we lay-to, with the ships heads to the northward.   Lat. at noon, 21 deg. 29 min.

The 26th we again bore away W. S. W. and so continued all day.

The 27th continued the same course all day. At night shortened sail, and hauled up to N. N. W.

Early on the 28th we were surprised by breakers close under our bows.   Made the signal to the Discovery; and immediately tacked to the southward.   At 7 we wore ship, and again stood to the N. W.   At ten, saw breakers from N. E. by E. to W. by S. the nearest distant about a mile.   We sounded at 54 fathom, and bore away W. S. W. keeping a pro-

per

per diftance from the reefs, and coafting along till we paffed them. About noon, the S. W. end bore from us N. N. W. diftant about 2 miles, lat. 22 deg. 30 min. long. 135 deg. 17 min. 23 fec. We then made fail N. N. W. which courfe we continued all night.

On the 29th, about 8 A. M. we came in fight of a whole fleet of fmall craft, which we took to be fifhing veffels. They were at a great diftance, and not one of them left their employment to come near us. Lat. 21 deg. 58 min. We were now only diftant from Mocao, the port to which we were bound, about 26 leagues

On the 30th we wore fhip, and ftood to the fouthward, and about 11 in the morning, the man at the maft-head called out Land, bearing W. $\frac{1}{2}$ S. diftant about 3 leagues. This proved one of the northernmoft of the Ladrone Iflands, As foon as we came within diftance, we fired two guns for a pilot, and one came prefently along-fide, and our Captain agreed for 35 dollars to carry us into Mocao.

December 1, about two in the afternoon, after a paffage of one and twenty days, we caft anchor within four miles of the harbour, where we were met by two Chinefe gentlemen, who told us of the French war, and of his majefty's fhip the Sea-horfe having left that place about the time we left Kamfhatfka. About 8 in the evening our boats were manned, and our 3d

Lieut.

Lieut. went to the Englifh factory there for news, and about ten returned with the magazines and news-papers for 1776, 1777, 1778; being the lateft they had received. He likewife brought a confirmation of the French war, and of the continuance of the American war; and that five fail of Englifh fhips were now at Vampo, near Canton, in China.

On the 2d early in the morning we made fail, and anchored a-breaft of the ifland, and faluted the governor with 13 guns, which were anfwered with an equal number from the fort. We had fcarce dropt anchor, when we were vifited by two Englifh gentlemen, who after learning who we were and what we had been upon; perfuaded the Commodore to leave our then fituation and to moor the fhips in a fafer birth to the leeward of a fmall ifland about two miles diftant, where they might remain without danger.

It was now three years fince we had been in any port, where we could converfe any otherwife than by figns; and before any one was fuffered to go afhore, the Commodore called all hands aft, and ordered them to deliver up their journals, and every writing, remark, or memorandum that any of them had made of any particular refpecting the voyage, on pain of the fevereft punifhment in cafe of concealment, in order that all thofe journals, writings, remarks or memorandums, refpecting the voyage, might be fealed up, and directed to the Lords of the Admiralty. At the fame time requiring that every chart
of

of the coasts, or of any part of any of the coasts where we had been, or draught of any thing curious might be delivered up in like manner, in order to accompany the journals, &c. all which was complied with ; and the papers were made up and sealed accordingly in sight of the whole crew, the papers of the commissioned officers by themselves, the papers of the non-commissioned officers by themselves, and the papers of the marines and common men by themselves. The boats were then ordered out and sent to Mocao for fresh provisions, which next day were dealt out to the ships companies at full allowance. But before these could return, there came from the town boats with beef, veal, pork, ducks, geese, turnips, carrots, lemons, oranges, and every other article of provisions which the island produced ; some as presents to the Captains and officers ; but by far the greatest part to make their market.

Being now safely moored, the first thing that claimed the attention of the Commodore, was to provide as well as he could for the safety of the crews in their return home. The news of a French war, without letting us know at the same time the order issued by the French king in our favour, gave us much concern. Our ships were ill fitted for war ; the decks fore and aft being finished flush had no covering for men or officers ; it was therefore thought necessary to strengthen the stanchions and rails, and to raise a kind of parapet, musket-proof on both

E e 4

decks; and likewife to ftrengthen the cabbins
as much as poffible, in cafe of action. And as
it was agreed that both fhips could carry more
guns if any were to be purchafed, the Commodore was for taking the fhips to Canton, till
perfuaded from it by fome gentlemen belonging
to the Englifh factory, who undertook to
negociate the bufinefs without giving umbrage
to the Chinefe, who certainly would, they faid,
be offended at the appearance of fhips of war
in their river, and would oppofe their progrefs ;
reminding him at the fame time of the difagreeable difpute in which Commodore Anfon was
formerly involved on a fimilar occafion; and
how hurtful it was to the Company's commerce
for feveral years after. Upon thefe reprefenta-
tions the Commodore relinquifhed his defign,
and Capt. King, with other officers, were fent
in a Company's fhip, affifted by one or two
gentlemen belonging to the factory, to Canton,
to purchafe cannon and fuch other ftores as were
not to be had at Mocao.

On the 18th they fet fail, and at the fame
time two Portuguefe veffels from the harbour
of Macao, came and anchored clofe by us.
They were bound to Bengal and Madrafs, and
very readily affifted us with ropes for running
rigging, fome canvas, and with 60 fathom of
cable. They likewife exchanged four fmall
cannon and fome fhot with the Difcovery for
a fpare anchor.

The 25th being Chriftmas day, was kept, as

is ufual with Englifh failors, in jollity and mirth;
and what added to the pleafure of the day there
was not a man ill in either fhip.

On the 28th the Commodore received a letter from Capt. King, with an account of the
difafters that had happened in the paffage, having loft two anchors and their boat, and were
feveral times in danger of running afhore; that
they did not arrive at Canton till the 24th;
but that he hoped foon to return with the cannon and ftores, for which he had bargained,
though at a great price.

Here they learnt that the fkins we had
brought with us from the N. W. continent of
America, were of nearly double the value at
Canton, as at Kamfhatfka.

Early on the 29th there came into the harbour of Macao a Spanifh galoon from Manilla,
faid to have more than four millions of treafure
on board; and before we left our ftation there
came in another worth double that fum. We
were unacquainted with the Spanifh war, or
thefe fhips, had we been properly commiffioned, might eafily have been captured. It is aftonifhing, that none of our cruifers have ever
lain in wait for thefe fhips, as their voyage is
annual, and their courfe known.

The fame evening a quarrel happened between
a party of our failors, on fhore with leave, and
fome of the town's people, in which feveral were
dangeroufly wounded on both fides; and Mr.
Burney, 1ft Lieut. of the Refolution, had a

dagger

dagger run through his left arm in endeavouring to put an end to the fray. For this infult
the Governor fent to demand fatisfaction; but
upon examination the town's-people were found
to be the aggreffors. The Governor made a
very handfome apology for his miftake, and
the affair ended without any ferious confequences.

We were now vifited daily by ftrangers who
came out of curiofity to fee fhips that had been
fo many years upon difcovery; and every one
was anxious to learn what he could concerning
our courfe, but that we were not at liberty to
tell. Among the reft came two French fpies,
as we imagined; but not being able to make
out any thing criminal againft them, they were
fuffered to depart. The fufpicion arofe from
fome of our men, who having particularly
marked them, infifted that they had formerly
failed with them in the French fervice. Nothing remarkable till

Jan. the 8th, 1780, when Capt. King, with
the officers that accompanied him, arrived in
the Company's veffel, with the cannon, ammunition, and ftores from Canton. Thefe
being fhipped, nothing remained to be done,
but to take on board the live ftock which the
Commodore and Officers had purchafed for their
own ufe, and nine head of cattle to be killed
at fea for the ufe of the fhip's company, the
beef

beef and pork which we brought from England being now scarce eatable. Provisions of all kinds were here very dear, and very indifferent; but what made us amends was the price they gave for our beaver-skins, on which they set a great value.

On the 11th of January we unmoored, and the wind being fair, came to sail with a pleasant breeze; but the wind dying away in the evening, we cast anchor, and in the night John Cave, quarter-master, and Robert Spencer, ran away with the great cutter. And

On the 12th we were the whole day detained in endeavouring to recover them; but to no purpose.

On the 13th we passed the fort, and saluted the garrison with 13 four pounders, which they answered with an equal number.

We had now nothing but a beaten tract to pass in our way to our long-wished for native country.

On the 20th we made the little group of islands known by the name of Pulo Condore, in lat. 8 deg. 40 min. N. at one of which we anchored, and found it inhabited. Here we both wooded and watered, and the carpenters felled some large trees, which were afterwards sawed on board. The trees on these islands are chiefly cedar, iron wood, mangrove, manchiconella and box. Some nutmeg trees there were, but of a wild kind, that bear a fruit without

out tafte or fmell. In purfuit of game, of which there was plenty, our gentlemen fell in with a party of natives, one of whom accompanied them to the fhips. We made him underftand, that we wanted provifions; and he had not left us long, before more than 20 boats came round the ifland laden with fruits, fowls, ducks, and other provifions, which they readily exchanged for any thing we offered them, though they were not wholly unacquainted with the ufe of money; for being informed, that buffaloes were on the ifland, we purchafed feven, three of them of a large fize, for four dollars. Here we found the cabbage-tree and other fucculent greens, with which our people made very free without afking queftions.

On the 28th we unmoored, and on

The 31ft made the ifland of Banca, and having paffed the ftraits

On the 5th of February we made the ifland of Sumatra, where we faw a large fhip lying at anchor, and

On the 7th paffed the ifland of Java, where we faw two more. We made the fignal to the Difcovery to prepare for action, and we did the fame, hoifting Englifh colours. It was fome time before they fhewed any, but at length they hoifted Dutch colours. We fent our boat on board, and received the firft news of a Spanifh war. We purfued our courfe, and

On

On the 11th we made the island of Coco-terra. Here, from a healthy ship's company, several of our people fell ill of the flux, and so continued for some time; however, having got plenty of good water on board, we sailed

On the 13th, directing our course to Prince's island.

On the 15th we entered the bay of Prince's Island, where Capt. Cook, when he commanded the Endeavour, anchored in his return to Europe. Here we purchased turtles, fowls, and some deer; and here we laid in store of cocoa-nuts, plantains, and other vegetables; and having compleated our stock of water set sail

On the 18th, directing our course for the Cape of Good Hope. Nothing remarkable till

The 25th of March, when we were attacked by a severe storm, attended with thunder, lightning and rain, which lasted five days without intermission.

On the 7th of April we were alarmed by finding our rudder-head almost twisted off. We got the pennants fixed to steer with tackles, it being the carpenter's opinion it could not last till our arrival at the next port. However, by proper application it lasted till we arrived at the Cape.

On the 9th we fell in with Cape Lagullas, where about 9 in the morning we saw a small vessel cruising, which proved to be the East-India Company's Snow, Betsey, looking out

for

for the Eaſt India fleet. She left England the 5th of November, and Falſe Bay on the 4th inſtant. She confirmed the account we had received of the Spaniſh war. We exchanged ſome trifles, and ſoon parted. And

On the 12th we entered Bay Falſe, came to, and moored the ſame day, after having ſaluted the fort with 13 guns, which was anſwered by the ſame number. We had ſcarce dropt an-chor, when the Governor came on board, bringing with him a packet of letters for Capt. Cook, which had lain there ever ſince the be-ginning of 1779; he had heard of the death of Capt. Cook by a Dutch veſſel, and expreſſed great concern for that unhappy event; aſking a thouſand queſtions concerning the particulars.

The firſt care of our Commodore was to provide for the ſick; and by three in the after-noon they were all landed, and ſent to the hoſpital under the care of the Surgeon's mate: All hands were next ſet to their different em-ployments, ſome to wood and water, and ſome to compleat the repairs. Theſe they forwarded with the utmoſt expedition, every one being eager to get to his native country. Of the repairs, the Reſolution's rudder was the moſt material. The firſt thing therefore to be done was to unhinge it and get it on ſhore: and though this was immediately put in hand, it was

The

The 27th before it was reſtored again to its place.

By the 29th, the ſick, who were numerous when we arrived at the Cape, we having 16 ill of the flux, were pretty well recovered: the repairs were in forwardneſs, and the ſtores ready to be taken on board at a moment's no-tice, when news was brought us, that an ex-preſs was arrived at Table Bay from England, in the Sibbald frigate, which had only been ten weeks from Plymouth, and that ſhe was to return again as ſoon as ſhe had delivered her diſpatches. Both Captains went inſtantly to learn the contents, and on their return, orders were given to prepare as faſt as poſſible to ſail. This was joyful news. The ſubſtance of theſe diſpatches related chiefly to the courſe the Eaſt-Indiamen were to ſteer, to fall in with the con-voy appointed to meet them; with ſome in-ſtructions for our Commodore, reſpecting the papers that were to be tranſmitted to the Ad-miralty, which were all put on board the fri-gate, and Mr. Portlock, maſter's mate, em-barked along with them.

On the 30th they ſet ſail; but it was

The 7th of May before we were in readineſs to follow. About noon, on that day, the ſig-nal was made for unmooring. We had now 120 live ſheep on board, and the Diſcovery a like proportion. We had all other proviſions in equal plenty, and we had likewiſe a healthy

crew

crew in high spirits, wishing for nothing but a fair wind to shorten our voyage; but that was not yet to be obtained. We had scarce saluted the garrison on taking leave, when the wind died away, and a great swell ensued, which continued till

The 9th, when the snow came in sight, which we spoke with on the 8th of April. We sent our pinnace for news from sea; but she had seen only one sail pass since we first spoke with her.

On the 19th of April their whole crew were near being blown up, by the snow's taking fire forwards: the ship was much damaged, and they were putting into the Cape to refit, and then were bound for St. Helena.

On the 12th we made sail, and pursued our course home, without any material occurrence till

The 10th of June, when the Discovery's boat brought us word that, in exercising the great guns, the carpenter's mate had his arm shattered in a shocking manner, by part of the wadding being left in after a former discharge; another man was slightly wounded at the same time.

On the 12th it began to blow very hard, and so continued till next day, when the Discovery sprung her main-top-mast; and we were obliged to lie-to till another was put up.

On

On the 13th we croſſed the line to the north-ward, and obſerved a water-ſpout to the N. W. at no great diſtance ; and for the remainder of the month had fine weather. Thermom. from 80 to 78 $\frac{1}{2}$.

July the 1ſt we had the Diſcovery's people on board to compare time, lat. at noon 20 deg. N. Long. 34 W.

On the 13th the ſhip's birth day was cele-brated on board, and double allowance given to the whole crew, who were at this time in perfect health.

On the 27th at day-light, the Diſcovery made the ſignal for ſeeing a ſail. We inſtant-ly began to clear ſhip in caſe of an enemy, and höiſted Engliſh colours ; and on our near ap-proach the ſail did the ſame. She was bound to the ſouthward, and we purſued our courſe.

On the 1ſt of Auguſt juſt at ſun ſet we ſaw a ſail at a great diſtance to the weſtward ; but in the morning ſhe was quite out of ſight. We were then in lat. 43 deg. 56 min. N.

On the 7th we were in lat. 48 deg. long. 10 deg. 10 min. W. a heavy gale with rain.

On the 9th the wind ſhifted to the eaſtward, when we ſhaped our courſe to the north of Ice-land. Blew hard all day.

On the 21ſt being then in lat. 58 deg. 4 min. N. long. 9 deg. 6 min. ſaw a ſail ſtanding to the ſouthward, when we made the Diſcovery's

F f

ſignal

fignal to chace ; but the gale continuing, could not come near enough to hale her. In the evening the man at the maft head called out land diftant about 3 leagues.

Early on the 22d made the fignal for a pilot, and at eight o'Clock a pilot came off, and by eleven we were fafely moored in the harbour of Strumnefs, in the north of Scotland. We were foon vifited by the gentlemen in the neighbourhood.

On the 23d frefh beef and greens were ferved in plenty to both fhips companies ; and the fame day our paffengers went on fhore, and fet out for London. The Captains and Officers went likewife on fhore, and the men had liberty to divert themfelves by turns during our ftay.

By the 29th we had got wood and water enough on board to ferve us to London ; and at noon the fignal was made to weigh ; but the wind coming about, and blowing frefh from the S. E. obliged us not only to relinquifh our defign for the prefent, but detained us till the 19th of September.

On the 20th of September Capt. King of the Difcovery, Mr. Bailey our aftronomer, and Mr. Webber, left the fhips, and fet out for London, and Mr. Burney, 1ft Lieut. of the Refolution, took the command of the Difcovery in the abfence of Capt. King.

During our ftay the fhips were vifited by gentlemen from all the iflands round ; and by the

the Apollo Frigate and her confort; they brought in a prize valued at 10,000 l. and both Captains came to vifit Capt. Gore on board the Refolution, who now was taken very ill, and fo continued to the end of the voyage. The fame afternoon, the wind came round in our favour, when the fignal was made for unmooring, and both fhips got under way. At night we came to an anchor with the tide.

On the 23d Samuel Johnfon, ferjeant of marines, died, and next morning his corpfe was committed to the deep.

On the 25th the wind came again to the eaftward, and continued againft us moft of our paffage.

On the 28th we paffed by Leith, off which we again fpoke with his Majefty's fhip Apollo.

On the 29th John Davis quarter-mafter, died. Our detention at Strumnefs proved unfortunate for thefe two men, who died in their paffage. Had the fhips arrived in a direct courfe, their friends would at leaft have had the fatisfaction of adminiftering all in their power to their recovery, which, to perfons who had been fo long abfent, would have been no fmall confolation.

On the 30th we came to an anchor off Yarmouth, in company with his Majefty's floops of war the Fly and Alderney. Our boats were immediately fent on fhore for provifions; and

for

for a fpare cable for our fmall bower, that we had being near worn out. We lay here till

The 2d of October, when we weighed and failed.

On the 4th we came too at the Nore. And

On the 6th dropt our anchors at Deptford, having been abfent juft four years, three months and two days.

FINIS.

DIRECTIONS *for placing the* CUTS.

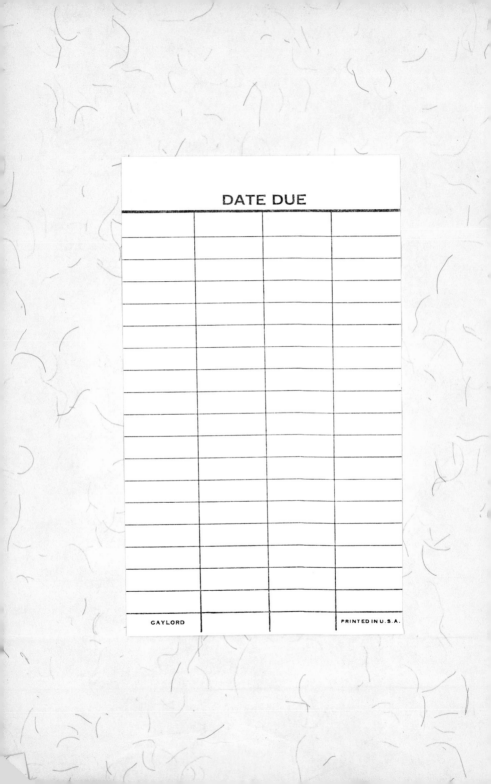

DATE DUE

GAYLORD   PRINTED IN U.S.A.